10/20

Fodor's

KAUAI

D0449611

Welcome to Kauai

Little did we realize that the emergence of a novel coronavirus in early 2020 would abruptly bring almost all travel to a halt. Although our Fodor's writers around the world have continued working to bring you, our readers, the best of the destinations they cover, we still anticipate that more than the usual number of businesses will close permanently in the coming months, perhaps with little advance notice. We don't expect that things will return to "normal" for some time. As you plan your upcoming travels to Kauai, please reconfirm that places are still open and let us know when we need to make updates by writing to us at editors@fodors.com.

TOP REASONS TO GO

- **Beaches:** Pristine strips of sand and palm-fringed shores make vacation dreams real.

- **Napali Coast:** Its towering cliffs astonish all who see them from land, sea, or air.

- **Outdoor Fun:** Kauai offers great surfing and snorkeling, plus top-notch golf and hiking.

- **Charming Towns:** Artsy Hanapepe, colorful Hanalei, historic Koloa, and more.

- **Kayaking:** Paddling on a river is a tranquil way to discover the island's allure.

- **Scenic Drives:** The North Shore's Highway 560, the West Side's Waimea Canyon Drive.

Contents

Fodor's Features

MAPS

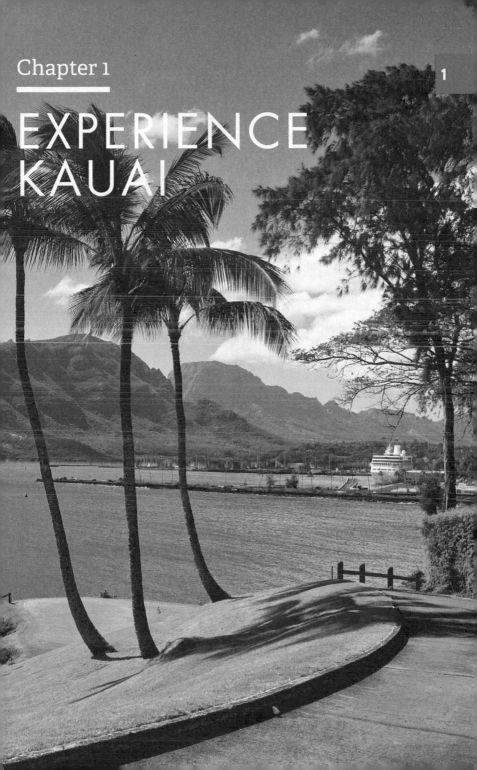

Chapter 1

EXPERIENCE KAUAI

24 ULTIMATE EXPERIENCES

Kauai offers terrific experiences that should be on every traveler's list. Here are Fodor's top picks for a memorable trip.

1 Hike the Kalalau Trail

Winding 11 taxing miles along rugged Napali Coast, this is one of the world's most outrageous hikes. The first 2 miles to Hanakapiai Beach is fairly moderate; the two- to three-day round-trip hike includes camping along the way (permit required). (Ch. 7)

2 Coastal Sunset Sail

Kauai sunsets are sublime, and perhaps the best way to experience that magical hour of the day is by boat, facing stunning Napali Coast. (Ch. 7)

3 Relax on Poipu Beach

Popular with tourists and locals, uncrowded Poipu Beach has calm waters ideal for snorkeling, and you might just spot an endangered Hawaiian monk seal. (Ch. 5)

4 Mountain Tubing

A century ago, Lihue Plantation dug waterways to irrigate its fields. Now you can take a tubing tour via the waterways for a glimpse of Kauai's hidden interior. (Ch. 7)

5 Sunrise on the Royal Coast

Kauai's Royal Coconut Coast—Lydgate State Park and the Ke Ala Hele Makalae biking/walking path are great vantage points—is the perfect place to watch the sunrise. (Ch. 4, 7)

6 Seek out the Menehune

The mythical Menehune are said to be descendants of the island's first settlers. Their "work" is found throughout Kauai, including Alekoko Fishpond near Lihue. (Ch. 4)

7 Learn Island History

The island's most important receptacle of island culture and history, Kauai Museum covers topics like geological formation and Hawaiian kings. (Ch. 4)

8 Admire the Spouting Horn

Shooting water as high as 50 feet, Kauai's version of Old Faithful was once guarded by a lizard. Today, you can still hear her roar. (Ch. 5)

9 Go Deep Sea Fishing

The deep Pacific waters surrounding Kauai are teaming with fish. Charters, most of which depart from Lihue, visit the best spots and provide all the gear. (Ch. 7)

10 Hanalei Valley Views

In a land of stellar vistas, the North Shore's Hanalei Valley stands out; head to the viewpoint on Highway 56 just outside the town of Hanalei. (Ch. 3)

11 Helicopter Vistas

Kauai's interior is best seen via helicopter. Tours give access to breathtaking scenery like Waimea Canyon and Waialeale Crater. (Ch. 7)

12 Visit Sacred Heiaus

Remains of sacred structures of the Kauai kingdom are found in Wailua along Route 580 between the mouth of the Wailua River and Mount Waialeale. (Ch. 4)

13 Kapaa Town

Meander through Kapaa town the first Saturday evening of each month as merchants show off their wares, food trucks sizzle, bands play, and locals "talk story." (Ch. 4)

14 Eat Shave Ice

The Hawaiian version of a snow cone—shave (never shaved) ice topped with a sugary syrup and condensed milk—is found throughout Kauai. (Ch. 4)

15 Sun-Kissed Farmers' Markets

Known as the Garden Isle, Kauai's numerous farmers' markets have the freshest fruits. (Ch. 4, 7)

16 Cocktails Overlooking Bali Hai

Order a tropical cocktail at the Happy Talk Lounge and enjoy an enchanting sunset over Hanalei Bay. (Ch. 3)

17 Bird- and Whale-Watching

The northernmost point of the inhabited Hawaiian Isles, Kilauea Point has stunning ocean and coast views and amazing opportunites for bird- and whale- watching. (Ch. 3, 7)

18 Waimea Canyon

A vast canyon on the island's West Side, this geologic wonder measures a mile wide, more than 10 miles long, and 3,567 feet deep. (Ch. 6, 7)

19 Attend a Luau

Guests are treated to Hawaiian-style storytelling, complete with hula dancing, traditional knife dancing, and fire poi ball throwing at traditional luaus. (Ch. 3-5)

20 Old Koloa Town

In 1835 Koloa's first sugar mill ushered in Hawaii's era of sugar production. Today, many of these historic buildings are shops and restaurants. (Ch. 5)

21 Art in Hanapepe

Established over a century ago, Hanapepe is filled with bougainvillea-draped, plantation-style buildings that contain restaurants, boutiques, and art galleries. (Ch. 6)

22 World-Class Golf

Breathtaking beauty, quality, and a vast number of thrilling, heart-stopping holes helps Kauai remain one of Hawaii's top golf destinations. (Ch. 7)

23 Kayaking to Secret Falls

One of Hawaii's few navigable rivers, kayaking Wailua River leads you into a mystical realm of lush rain forests, velvety green mountains, and secret, crystal-clear waterfalls. (Ch. 4, 7)

24 Snorkel at Kee Beach

Kauai has many snorkeling beaches, but Kee is one of the best, especially for beginners and kids. Spot parrotfish, unicorn fish, and green sea turtles. (Ch. 3, 7)

WHAT'S WHERE

1 **North Shore.** Dreamy beaches, verdant mountains, breathtaking scenery, and abundant rain, waterfalls, and rainbows characterize the North Shore, which includes Kilauea, Princeville, Hanalei, and Haena.

2 **East Side.** This is Kauai's commercial and residential hub, dominated by the island's largest town, Kapaa. The airport, main harbor, and government offices are found in the county seat of Lihue.

3 **South Shore.** Peaceful landscapes, sunny weather, and beaches that rank among the best in the world make the South Shore the resort capital of Kauai. The Poipu resort area is here, along with the main towns of Koloa and Lawai.

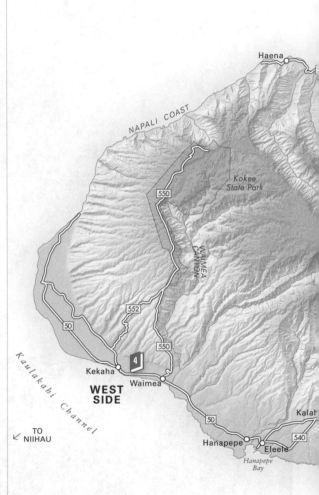

4 West Side. Dry, sunny, and sleepy, the West Side includes the historic towns of Hanapepe, Waimea, and Kekaha. The area's ideal for outdoor adventurers as it's the entryway to the Waimea Canyon and Kokee State Park and the departure point for most Napali Coast boat trips.

■ TIP→ On Kauai, the directions "mauka" (toward the mountains) and "makai" (toward the ocean) are often used. Locals tend to refer to highways by name rather than by number.

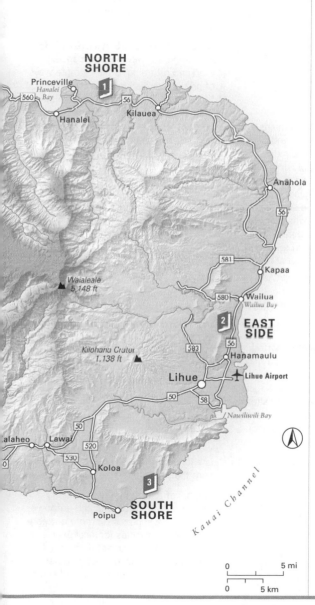

Kauai Today

Hawaiian culture and tradition have experienced a renaissance over the last few decades. There's a real effort to revive traditions and to respect history as the Islands go through major changes. New developments often have a Hawaiian cultural expert on staff to ensure cultural sensitivity and to educate newcomers. Kauai public, private, and charter schools now offer full-time coursework in the Hawaiian language.

Nonetheless, development remains a huge issue for all Islanders—land prices are still skyrocketing, putting many areas out of reach for locals. Approximately 45% of recent new housing on Kauai is bought by off-island purchasers, often as second homes. Traffic is also a major problem on aging Kauai roads that were not designed to accommodate all the new drivers and the surge in tourism. Plus, the Islands' limited natural resources are being seriously depleted.

SUSTAINABILITY

Although sustainability is an effective buzzword and authentic direction for the Islands' dining establishments, 90% of Hawaii's food and energy is imported. However, solar power is making a major inroad in power production: on some sunny days, for a few hours, the Kauai electric grid is 100% powered by alternative energy sources. In fact, Kauai leads the state in alternative energy solutions, including hydro.

For many years, most of Kauai's land was used for mono-cropping of pineapple or sugarcane. As a result, sugarcane is now a memory, and pineapple production has dropped precipitously. Dole, once the largest pineapple company in Hawaii, closed its plants in 1991, and after 90 years, Del Monte stopped pineapple production in 2008. But the Islands have perfected a sugar pineapple that is much less acidic than the previously available ones. Although imports have negatively affected market share, they have also set the stage for great agricultural change to be explored.

BACK-TO-BASICS AGRICULTURE

Emulating the way Hawaiian ancestors lived and returning to their simple ways of growing and sharing a wide variety of foods have become statewide initiatives. Many Kauai locals buy all their fruit and produce from the numerous farmers' markets, which often feature exotic in-season crops at reasonable prices.

Localized efforts such as the Hawaii Farm Bureau Federation are collectively aiding the organic and sustainable agriculture renaissance. The seed of this movement is thriving in the form of farmers' markets and partnerships among restaurants and local farmers. From home-cooked meals and casual plate lunches to fine-dining cuisine and an abundance of new food trucks, sustainability trailblazers in Kauai's kitchens are enriching the island's culinary tapestry.

TOURISM AND THE ECONOMY

The $17 billion tourism industry represents more than a third of Hawaii's state income. Naturally, this dependency has caused economic hardship during the coronavirus outbreak in spring of 2020. Restaurants, hotels, shops, and even cultural institutions were forced to close. If you're planning a visit, remember to call ahead to verify open hours, and to make sure that the property is still in operation.

The belief that the tourism industry should protect, promote, and empower local culture and provide more entrepreneurial opportunities for local people has become more important than ever. More companies are incorporating authentic Hawaiiana in their programs and aim not only to provide a commercially viable tour but also to ensure that the visitor leaves feeling connected to his or her host.

The concept of *kuleana,* a word denoting both privilege and responsibility, is a traditional Hawaiian value. The privilege of living in such a sublime place comes with the responsibility to protect it.

SOVEREIGNTY

Political issues of sovereignty continue to divide Native Hawaiians, who have formed myriad organizations around the issue, each operating with a separate agenda and lacking one collectively defined goal. Ranging from achieving complete independence to solidifying a nation within a nation, existing sovereignty models remain fractured and their future unresolved.

The introduction of the Native Hawaiian Government Reorganization Act of 2009 attempts to set up a legal framework in which Native Hawaiians can attain federal recognition and coexist as a self-governed entity, similar to Native American status. Also known as the Akaka Bill, after former Senator Daniel Akaka of Hawaii, this bill has been presented before Congress and is still pending.

RISE OF HAWAIIAN PRIDE

After the overthrow of the monarchy in 1893, a process of Americanization began. Traditions were silenced in the name of citizenship. Teaching the Hawaiian language was banned from schools, and children were distanced from their local customs.

But Hawaiians are resilient people, and with the rise of the civil rights movement they began to reflect on their own national identity, bringing an astonishing renaissance of the Hawaiian culture to fruition.

The people rediscovered language, hula, chanting, and even the traditional Polynesian arts of canoe building and wayfinding (navigation by the stars without use of instruments). This cultural resurrection is now firmly established in today's Hawaiian culture, with a palpable pride that exudes from Hawaiians young and old.

The election of former President Barack Obama increased Hawaiian pride. The president's strong connection and commitment to Hawaiian values of diversity, spirituality, family, and conservation have restored confidence that Hawaii can inspire a more peaceful, tolerant, and environmentally conscious world.

CHANGES ON THE NORTH SHORE

In 2018, Kauai's North Shore experienced epic rainfall, with Hanalei absorbing 50 inches of rain in one 24-hour period. The flooding cut off the only road west of Princeville for long periods, and residents were forced to make many daily adjustments. The silver lining? While many areas were forced to close for repairs, many of the North Shore's parks took the time to make improvements. Haena State Park, Kee Beach, and Kalalau Trail are now cleaner and calmer. That's in part due to new park fees for non-residents; it's $1 to hike to Hanakapiai Valley, for example, and $5 to park. There's also a limit on the number of vehicles allowed in the park per day, with only 70 parking spots for visitors, cutting down on crowds. It's wise to purchase all shuttle, entry, and parking permits well in advance. The best option for many is to take the new North Shore Shuttle ($15 round trip), which includes all fees and leaves from Princeville and rumbles to Kee with stops along the way.

Kauai's Best Beaches

HANALEI BEACH PARK
One of the most legendary beaches on Kauai and the largest bay on the island's North Shore, this 2-mile family-friendly beach features a long pier that's ideal for admiring the exceptional views. It's also great for water activities, such as paddleboarding, snorkeling, and swimming. (Ch. 3)

MAHAULEPU BEACH
This isolated beach is pristine and wild, from its windswept cliffs to the waves crashing on the shore. There are no lifeguards and the surf can be dangerous, so trek along Mahaulepu Heritage Trail instead, spotting blowholes, lava tubes, and tide pools along the rocky coastline. (Ch. 5)

KEALIA BEACH
East-facing Kealia is the spot to catch a sunrise on Kauai and a good lookout point for spotting whales during the winter. With strong waves, wind swell, and rough currents during most of the year, it's ideal for surfing and body boarding, or for biking along the Coastal Path. (Ch. 4)

ANINI BEACH
Although there are no lifeguards on this golden-sand, 3-mile beach, Anini is considered one of the safest places to swim on the island's North Shore during summer. Naturally protected by an expansive coral reef—the largest in all of Hawaii—it offers exceptional snorkeling, too. Windsurfers and campers also love this beach. (Ch. 4)

POLIHALE STATE PARK
Hawaii's longest stretch of sandy beach is situated on the westernmost point of the island and is well known for its spectacular sunset views. If you're seeking privacy, this 2-mile white-sand beach has high dunes and plenty of shade, an ideal getaway for the afternoon. Swimming is only recommended in the area here known as "Queen's Pond," which is a tranquil sheltered cove. Keep in mind this remote area is for the adventurous only: it has a bumpy access road that's a dusty 5 miles long and best navigated with a four-wheel drive vehicle (Ch. 6).

LYDGATE BEACH
This laid-back, family-friendly beach is popular in eastern Kauai and offers an easy and relaxing beach experience. It's especially fun for children because it features an adjacent pool area that's protected from the larger waves by a rock wall. Lifeguards watch over the snorkelers who flock to the top spot to view tropical fish and other marine life. (Ch. 4)

Haena Beach Park (Tunnels Beach)

HAENA BEACH PARK (TUNNELS BEACH)
Earning its nickname from the underwater lava tunnels offshore, this beach with calm, turquoise waters has ideal conditions for snorkeling and is teeming with marine life. Just around the bend is a scenic yet lively stretch of pale yellow sand. (Ch. 3)

ANAHOLA BEACH PARK
Situated on Kauai's eastern shore, this sugar-white beach is a hotspot for the local crowd on weekends and offers plenty of shade as well as gorgeous mountain views of Kalalea. Although it's slightly off the beaten track, Anahola is a family-friendly, guarded beach, but it's important to note that swimming is protected in specific areas only. This destination is a draw for those who enjoy camping and picnics. (Ch. 4)

KALAPAKI BEACH
This lively, beautiful beach area in Lihue in front of the sprawling Marriott Beach Club provides protected swimming with an abundance of options and plenty of convenient amenities. Featuring smaller, forgiving waves and a sandy ocean floor, the area is ideal for most water activities, including beginner surf and stand-up paddleboarding lessons. Steps away from the sand, there are a number of shops that sell standard beach supplies and local products, as well as cafes to grab lunch or a quick snack. (Ch. 4)

POIPU BEACH PARK
Popular Poipu is situated on the island's south shore with a prime location in front of several major hotels. The wide, often noisy, beach is optimal for snorkeling and swimming and is a fun spot for beginner surf lessons. (Ch. 5)

Kauai's Natural Wonders

HANALEI RIVER VALLEY

With cascading waterfalls, sprawling taro fields, and the island's famous Hanalei River, the valley's beauty stretches for nearly 1,000 acres. Get a panoramic view from the Hanalei Valley Lookout or kayak for a close-up. (Ch. 3)

SPOUTING HORN

A popular island landmark near Poipu Beach on Kauai's South Shore, Spouting Horn is a blowhole that shoots ocean water into the air (often to an impressive 50 feet high) à la Old Faithful. This natural wonder is created from the pressure of ocean water being forced into an undersea lava tube. If you're lucky, you might spot a sea turtle or a whale during winter. (Ch. 5)

KALALAU TRAIL

This rugged hike winds about 11 miles through the magnificent Napali Coast State Wilderness Park, offering stunning views of the Pacific Ocean. Suited for experienced hikers only, the challenging path traverses rocky mountain streams, crosses five valleys, and passes majestic waterfalls. Twisting along the high cliffs, the trail ends at Kalalau Beach. (Ch. 3)

QUEEN'S BATH

This picturesque tide pool surrounded by volcanic rock is a gorgeous place to admire the natural, rugged scenery. However, it's also dangerous due to crashing waves and a slippery trail. For that reason, avoid swimming here—it's a spot best viewed from above. (Ch. 3)

KILAUEA POINT NATIONAL WILDLIFE REFUGE

Bird-watchers adore this scenic reserve situated on an ancient dormant volcano, as it's home to a variety of diverse waterfowl and plenty of other wildlife. Visitors can also tour the nearby lighthouse and spot turtles, whales, and monk seals. (Ch. 3)

WAILUA RIVER AND FALLS

Flowing past ancient temples, this 20-mile-long meandering river ends in two spectacular and awe-inspiring waterfalls: Opaekaa Falls and Wailua Falls. Hiking here will require hours (or perhaps days), or you can drive to the Wailua Falls and the Opaekaa Falls overlooks. (Ch. 4)

KOKEE STATE PARK

Located north of Waimea Canyon, Kokee State Park offers breathtaking views along verdant pathways that ascend over 4,000 feet. With 45 miles of hiking trails and diverse terrain home to forests, wildflowers, and lush valleys, this peaceful area is popular with campers. The park offers something for everyone, so day-trippers can choose an easy or moderate trail. (Ch. 6)

WAIMEA CANYON STATE PARK

Considered the "Grand Canyon of the Pacific," this awe-inspiring natural wonder is over 3,000 feet deep and stretches nearly 14 miles. Take in its brilliant dark pink and emerald hues at numerous scenic lookout points offering photo ops across the valley. (Ch. 6)

NOUNOU MOUNTAIN (SLEEPING GIANT)

Resembling a man resting on his back, this magnificent mountain range has several trails to choose from, but the East Trail is considered the most moderate, with parking close by. You can hike the 2-mile ascent to the top (across the giant's body to the area that would be his "forehead") and soak in some unobstructed island vistas. (Ch. 4)

NAPALI COAST

This iconic stretch of Kauai's dramatic coastline features cliffs that soar nearly 4,000 feet above the Pacific Ocean. The breathtaking natural wonder is best admired at a distance, either from the water (ideally by catamaran or sailboat) or from the air by helicopter. (Ch. 3)

Flora and Fauna in Hawaii

KUKUI
The kukui, or candlenut, is Hawaii's state tree. Hawaiians had many uses for kukui. Oil was extracted from its nuts and burned as a light source and also rubbed on fishing nets to preserve them. The juice from the husk's fruit was used as a dye. The small kukui blossoms and nuts also had medicinal purposes.

PLUMERIA
This fragrant flower is named after Charles Plumier, the noted French botanist who discovered it in Central America in the late 1600s. Plumeria come in shades of white, yellow, pink, red, and orange. The hearty, plentiful blossoms are frequently used in lei.

HUMPBACK WHALES
Each year, North Pacific humpback whales make the long journey to Hawaii from Alaska. With its warm waters, Hawaii's shores provide the ideal place for the marine mammals to mate, birth, and nurse their young. They arrive between November and May, and their presence is an anticipated event for many. You can see them up close during whale-watching boat tours.

GARDENIA
The gardenia is a favorite for lei makers because of its sweet smell. The plant is native to tropical regions throughout China and Africa, but there are also endemic gardenia in Hawaii. The nanu gardenia are found only in the Islands and have petite white blossoms.

HONU
The honu, or Hawaiian green sea turtle, is a magical sight. The graceful reptile is an endangered and protected species in Hawaii. It's easier to run across honu during a snorkeling or scuba diving excursion, but they occasionally can be spotted coming to the ocean's surface.

MONK SEAL

Known as the *ilio holo I ka uaua*, or, "dog that runs in rough water," monk seals are endemic to Hawaii and critically endangered. Most of these mammals, which can grow more than seven feet long and weigh more than 600 pounds, live in remote, uninhabited Northwestern Hawaiian Islands.

TROPICAL FISH

Approximately 25% of the fish species in the Islands are endemic. Snorkeling in Hawaii is a unique, fun opportunity to see colorful fish, big and small. Interestingly, Hawaii's state fish, the tongue-twister *humuhumunukunukuapuaa*, or reef trigger, is not endemic to the state.

NENE GOOSE

Pronounced *nay-nay*, the endemic nene goose (the state bird) is the rarest in the world. Thanks to preservation efforts, the goose, which is a descendent of the Canadian goose, has been bred back from the edge of extinction and reintroduced into the wild.

HIBISCUS

In 1923, the Territory of Hawaii passed a law designating hibiscus as Hawaii's official flower. While there are more than 30 introduced species of the large, colorful flowers throughout the Islands, there are five endemic types. In Hawaiian, the endemic hibiscus has yellow blossoms and is known as mao hau hele, which means the "traveling green tree."

PIKAKE

These small, delicate blossoms are known for their hypnotic sweet scent. The jasmine flower was introduced from India and was a favorite of Princess Kaiulani. Pikake, which is the Hawaiian word for the blossom as well as peacock—another favorite of the princess—is the subject of many mele or Hawaiian songs.

What to Eat and Drink in Hawaii

SHAVE ICE
Shave ice is simple in its composition—fluffy ice drizzled in Technicolor syrups. Shave ice traces its roots to Hawaii's plantation past. Japanese laborers would use the machetes from their field work to finely shave ice from large frozen blocks and then pour fruit juice over it.

MUSUBI
Musubi are Hawaii's answer to the perfect snack. Portable, handheld, and salty, musubi are a great go-to any time of day. The local comfort food is a slice of Spam encased in packed white rice and snugly wrapped with nori, or dried seaweed. Available everywhere, musubi are usually just a few dollars.

MAI TAI
When people think of a Hawaiian cocktail, the colorful Mai Tai often comes to mind. It's the unofficial drink to imbibe at a luau and refreshingly tropical. This potent concoction has a rum base and is traditionally made with orange curaçao, orgeat, fresh squeezed lime juice, and simple syrup.

HAWAIIAN PLATE
The Hawaiian plate comprises the delicious, traditional foods of Hawaii, all on one heaping plate. You can find these combo meals anywhere from roadside lunch wagons to five-star restaurants. Get yours with the melt-in-your-mouth shredded kalua pig, pork, or chicken *laulau* (cooked in ti leaves) with *lomi* salmon (diced salmon with tomatoes and onions) on the side and the coconut-milk haupia for dessert. Most Hawaiian plates come with the requisite two scoops of white rice. Don't forget to try *poi*, or pounded and cooked taro. For an authentic plate, visit Helena's Hawaiian Food on Oahu; just be sure to get there early.

POKE
In Hawaiian, *poke* is a verb that means to slice and cut into pieces. It perfectly describes the technique Hawaiians have used for centuries to prepare poke the dish. The cubed raw fish, most commonly ahi, or tuna, is traditionally tossed with Hawaiian sea salt, imu kohu, seaweed, inamona, or crushed, roasted kukui nuts. Today, there are countless varieties of poke across the Islands. It's a must try when visiting Hawaii. On Oahu, Ono Seafood, a no-frills, take-out eatery serves made-to-order poke.

MANAPUA
When *kamaaina*, or Hawaii residents, are invited to a potluck, business meeting, or even an impromptu party, you'll inevitably see a box filled with manapua.

Poke

Inside these airy white buns are pockets of sweet char siu pork. Head to Oahu's Chinatown in Honolulu, and you'll find Chinese restaurants with manapua on their menus, as well as manapua take-out places serving a variety of fillings. There's sweet potato, curry chicken, *lup cheong* (or Chinese sausage), even sweet flavors such as custard and ube, a purple yam popular in Filipino desserts.

SAIMIN

This only-in-Hawaii noodle dish is the culinary innovation of Hawaii plantation workers in the late 1800s who created a new comfort food with ingredients and traditions from their home countries.

MALASADA

Malasadas are a beloved treat in Hawaii. The Portuguese pastries are about the size of a baseball and are airy, deep-fried, and dusted with sugar. In Honolulu, on Oahu, Lenard's Bakery is a well-known purveyor of these delicious desserts.

LOCO MOCO

Loco moco is one of Hawaii's classic comfort-food dishes. The traditional loco moco consists of white rice topped with a hamburger patty and fried eggs and generously blanketed in rich, brown gravy. Cafe 100 in Hilo on Hawaii Island is renowned as the home of the loco moco. The 74-year-old café's original loco moco is one of the most popular, and at the amazing price of $4.35.

KONA COFFEE

In Kona, on Hawaii Island, coffee reigns supreme. There are roughly 600 coffee farms dotting the west side of the island, each producing flavorful coffee grown in the rich, volcanic soil. Kona coffee is typically harvested from August to December.

What to Buy in Hawaii

LEI
As a visitor to Hawaii, you will likely receive a lei, either a shell, kukui nut, or the fragrant flower variety, as a welcome to the Islands. Kamaaina or Hawaii residents mark special occasions by gifting lei.

MACADAMIA NUT CANDY
Macadamia are native to Australia, but the gumball-sized nut remains an important crop in Hawaii. It was first introduced in the late 1880s as a windbreak for sugar cane crops. Today, mac nuts, as they are colloquially known, are a popular local food, especially in desserts. They are easily found at convenience and grocery stores.

LAUHALA
The hala tree is most known for its long, thin leaves and the masterful crafts that are created from them. Lauhala weavers make baskets, hats, mats, jewelry, and more, using intricate patterns.

JEWELRY
Island-inspired jewelry is a unique and personalized gift. There are several styles from which to choose, including pieces featuring Tahitian pearls, shells like the dainty orange and pink sunrise shell, and gold Hawaiian heirloom necklaces and bangles with black Old English lettering.

ALOHA WEAR
Aloha wear in Hawaii has come a long way from the cheap fabrics with the too bright and kitsch patterns (although those still exist). Local designers have been creating stylish, modern Aloha shirts, dresses, and more with soft, sleek prints that evoke Island botanicals, heritage, and tradition. Hawaii residents sport Aloha wear for everything from work to weddings.

KONA COFFEE
Reminiscence about your wonderful Hawaii getaway each time you brew a cup of Kona coffee. Authentic Kona coffee is renowned throughout the world for its heady aroma and full-bodied flavor. Stores and cafés sell bags of varying sizes.

HAWAIIAN SEA SALT
A long tradition of harvesting salt beds by hand continues today on the islands of Kauai and Molokai. The salt comes in various colors, including inky black and brick red; these distinctive colors come from the salt reacting and mixing with activated charcoal and alaea, or volcanic clay.

BIG ISLAND HONEY
With its temperate climate and bountiful foliage, honeybees love Hawaii. The island's unique ecosystem results in robust honey flavors, including the nutty macadamia nut blossom honey or the ohia lehua variety, made from the endemic tree.

UKULELE
In Hawaiian, *ukulele* means "the jumping flea." The small instrument made its way to the Islands in the 1880s via Portuguese immigrants who brought with them the four-string, guitar-like machete. It is renowned as a solo instrument today, with artists like Jake Shimabukuro and Taimane Gardner popularizing it.

KOA WOOD
If you're looking for an heirloom keepsake from the Islands, consider a Koa wood product. Grown only in Hawaii, the valuable Koa wood is some of the world's rarest and hardest wood. Hawaiians traditionally made surfboards and canoes from Koa trees.

What to Read and Watch

HAWAIIAN MYTHOLOGY, BY MARTHA BECKWITH

This exhaustive work of ethnology and folklore was researched and collected by Martha Beckwith over decades and published when she was 69. *Hawaiian Mythology* is a comprehensive look at the Hawaiian ancestral deities and their importance throughout history.

HAWAII'S STORY BY HAWAII'S QUEEN, BY LILIUOKALANI

This poignant book, by Queen Liliuokalani, chronicles the 1893 overthrow of the Hawaiian monarchy and her plea for her people. It's an essential read to understand the political undercurrent and the push for sovereignty that exists in the Islands more than 125 years later.

MARK TWAIN'S LETTERS FROM HAWAII, BY MARK TWAIN

When Samuel Clemens was 31 in 1866, he sailed from California and spent four months in Hawaii. He eventually mailed 25 letters to the *Sacramento Union* newspaper about his experiences. Along the way, Twain sheds some cultural biases as he visits the Kilauea volcano, meets with Hawaii's newly formed legislators, and examines the sugar trade.

SHOAL OF TIME: A HISTORY OF THE HAWAIIAN ISLANDS, BY GAVAN DAWS

Perhaps the most popular book of this best-selling Honolulu author is *Shoal of Time*. Published in 1974, this account of modern Hawaiian history details the colonization of Hawaii and everything that was lost in the process.

MOLOKAI, BY ALAN BRENNERT

Alan Brennert's debut novel, set in the 1890s, follows a Hawaiian woman who contracts leprosy as a child and is sent to the remote, quarantined community of Kalaupapa on the island of Molokai where she then lives. The Southern California–based author was inspired to write the book during his visits to Hawaii.

THE DESCENDANTS

Based on the book by local author, Kaui Hart Hemmings, the film adaptation starring George Clooney and directed by Alexander Payne was filmed on Oahu and Kauai. It spotlights a contemporary, if not upper-class, family in Hawaii as they deal with family grief and landholdings in flux.

50 FIRST DATES

The majority of this 2004 Drew Barrymore–Adam Sandler rom-com was shot on Oahu. While the plot is simultaneously cute and cheesy, *50 First Dates* highlights the beauty of Hawaii. You can pick out several picturesque island places, including the rolling Kualoa Ranch and Waimanalo, Makapuu, and Kaneohe Bay, all on Oahu's rustic east side.

BLUE HAWAII

The 1961 musical features the hip-shaking songs and moves by Elvis Presley, who plays tour guide Chadwick Gates. Elvis famously sings *Ke Kali Nei Au*, or *The Hawaiian Wedding Song*, at the iconic and now-shuttered Coco Palms Resort on Kauai. (The resort has remained closed since 1992 following Hurricane Iniki.)

MOANA

The release of *Moana* in 2016 was celebrated by many in Hawaii and the Pacific for showcasing Polynesian culture. The now-beloved animated movie, which includes the story of the demigod Maui, features the voice talents of Aulii Cravalho and Dwayne Johnson. In 2018, *Moana* was re-recorded and distributed in Olelo Hawaii, or the Hawaiian language, with Cravalho reprising her role. It marked the first time a Disney movie was available in Hawaiian.

Kids and Families

CHOOSING A PLACE TO STAY

Resorts: The Kauai Marriott Resort is a good choice on the East Side, and on the South Shore both the Grand Hyatt Kauai and Sheraton Kauai Resort have kids' programs. North Shore hotel guests can take their *keiki* (children) to the Anaina Hou Community Park playground, located behind the mini-golf course on the main highway just outside Kilauea.

Condos: Condo rentals are a fantastic value for families. On the North Shore, there are numerous condo resort choices in Princeville, including Hanalei Bay Resort, with eight tennis courts and two pools. On the South Shore, Outrigger Kiahuna Plantation is a family favorite, with an excellent location that includes a swimmable beach adjacent to a grassy field great for picnics.

Transit Vacation Rentals (TVRs): The new kids on the block are rentals in homelike dwellings licensed for tourism. These rentals, and others that are "under the table," have in essence created another resort area along the North Shore—think private home with exclusive beach access. Make sure your renter is operating legally before paying.

OCEAN ACTIVITIES

On the Beach: There are several beaches in Kauai that are nearly as safe as a pool—Anini Beach near the boat ramp and Hanalei Beach Park on the North Shore, Lydgate State Park and Kalapaki Beach on the East Side, Poipu Beach Park on the South Shore, and Salt Pond Beach Park on the West Side.

On the Waves: Surf lessons are a great idea for older kids, especially if Mom and Dad want a little quiet time. The Blue Seas Surfing School is best for beginners, and you can book you or your kids a private 1½-hour lesson for $75.

The Underwater World: If your kids are ready to try snorkeling, Kauai is a great place to introduce them to the underwater world. Get your kids used to the basics at Lydgate State Park on the island's East Side, where there's no threat of a current. On its guided snorkel tours, SeaFun Kauai will show kids of all ages how to identify marine life and gives great beginner instruction.

LAND ACTIVITIES

On the North Shore, kids will love Na Aina Kai, a garden with a 16-foot-tall Jack and the Beanstalk bronze sculpture, gecko maze, tree house, kid-size train, and tropical jungle, and on the East Side is Smith's Tropical Paradise, a 30-acre botanical garden.

Horseback riding is a popular family activity, and most of the tours on Kauai move slowly, so no riding experience is required.

ATV tours are the activity of choice when it rains. Try Kauai ATV Tours, which has two-passenger "Mud Bugs" to accommodate families with kids ages five and older.

AFTER DARK

At night, younger kids get a kick out of luau, and many shows incorporate young audience members. Older kids might find it all a bit lame, but there are a handful of new shows in the Islands that are more modern, incorporating acrobats, lively music, and fire dancers. If you're planning on hitting a luau with a teen in tow, we highly recommend going the modern route—try Luau Kalamaku in Lihue. The best luau for young kids on Kauai is Smith's Tropical Paradise, in Wailua. A tram tour takes families through the botanical garden before dinner, and the show starts with some high-tech pyrotechnics.

Weddings and Honeymoons

There's no question that Hawaii is one of the country's foremost honeymoon destinations. Romance is in the air here, and the white, sandy beaches, turquoise water, swaying palm trees, balmy tropical breezes, and brilliant sunshine put people in the mood for love. So it goes without saying that Kauai has also become a popular wedding destination, especially as new resorts and hotels entice visitors, and same-sex marriage is legal. Once the knot is tied, why not stay for the honeymoon?

THE BIG DAY

Choosing the Perfect Place. You really have two choices to make: the ceremony location and where to have the reception. For the former, Kauai boasts stunning beaches, sea-hugging bluffs, gardens, private residences, resort lawns, and, of course, places of worship. As for the reception, there are these same choices, as well as restaurants and even a luau. If you decide to go outdoors, make sure to have a backup plan for inclement weather.

Finding a Wedding Planner. If you're planning to invite more than an officiant and your loved one to your wedding ceremony, seriously consider a Kauai wedding planner who can help select a location, design the floral scheme, and recommend a florist and photographer. They can also plan the menu and choose a restaurant, caterer, or resort, and suggest any Hawaiian traditions to incorporate into your ceremony.

Getting Your License. There's no waiting period in Hawaii, no residency or citizenship requirements, and no required blood test or shots. You can apply and pay the fee online; however, both partners must appear together in person before a marriage-license agent to receive the marriage license (the permit to get married) at the State Department of Health in Lihue. You'll need proof of age—the

legal age to marry is 18. Upon approval, a marriage license is immediately issued and costs $60. After the ceremony, your officiant will mail the marriage certificate to the state. Approximately four months later, you will receive a copy in the mail. For more detailed information, visit ⊕ *marriage.ehawaii.gov.*

Also—this is important—the person performing your wedding must be licensed by the Hawaii Department of Health, even if he or she is a licensed officiant. Be sure to ask.

Wedding Attire. In Hawaii, basically anything goes, from long, formal dresses with trains to white bikinis. For men, a pair of solid-colored slacks with a nice aloha shirt is appropriate. If you're planning a wedding on the beach, barefoot is the way to go.

Local Customs. The most obvious traditional Hawaiian wedding custom is the lei exchange, in which the bride and groom take turns placing a lei around the neck of the other—with a kiss. Bridal lei are usually floral, whereas the groom's is typically made of *maile,* a green leafy garland. Brides often also wear a *lei poo,* a circular floral headpiece.

THE HONEYMOON

Do you want champagne and strawberries delivered to your room each morning? A breathtaking swimming pool in which to float? A five-star restaurant in which to dine? Then a resort is the way to go. A small inn is also good if you're on a tight budget or don't plan to spend much time in your room. The lodging accommodations are almost as plentiful as the beaches.

HAWAIIAN CULTURAL TRADITIONS HULA, LEI, AND LUAU

HULA: MORE THAN A FOLK DANCE

Hula has been called "the heartbeat of the Hawaiian people" and also "the world's best-known, most misunderstood dance." Both are true. Hula isn't just dance. It is storytelling.

Chanter Edith McKinzie calls it "an extension of a piece of poetry." In its adornments, implements, and customs, hula integrates every important Hawaiian cultural practice: poetry, history, genealogy, craft, plant cultivation, martial arts, religion, protocol. So when 19th-century Christian missionaries sought to eradicate a practice they considered depraved, they threatened more than just a folk dance.

With public performance outlawed and private hula practice discouraged, hula went underground for a generation. The fragile verbal link by which culture was transmitted from teacher to student hung by a thread. Even increasing literacy did not help because hula's practitioners were a secretive and protected circle.

As if that weren't bad enough, vaudeville, Broadway, and Hollywood got hold of the hula, giving it the glitz treatment in an unbroken line from "Oh, How She Could Wicky Wacky Woo" to "Rock-A-Hula Baby." Hula became shorthand for paradise: fragrant flowers, lazy hours. Ironically, this development assured that hundreds of Hawaiians could make a living performing and teaching hula. Many danced *auana* (modern form) in performance; but taught *kahiko* (traditional), quietly, at home or in hula schools.

Today, decades after the cultural revival known as the Hawaiian Renaissance, language immersion programs have assured a new generation of proficient chanters, songwriters, and translators. Visitors can see more, and more authentic, traditional hula than at any other time in the last 200 years.

Like the culture of which it is the beating heart, hula has survived.

Lei *poo*. Head lei. In *kahiko*, greenery only. In auana, flowers.

Face emotes appropriate expression. Dancer should not be a smiling automaton.

Shoulders remain relaxed and still, never hunched, even with arms raised. No bouncing.

Eyes always follow leading hand.

Lei. Hula is rarely performed without a shoulder lei.

Traditional hula skirt is loose fabric, smocked and gathered at the waist.

Arms and hands remain loose, relaxed, below shoulder level—except as required by interpretive movements.

Hip is canted over weight-bearing foot.

Knees are always slightly bent, accentuating hip sway.

Kupee. Ankle bracelet of flowers, shells, or foliage.

In kahiko, feet are flat. In auana, they may be more arched, but not tiptoes or bouncing.

BASIC MOTIONS

Speak or Sing

Moon or Sun

Grass Shack or House

Mountains or Heights

Love or Caress

At backyard parties, hula is performed in bare feet and street clothes, but in performance, adornments play a key role, as do rhythm-keeping implements such as the pahu drum and the *ipu* (gourd).

In hula *kahiko* (traditional style), the usual dress is multiple layers of stiff fabric (often with a pellom lining, which most closely resembles *kapa*, the paperlike bark cloth of the Hawaiians). These wrap tightly around the bosom but flare below the waist to form a skirt. In pre-contact times, dancers wore only kapa skirts. Men traditionally wear loincloths.

Monarchy-period hula is performed in voluminous muumuu or high-necked muslin blouses and gathered skirts. Men wear white or gingham shirts and black pants.

In hula *auana* (modern), dress for women can range from grass skirts and strapless tops to contemporary tea-length dresses. Men generally wear aloha shirts, but sometimes grass skirts over pants or even everyday gear.

SURPRISING HULA FACTS

■ Grass skirts are not traditional; workers from Kiribati (the Gilbert Islands) brought this custom to Hawaii.

■ In olden-day Hawaii, *mele* (songs) for hula were composed for every occasion—name songs for babies, dirges for funerals, welcome songs for visitors, celebrations of favorite pursuits.

■ Hula *mai* is a traditional hula form in praise of a noble's genitals; the power of the *alii* (royalty) to procreate gave mana (spiritual power) to the entire culture.

■ Hula students in old Hawaii adhered to high standards: scrupulous cleanliness, no sex, daily cleansing rituals, certain food prohibitions, and no contact with the dead. They were fined if they broke the rules.

WHERE TO WATCH

If you're interested in "the real thing," there are annual hula festivals on each island. Check the individual island visitors' bureaus websites at ⊕ *www.gohawaii.com*.

If you can't make it to a festival, there are plenty of other hula shows—at most resorts, many lounges, and even at certain shopping centers. Ask your hotel concierge for performance information.

ALL ABOUT LEI

Lei brighten every occasion in Hawaii, from birthdays to bar mitzvahs to baptisms. Creative artisans weave nature's bounty—flowers, ferns, vines, and seeds—into gorgeous creations that convey an array of heartfelt messages: "Welcome," "Congratulations," "Good luck," "Farewell," "Thank you," "I love you." When it's difficult to find the right words, a lei expresses exactly the right sentiment.

WHERE TO BUY THE BEST LEI

Most airports in Hawaii have lei stands where you can buy a fragrant garland upon arrival. Every florist shop in the Islands sells lei; you can also treat yourself to a lei while shopping for provisions at any supermarket or box store. And you'll always find lei sellers at crafts fairs and outdoor festivals.

LEI ETIQUETTE

■ To wear a closed lei, drape it over your shoulders, half in front and half in back. Open lei are worn around the neck, with the ends draped over the front in equal lengths.

■ Pikake, ginger, and other sweet, delicate blossoms are "feminine" lei. Men opt for cigar, crown flower, and ti leaf lei, which are sturdier and don't emit as much fragrance.

■ Lei are always presented with a kiss, a custom that supposedly dates back to World War II when a hula dancer fancied an officer at a U.S.O. show. Taking a dare from members of her troupe, she took off her lei, placed it around his neck, and kissed him on the cheek.

■ You shouldn't wear a lei before you give it to someone else. Hawaiians believe the lei absorbs your mana (spirit); if you give your lei away, you'll be giving away part of your essence.

ORCHID

Growing wild on every continent except Antarctica, orchids—which range in color from yellow to green to purple—comprise the largest family of plants in the world. There are more than 20,000 species of orchids, but only three are native to Hawaii—and they are very rare. The pretty lavender vanda you see hanging by the dozens at local lei stands has probably been imported from Thailand.

MAILE

Maile, an endemic twining vine with a heady aroma, is sacred to Laka, goddess of the hula. In ancient times, dancers wore maile and decorated hula altars with it to honor Laka. Today, "open" maile lei usually are given to men. Instead of ribbon, interwoven lengths of maile are used at dedications of new businesses. The maile is untied, never snipped, for doing so would symbolically "cut" the company's success.

ILIMA

Designated by Hawaii's Territorial Legislature in 1923 as the official flower of the island of Oahu, the golden ilima is so delicate it lasts for just a day. Five to seven hundred blossoms are needed to make one garland. Queen Emma, wife of King Kamehameha IV, preferred ilima over all other lei, which may have led to the incorrect belief that they were reserved only for royalty.

PLUMERIA

This ubiquitous flower is named after Charles Plumier, the noted French botanist who discovered it in Central America in the late 1600s. Plumeria ranks among the most popular lei in Hawaii because it's fragrant, hardy, plentiful, inexpensive, and requires very little care. Although yellow is the most common color, you'll also find plumeria lei in shades of pink, red, orange, and "rainbow" blends.

PIKAKE

Favored for its fragile beauty and sweet scent, pikake was introduced from India. In lieu of pearls, many brides in Hawaii adorn themselves with long, multiple strands of white pikake. Princess Kaiulani enjoyed showing guests her beloved pikake and peacocks at Ainahau, her Waikiki home. Interestingly, pikake is the Hawaiian word for both the bird and the blossom.

KUKUI

The kukui (candlenut) is Hawaii's state tree. Early Hawaiians strung kukui nuts (which are quite oily) together and burned them for light; mixed burned nuts with oil to make an indelible dye; and mashed roasted nuts to consume as a laxative. Kukui nut lei may not have been made until after Western contact, when the Hawaiians saw black beads from Europe and wanted to imitate them.

LUAU: A TASTE OF HAWAII

The best place to sample Hawaiian food is at a backyard luau. Aunts and uncles are cooking, the pig is from a cousin's farm, and the fish is from a brother's boat.

But even locals have to angle for invitations to those rare occasions. So your choice is most likely between a commercial luau and a Hawaiian restaurant.

Some commercial luau are less authentic; they offer little of the traditional diet and are more about umbrella drinks, spectacle, and fun.

For greater culinary authenticity, folksy experiences, and rock-bottom prices, visit a Hawaiian restaurant (most are in anonymous storefronts in residential neighborhoods). Expect rough edges and some effort negotiating the menu.

In either case, much of what is known today as Hawaiian food would be as foreign to a 16th-century Hawaiian as risotto or chow mien. The pre-contact diet was simple and healthy—mainly raw and steamed seafood and vegetables. Early Hawaiians used earth ovens and heated stones to cook seafood, taro, sweet potatoes, and breadfruit and seasoned their food with sea salt and ground kukui nuts. Seaweed, fern shoots, sweet potato vines, coconut, banana, sugarcane, and select greens and roots rounded out the diet.

Successive waves of immigrants added their favorites to the ti leaf–lined table. So it is that foods as disparate as salt salmon and chicken long rice are now Hawaiian—even though there is no salmon in Hawaiian waters and long rice (cellophane noodles) is Chinese.

AT THE LUAU: KALUA PORK

The heart of any luau is the *imu*, the earth oven in which a whole pig is roasted. The preparation of an imu is an arduous affair for most families, who tackle it only once a year or so, for a baby's first birthday or at Thanksgiving, when many Islanders prefer to imu their turkeys. Commercial luau operations have it down to a science, however.

THE ART OF THE STONE

The key to a proper imu is the *pohaku*, the stones. Imu cook by means of long, slow, moist heat released by special stones that can withstand a hot fire without exploding. Many Hawaiian families treasure their imu stones, keeping them in a pile in the backyard and passing them on through generations.

PIT COOKING

The imu makers first dig a pit about the size of a refrigerator, then lay down *kiawe* (mesquite) wood and stones, and build a white-hot fire that is allowed to burn itself out. The ashes are raked away, and the hot stones covered with banana and ti leaves. Well-wrapped in ti or banana leaves and a net of chicken wire, the pig is lowered onto the leaf-covered stones. Laulau (leaf-wrapped bundles of meats, fish, and taro leaves) may also be placed inside. Leaves—ti, banana, even ginger—cover the pig followed by wet burlap sacks (to create steam). The whole is topped with a canvas tarp and left to steam for the better part of a day.

OPENING THE IMU

This is the moment everyone waits for: The imu is unwrapped like a giant present and the imu keepers gingerly wrestle out the steaming pig. When it's unwrapped, the meat falls moist and smoky-flavored from the bone, looking just like Southern-style pulled pork, but without the barbecue sauce.

WHICH LUAU?

Most resort hotels have luau on their grounds that include hula, music, and, of course, lots of food and drink. Each island also has at least one "authentic" luau. For lists of the best luau on each island, visit the Hawaii Visitors and Convention Bureau website at ⊕ *www. gohawaii.com.*

MEA AI ONO:
GOOD THINGS TO EAT.

LAULAU
Steamed meats, fish, and taro leaf in ti-leaf bundles: fork-tender, a medley of flavors; the taro resembles spinach.

LOMI LOMI SALMON
Salt salmon in a piquant salad or relish with onions and tomatoes.

POI
Poi, a paste made of pounded taro root, may be an acquired taste, but it's a must-try during your visit.

Consider: The Hawaiian Adam is descended from *kalo* (taro). Young taro plants are called "keiki"–children. Poi is the first food after mother's milk for many Islanders. Ai, the word for food, is synonymous with poi in many contexts.

Not only that, we love it. "There is no meat that doesn't taste good with poi," the old Hawaiians said.

But you have to know how to eat it: with something rich or powerfully flavored. "It is salt that makes the poi go in," is another adage. When you're served poi, try it with a mouthful of smoky kalua pork or salty lomi lomi salmon. Its slightly sour blandness cleanses the palate. And if you don't like it, smile and say something polite. (And slide that bowl over to a local.)

Laulau

Lomi Lomi Salmon

Poi

E HELE MAI AI! COME AND EAT!

Local-style Hawaiian restaurants tend to be inconveniently located in well-worn storefronts with little or no parking, outfitted with battered tables and clattering Melmac dishes, but they personify aloha, invariably run by local families who welcome tourists who take the trouble to find them.

Many are cash-only operations and combination plates, known as "plate lunch," are a standard feature: one or two entrées, two scoops of steamed rice, one scoop of macaroni salad, and—if the place is really old-style—a tiny portion of coarse Hawaiian salt and some raw onions for relish.

Most serve some foods that aren't, strictly speaking, Hawaiian, but are beloved of kamaaina, such as salt meat with watercress (preserved meat in a tasty broth), or *akubone* (skipjack tuna fried in a tangy vinegar sauce).

The History of Hawaii

Hawaiian history is long and complex; a brief survey can put into context the ongoing renaissance of native arts and culture.

THE POLYNESIANS

Long before both Christopher Columbus and the Vikings, Polynesian seafarers set out to explore the vast stretches of the open ocean in double-hulled canoes. From western Polynesia, they traveled back and forth between Samoa, Fiji, Tahiti, the Marquesas, and the Society Isles, settling on the outer reaches of the Pacific, Hawaii, and Easter Island as early as AD 300. The golden era of Polynesian voyaging peaked around AD 1200, after which the distant Hawaiian Islands were left to develop their own unique cultural practices and subsistence in relative isolation.

The Islands' symbiotic society was deeply intertwined with religion, mythology, science, and artistry. Ruled by an *alii*, or chief, each settlement was nestled in an *ahupuaa*, a pie-shape land division from the uplands where the alii lived, through the valleys and down to the shores where the commoners resided. Everyone contributed, whether it was by building canoes, catching fish, making tools, or farming land.

A UNITED KINGDOM

When the British explorer Captain James Cook arrived in 1778, he was revered as a god. With guns and ammunition purchased from Cook, the Big Island chief, Kamehameha the Great, gained a significant advantage over the other alii. He united Hawaii into one kingdom in 1810, bringing an end to the frequent interisland battles that dominated Hawaiian life.

Tragically, the new kingdom was beset with troubles. Native religion was abandoned, and *kapu* (laws and regulations) were eventually abolished. The European explorers brought foreign diseases with them, and within a few short decades the Native Hawaiian population was decimated.

New laws regarding land ownership and religious practices eroded the underpinnings of precontact Hawaii. Each successor to the Hawaiian throne sacrificed more control over the island kingdom. As Westerners permeated Hawaiian culture, Hawaii became more riddled with layers of racial issues, injustice, and social unrest.

MODERN HAWAII

In 1893, the last Hawaiian monarch, Queen Liliuokalani, was overthrown by a group of Americans and European businessmen and government officials, aided by an armed militia. This led to the creation of the Republic of Hawaii, and it became a U.S. territory for the next 60 years. The loss of Hawaiian sovereignty and the conditions of annexation have haunted the Hawaiian people since the monarchy was deposed.

Pearl Harbor was attacked in 1941, which pulled the United States immediately into World War II. Tourism, from its beginnings in the early 1900s, flourished after the war and naturally inspired rapid real estate development in Waikiki. In 1959, Hawaii officially became the 50th state. Statehood paved the way for Hawaiians to participate in the American democratic process, which was not universally embraced by Hawaiians. With the rise of the civil rights movement in the 1960s, Hawaiians began to reclaim their own identity, from language to hula.

Chapter 2

TRAVEL SMART

Updated by
Charles E. Roessler

★ **CAPITAL:**
Honolulu (capital of Hawaii)

👤 **POPULATION:**
73,000

💬 **LANGUAGE:**
Hawaiian and English

$ **CURRENCY:**
USD

☎ **AREA CODE:**
808

⚠ **EMERGENCIES:**
911

🚗 **DRIVING:**
On the right

⚡ **ELECTRICITY:**
120-220 v/60 cycles; plugs
have two or three rectangu-
lar prongs

🕐 **TIME:**
Five hours behind New York;
six during daylight saving
time

🌐 **WEB RESOURCES:**
gohawaii.com
dlnr.hawaii.gov
kauai.com

✈ **AIRPORT:**
LIH

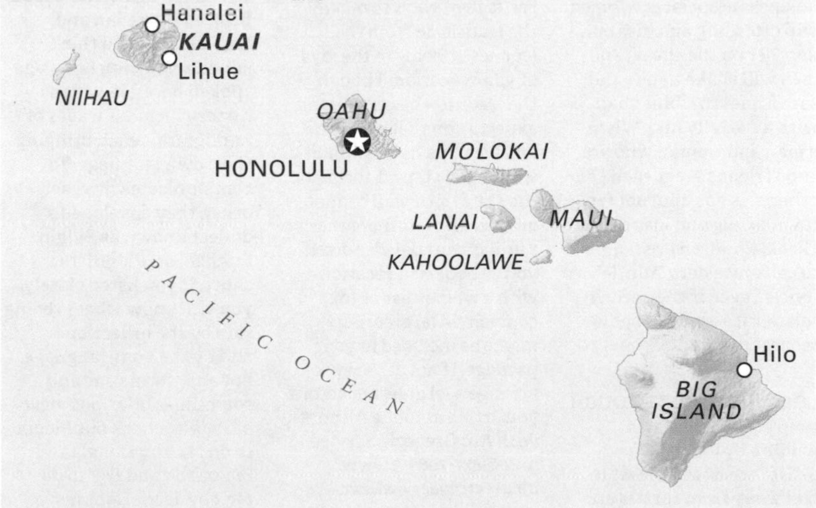

Hanalei
KAUAI
Lihue

NIIHAU

OAHU
⭐
HONOLULU

MOLOKAI

LANAI
MAUI

KAHOOLAWE

P A C I F I C   O C E A N

Hilo
*BIG
ISLAND*

Know Before You Go

Do they really hand you a lei when you arrive? What are some common Hawaiian phrases? Is swimming at the beaches safe? How about the water quality? Traveling to Kauai is an easy adventure, but we've got tips to make your trip seamless and more meaningful. Below are all the answers to FAQs about Kauai and Hawaii.

DON'T CALL IT "THE STATES"

Hawaii was admitted to the Union in 1959, so residents can be somewhat sensitive when visitors refer to their own hometowns as "back in the States." Instead, refer to the contiguous 48 states as "the mainland." When you do, you won't appear to be such a *malihini* (newcomer).

WELCOME ISLAND-STYLE GREETINGS

Hawaii is a friendly place, and this is reflected in the day-to-day encounters with friends, family, and even business associates. Women will often hug and kiss one another on the cheek, and men will shake hands and sometimes combine that with a friendly hug. When a man and woman who are good friends greet each other, it is not unusual for them to hug and kiss on the cheek. Children are taught to call any elders "auntie" or "uncle," even if they aren't related; it's a way to show respect.

LOOK, BUT DON'T TOUCH

Help protect Hawaii's wildlife by loving it from a distance. Stay at least 10 feet away from turtles and 100 feet from monk seals, wherever you encounter them. Though they may not look it, coral are alive and fragile; harming them also harms the habitat for reef fish and other marine life. Avoid touching or stepping on coral, and take extra care when entering and exiting the water.

ENJOY A FRESH FLOWER LEI

When you walk off a long flight, nothing quite compares with a Hawaiian lei greeting. The casual ceremony ranks as one of the fastest ways to make the transition from the worries of home to the joys of your vacation. Though the tradition has created an expectation that everyone receives this floral garland when they step off the plane, the state of Hawaii cannot greet each of its more than 8 million annual visitors. If you've booked a vacation with a wholesaler or tour company, a lei greeting might be included in your package. If not, it's easy to arrange a lei greeting before you arrive at Lihue Airport with Alii Greeting Service ☎ *808-877-7088* ⊕ *www. aliigreetingservice.com*. A plumeria lei is considered standard and costs about $25 per person. You can also tuck a single flower behind your ear; a flower behind the left ear means you are in a relationship or unavailable, while the right ear indicates you are looking for love.

APPRECIATE THE HAWAIIAN LANGUAGE

While Hawaiian and English are both official state languages, the latter is used widely. Making the effort to learn some Hawaiian words can be rewarding, however. Hawaiian words you are most likely to encounter during your visit to the Islands are *aloha* (hello and good-bye), *mahalo* (thank you), *keiki* (child), *haole* (Caucasian or foreigner), *mauka* (toward the mountains), *makai* (toward the ocean), and *pau* (finished, all done). If you'd like to learn more Hawaiian words, check out ⊕ *www. wehewehe.org*.

LISTEN FOR HAWAII'S UNOFFICIAL LANGUAGE

Besides Hawaiian and English, there's a third (albeit unofficial) language spoken here. Hawaiian history includes waves of immigrants, each bringing their own language. To communicate with each other, they developed a dialect known as Pidgin English, or "Pidgin" for short. If you listen closely, you will know what is being said by the inflections and by the body language. For an informative and sometimes hilarious view of Pidgin, check out *Pidgin to da Max* by Douglas Simonson and *Fax to da Max* by Jerry Hopkins.

Both are available at most local bookstores in the Hawaiiana sections and at variety stores. While it's nice to appreciate this unique language, it's not wise to emulate it, as it can be considered disrespectful.

BE MINDFUL OF LOCAL CUSTOMS

If you've been invited to the home of friends living in Hawaii (an ultimate compliment), bring a small gift and take off your shoes when you enter their house. Try to take part in a cultural festival during your stay in the Islands; there is no better way to get a glimpse of Hawaii's ethnic mosaic.

CHECK THE WEATHER

Kauai's environment can change in an instant, and with little or no warning. Strong ocean currents, flash floods (like those that ravaged the North Shore in 2018), and rockslides are a real threat, especially during extreme weather events. If you're hiking, you'll want to check wind and rain conditions. Hurricane season runs from June to November.

SWIMMING ISN'T ALWAYS SAFE

Unfortunately, Kauai has the highest drowning rate in the state due to rocky shores, big waves, wind, and unseen rip currents. Even strong swimmers should stick to beaches with a lifeguard who knows the local currents and tides. Be particularly cautious and always check conditions before you head out at ⊕ *hawaiibeachsafety.com/ kauai*.

THE WATER IS GREAT; THE FOOD IS OKAY

Kauai's tap water is highly rated as it is naturally filtered through volcanic rock and has no odd taste or odor. The food, however, is not on anyone's bucket list. It's all safe to eat, of course, but the typical island fare is nothing too fancy. Still, there are one-of-a-kind food trucks and local holes-in-the-wall, and you must try local *lau lau* (taro leaves and kalua pig) and *poke* (raw ahi tuna bowl).

PRICES ARE HIGHER HERE

Almost everything is shipped in to Kauai, meaning you'll see higher prices than you're used to at the grocery store. On the other hand, the local food is usually fresh and healthy, and you can always find the best deals by talking to a local.

STREET NAMES ARE RARELY USED

You're more likely to hear "Turn right at the Shell station" or "Turn *makai* (toward the ocean) at the big mango tree" rather than an address. It's best to have a clear idea where you are going before you take off. The town areas off the highway use incredibly complicated address-numbering systems, so be prepared, especially in developments like Princeville.

MIND YOUR (ROAD) MANNERS

It's a good policy not to pass another car on any of the roads as visibility is often diminished by the

ever-present guinea grass, an invasive weed that lines the roads and ruins many a vista. Most local drivers are courteous, and they appreciate the same from you. You might spot the iconic "Slow down, this ain't the mainland" bumper sticker. So, no tailgating, please.

CHICKENS ARE EVERYWHERE

Kauai's unofficial bird roams the island everywhere, all the time. They beg for food at the beach, jump onto your picnic table, and, most annoyingly for the tired traveler, start crowing before dawn.

RENEWABLE ENERGY IS A PRIORITY

Kauai shines a light for the rest of the state and the country as it speeds toward renewable energy independence. By 2019, the electricity co-op obtained 55% of its power from renewable solar and hydro energy, some days hitting 100%. The island's goal is to reach 100% renewable energy in two decades.

USE REEF-SAFE SUNSCREEN

Sunscreens containing oxybenzone and and octinoxate, ingredients that can harm coral reefs and marine ecosystems, are banned in Hawaii effective January 2021. Protect the environment—and your skin—by using a product that's certified marine safe, such as TropicSport.

Getting Here

Air

Flying time is about 10 hours from New York, 8 hours from Chicago, and 5 hours from Los Angeles.

Some of the major airline carriers serving Hawaii fly directly from the U.S. mainland to Kauai, allowing you to bypass connecting flights out of Honolulu. Although Lihue Airport is smaller and more casual than Honolulu International, it can also be quite busy during peak times.

Plants and plant products are subject to regulation by the Department of Agriculture, both on entering and leaving Hawaii. Upon leaving the Islands, you'll have to have your bags x-rayed and tagged at one of the airport's agricultural inspection stations before you proceed to check-in. Pineapples and coconuts with the packer's agricultural inspection stamp pass freely; papayas must be treated, inspected, and stamped. All other fruits are banned for export to the U.S. mainland. Flowers pass—except for gardenias, rose leaves, jade vine, and mauna loa. Also banned are insects, snails, soil, cotton, cacti, sugarcane, and all berry plants.

You'll have to leave dogs and other pets at home. A 120-day quarantine is imposed to keep out rabies, which is nonexistent in Hawaii. If specific pre- and post-arrival requirements are met, animals may qualify for a 30-day or 5-day-or-less quarantine.

AIRPORTS

On Kauai, visitors fly into Lihue Airport, on the East Side of the island. Visitor information booths are outside each baggage-claim area. Visitors will also find news- and lei stands, an HMS Host restaurant, and a Travel Traders gift shop at the airport.

For most domestic and international flights, however, Honolulu International Airport (HNL) is the main stopover. From Honolulu, there are interisland flights to Kauai departing regularly from early morning until evening. In addition, some carriers offer nonstop service directly from the U.S. mainland to Lihue Airport (LIH).

To travel interisland from Honolulu on Hawaiian Air you will depart from the connected interisland terminal. Southwest Airlines now flies out of Terminal 2, located in a separate structure adjacent to the main terminal building. A free bus service, the Wiki Wiki Shuttle, operates between terminals.

GROUND TRANSPORTATION

Marriott Kauai and Kauai Beach Resort provide airport shuttles to and from the Lihue Airport. In addition, travelers who've booked a tour with Kauai Island Tours, Roberts Hawaii, or Polynesian Adventure Tours will be picked up at the airport.

SpeediShuttle offers transportation between the airport and hotels, resorts, and time-share complexes on the island. There is an online reservation and fare quote system for information and bookings. Or, you can hire a taxi or limousine. Cabs are available curbside at baggage claim. Cab fares to locations around the island are estimated as follows: Poipu $35–$41, Wailua–Waipouli $17–$20, Lihue–Kukui Grove $10, Princeville–Haena $72–$95. Kauai Luxury Transportation and Tours offers service to Lihue Airport.

Uber and Lyft are somewhat recent arrivals on the island, but you can still expect to pay around $75–$80 for a ride from the airport to Princeville (approximately 30 miles).

FLIGHTS

Alaska Airlines has a daily Seattle–Lihue flight. American Airlines offers a daily, nonstop Los Angeles–Lihue flight, in addition to its service into Honolulu, Maui, and the Big Island. Delta has a Los Angeles–Lihue flight and also serves Oahu (Honolulu) and Maui. United Airlines provides direct service to Lihue Airport from Denver, Los Angeles, and San Francisco. The carrier also flies into Honolulu, Maui, and the Big Island. Hawaiian offers a daily, nonstop Los Angeles–Lihue flight; all other mainland flights require a connection in Honolulu except Southwest Airlines, which has limited direct flights to Lihue from Oakland.

INTERISLAND FLIGHTS

The arrival of Southwest Airlines's service has driven down prices of interisland flights, which had become expensive in recent years. Hawaiian Airlines and Southwest service Kauai regularly. In addition to offering a discount for booking online, free frequent-flier programs entitle you to rewards and upgrades the more you fly. Be sure to compare prices offered by all the interisland carriers. If you are somewhat flexible with your days and times for island-hopping, you should have no problem getting a round-trip ticket.

Bus

On Kauai, the County Transportation Agency operates the Kauai Bus, which provides service between Hanalei and Kekaha. It also provides limited service to the airport and to Koloa and Poipu. The fare is $2 for adults, and frequent-rider passes are available. The new North Shore Shuttle now operates between Princeville and Kee Beach. The fare is $15

round trip, free for children under two, and $5 for residents. A hop-on hop-off option takes you to seven stops along the way.

Car

The best way to experience all of Kauai's stunning beauty is to get in a car and explore. The 15-mile stretch of Napali Coast, with its breathtaking, verdant-green sheer cliffs, is the only outer part of the island that's not accessible by car. Otherwise, one main road can get you from Barking Sands Beach on the West Side to Haena on the North Shore.

Asking for directions will almost always get a helpful explanation from the locals, but you should be prepared for an island term or two. Instead of using compass directions, remember that Hawaii residents refer to places as being either *mauka* (toward the mountains) or *makai* (toward the ocean) from one another. Hawaii has a strict seat-belt law. All those riding in the vehicle must wear a seat belt. The fine for not wearing a seat belt is $112. There is also a law forbidding the use of handheld devices while driving. Jaywalking is common in the Islands, so please pay careful attention to the roads. It also is considered rude to honk your horn, so be patient if someone is turning or proceeding through an intersection.

While driving on Kauai, you will come across several one-lane bridges. If you are the first to approach a bridge, the car on the other side will wait while you cross. If a car on the other side is closer to the bridge, then you should wait while the driver crosses. If you're enjoying the island's dramatic views, pull over to the shoulder so you don't block traffic.

Getting Here

GASOLINE

You can count on having to pay more at the pump for gasoline on Kauai than on the U.S. mainland. There are no gas stations past Princeville on the North Shore, and no stations past Waimea on the West Side, so if you're running low, fuel up before heading out to the end of the road.

PARKING

Only recently has Kauai instituted parking fees for a few popular tourist areas, and these fees are collected for upkeep. Expect to pay a daily parking fee of $50 in order to enjoy parking at any of the county parks. Also, there is a $5 fee to park at Kee Beach as well as for the fantastic lookouts over Waimea Canyon on the way up to Kokee. This fee includes parking for all three outlooks. Otherwise, there are no parking meters, parking garages, parking tags, or paid parking. If there's room on the side of the road, you can park there. A good rule of thumb is if there are other cars parked in that area, it's safe to do the same.

ROAD CONDITIONS

Kauai has a relatively well-maintained highway running south from Lihue to Barking Sands Beach; a spur at Waimea takes you along Waimea Canyon Drive to Kokee State Park. A northern route also winds its way from Lihue to the end of the road at Haena, the beginning of rugged and roadless Napali Coast. Opt for a four-wheel-drive vehicle if dirt-road exploration holds any appeal.

CAR RENTAL

While on Kauai, you can rent anything from an econobox to a Ferrari. Rates are usually better if you reserve through a rental agency's website. It's wise to make reservations far in advance and make sure that a confirmed reservation guarantees you a car, especially if you're visiting during peak seasons or for major conventions or sporting events. Rates begin at about $25–$35 a day for an economy car with air-conditioning, automatic transmission, and unlimited mileage, depending on your pickup location. This does not include the airport concession fee, general excise tax, rental-vehicle surcharge, or vehicle license fee. When you reserve a car, ask about cancellation penalties. Many rental companies in Hawaii offer coupons for discounts at various attractions that could save you money later on in your trip.

In Hawaii you must be 21 years of age to rent a car, and you must have a valid driver's license and a major credit card. Those under 25 will pay a daily surcharge of $15–$25. Request car seats and extras such as GPS when you book. Hawaii's Child Restraint Law requires that all children three years and younger be in an approved child safety seat in the back-seat of a vehicle. Children ages four to seven must be seated in a rear booster seat or child restraint such as a lap and shoulder belt. Car seats and boosters range from $5 to $8 per day.

Your unexpired driver's license is valid for rental for up to 90 days.

Since the road circling the island is usually two lanes, allow plenty of time to return your vehicle so that you can make your flight. Traffic can be bad during morning and afternoon rush hour. Give yourself about two hours before departure time to return your vehicle.

🚗 Island Driving Times

It might not seem as if driving from the North Shore to the West Side, say, would take much time, as Kauai is smaller than Oahu, Maui, and certainly the Big Island. But it will take longer than you'd expect, and Kauai roads are subject to some heavy traffic, especially going through Kapaa and Lihue.

Island Driving Times

Haena to Hanalei	5 miles/15 mins
Hanalei to Princeville	4 miles/10 mins
Princeville to Kilauea	5 miles/10 mins
Kilauea to Anahola	8 miles/12 mins
Anahola to Kapaa	5 miles/10 mins
Kapaa to Lihue	10 miles/20 mins
Lihue to Poipu	13 miles/25 mins
Poipu to Kalaheo	8 miles/15 mins
Kalaheo to Hanapepe	4 miles/8 mins
Hanapepe to Waimea	7 miles/10 mins

🚗 Ride-Sharing

Ride-sharing apps like Uber and Lyft are newcomers to the Kauai transportation scene; they usually offer a slightly cheaper rate than traditional taxis or car services.

🚗 Taxi

Kauai has always had taxi service, though it's never been a major transportation choice. Upon arrival, you can catch a cab from the small lot near the baggage claim. Kauai Taxi, Sue's Northside Taxi, Princeville Taxi, and Poipu Taxi head the Kauai fleet.

2

Travel Smart   GETTING HERE

Essentials

🍴 Dining and Lodging

Hawaii is a melting pot of cultures, and nowhere is this more apparent than in its cuisine. From luau and "plate lunch" to sushi and steak, there's no shortage of interesting flavors and presentations.

There are several top-notch resorts on Kauai, as well as a wide variety of condos, vacation rentals, and bed-and-breakfasts to choose from. Selecting vacation lodging is a tough decision, but fret not—our expert writers and editors have done most of the legwork.

Looking for a tropical forest retreat, a big resort, or a private vacation rental? We'll give you all the details you need to book a place that suits your style. Quick tips: Reserve your room far in advance. Be sure to ask about discounts and special packages (hotel websites often have Internet-only deals).

What It Costs			
$	$$	$$$	$$$$
RESTAURANTS			
under $18	$18–$26	$27–$35	over $35
HOTELS			
under $180	$180–$260	$261–$340	over $340

➕ Health

In addition to being the Aloha State, Hawaii is known as the Health State. The life expectancy here is 83 years, the longest in the nation. Balmy weather makes it easy to remain active year-round, and the low-stress aloha attitude certainly contributes to general well-being. When you are visiting the Islands, however, there are a few health issues to keep in mind.

The Hawaii State Department of Health recommends that you drink 16 ounces of water per hour to avoid dehydration when hiking or spending time in the sun. Use sunscreen, wear UV-reflective sunglasses, and protect your head with a visor or hat for shade. If you're not acclimated to warm, humid weather, you should allow plenty of time for rest stops and refreshments. When visiting fresh-water streams, be aware of the tropical disease leptospirosis, which is spread by animal urine and carried into streams and mud. Symptoms include fever, headache, nausea, and red eyes and may not appear immediately. If left untreated, it can cause liver and kidney damage, respiratory failure, internal bleeding, and even death. To avoid this, don't swim or wade in freshwater streams or ponds if you have open sores, and don't drink from any freshwater streams or ponds, especially after heavy rains.

On the Islands, fog is a rare occurrence, but there can often be "vog," an airborne haze of gases released from volcanic vents on the Big Island. During certain weather conditions such as "Kona Winds," the vog can settle over the Islands and wreak havoc with respiratory and other health conditions, especially asthma or emphysema. If susceptible, stay indoors and get emergency assistance if needed.

The Islands have their share of bugs and insects that enjoy the tropical climate as much as visitors do. Most are harmless but annoying. When planning to spend time outdoors in hiking areas, wear long-sleeved clothing and pants and use mosquito repellent containing DEET. In very damp places you may encounter the

Where to Stay in Kauai

	LOCAL VIBE	PROS	CONS
The North Shore	Properties here have the "wow" factor with ocean and mountain beauty; laid-back Hanalei and Princeville set the high-end pace.	When the weather is good, this side has it all. Epic winter surf, gorgeous waterfalls, and verdant vistas create some of the best scenery in Hawaii.	Frequent winter rain (being green has a cost) means you may have to travel south to find the sun; expensive restaurants and shopping offer few deals.
The East Side	The most reasonably priced area to stay for the practical traveler; lacks the pizzazz of expensive resorts on North and South Shores; more traditional beach hotels.	The best travel deals show up here; more direct access to the local population; plenty of decent restaurants with good variety, along with delis in food stores.	Beaches aren't the greatest (rocky, reefy) at many of the lodging spots; congested traffic at times; some crime issues in parks.
The South Shore	Resort central; plenty of choices where the consistent sunshine is perfect for those who want to do nothing but play golf or tennis and read a book by the pool.	Beautiful in its own right; many enchanted evenings with stellar sunsets; summer surf a bit easier for beginners to handle.	Though resorts are lush, surrounding landscape is desert-like with scrub brush; construction can be brutal on peace of mind.
The West Side	There are few options for lodging in this mostly untouristed setting, with contrasts such as the extreme heat of a July day in Waimea to a frozen winter night up in Kokee.	A gateway area for exploration into the wilds of Kokee or for boating trips on Coast; main hub for boat and helicopter trips; outstanding sunsets.	Least convenient side for most visitors; daytime is languid and dry; river runoff can ruin ocean's clarity

Essentials

dreaded local centipede. On the Islands they usually come in one of three colors: brown, blue, or bright orange. They range from the size of a worm to an 8-inch cigar. Their sting is very painful, and the reaction is similar to bee- and wasp-sting reactions. If stung, immediately run very hot water over the wound for 20 minutes or so. When camping, shake out your sleeping bag before climbing in, and check your shoes in the morning, as the centipedes like cozy places. If planning on hiking or traveling in remote areas, always carry a first-aid kit and appropriate medications for sting reactions.

COVID-19

A novel coronavirus brought all travel to a virtual standstill in the first half of 2020. Although the illness is mild in most people, some experience severe and even life-threatening complications. Once travel started up again, albeit slowly and cautiously, travelers were asked to be particularly careful about hygiene and to avoid any unnecessary travel, especially if they are sick.

Older adults, especially those over 65, have a greater chance of having severe complications from COVID-19. The same is true for people with weaker immune systems or those living with some types of medical conditions, including diabetes, asthma, heart disease, cancer, HIV/AIDS, kidney disease, and liver disease. Starting two weeks before a trip, anyone planning to travel should be on the lookout for some of the following symptoms: cough, fever, chills, trouble breathing, muscle pain, sore throat, new loss of smell or taste. If you experience any of these symptoms, you should not travel at all.

And to protect yourself during travel, do your best to avoid contact with people showing symptoms. Wash your hands often with soap and water. Limit your

time in public places, and, when you are out and about, wear a cloth face mask that covers your nose and mouth. Indeed, a mask may be required in some places, such as on an airplane or in a confined space like a theater, where you share the space with a lot of people.

You may wish to bring extra supplies, such as disenfecting wipes, hand sanitizer (12-ounce bottles were allowed in carry-on luggage at this writing), and a first-aid kit with a thermometer.

Given how abruptly travel was curtailed in March 2020, it is wise to consider protecting yourself by purchasing a travel insurance policy that will reimburse you for any costs related to COVID-19 related cancellations. Not all travel insurance policies protect against pandemic-related cancellations, so always read the fine print.

Immunizations

There are no immunization requirements for visitors traveling to the United States for tourism.

Packing

Hawaii is casual: sandals, bathing suits, and comfortable, informal clothing are the norm. In summer, synthetic slacks and shirts, although easy to care for, can be uncomfortably warm.

One of the most important things to tuck into your suitcase is sunscreen, though it is readily available at most stores.

As for clothing in the Hawaiian Islands, there's a saying that when a man wears a suit during the day, he's either going for a loan or he's a lawyer trying a case. Only a few upscale restaurants require a jacket for dinner. The aloha shirt is accepted dress in Hawaii for business and most social occasions. Shorts are acceptable daytime attire, along with a T-shirt or polo shirt. There's no need to buy expensive sandals on the mainland—here you can get flip-flops for a couple of dollars and off-brand sandals for $20. Golfers should remember that many courses have dress codes requiring a collared shirt; call courses you're interested in for details. If you're not prepared, you can pick up appropriate clothing at resort pro shops. If you're visiting in winter, bring a sweater or light- to medium-weight jacket. A polar fleece pullover is ideal and makes a great impromptu travel pillow.

Passport

All visitors to the United States require a passport that is valid for six months beyond your expected period of stay.

Safety

Hawaii is generally a safe tourist destination, but it's still wise to follow the same common-sense safety precautions you would normally follow in your own hometown.

Be wary of those hawking "too good to be true" prices on everything from car rentals to attractions. Many of these offers are just a lure to get you in the door for time-share presentations. When handed a flier, read the fine print before you make your decision to participate.

Taxes

There's a 4.16% state sales tax on all purchases, including food. The state sales tax plus the hotel room tax add approximately 14% to your hotel bill. A $3-per-day road tax is also assessed on each rental vehicle.

Tipping

Tip cabdrivers 15% of the fare. Standard tips for restaurants and bar tabs run from 15% to 20% of the bill, depending on the standard of service. Bellhops at hotels usually receive $1 per bag, more if you have bulky items such as bicycles and surfboards. Tip the hotel room maid $1 per night, paid daily. Tip doormen $1 for assistance with taxis; tips for concierges vary depending on the service. For example, tip more for "hard-to-get" event tickets or dining reservations.

For single-day guided activities like a boat trip to Napali, a zip-lining tour, or surf lessons, you should tip each guide at least $10–$20 if you feel he or she enhanced your experience. Often, the tour company takes the bulk of your booking price, and the locals who are sharing their alohas with you are depending on your tips.

Tours

Globus has two Hawaii itineraries that include Kauai, one of which is an escorted cruise on Norwegian Cruise Lines's *Pride of America* that includes two days on the Garden Island. Tauck Travel offers an 11-night *Best of Hawaii* tour that includes two nights on Kauai with leisure time for either relaxation or exploration.

Escortedhawaiitours.com, owned and operated by Atlas Cruises & Tours, sells

Essentials

more than a dozen Hawaii trips ranging from 7 to 12 nights operated by various guided-tour companies including Globus and Tauck. Several of these trips include two to three nights on Kauai.

SPECIAL-INTEREST TOURS
BIRD-WATCHING

There are more than 150 species of birds that live in the Hawaiian Islands. Field Guides has a three-island (Oahu, Kauai, and the Big Island), 10-day guided bird-watching trip for 14 birding enthusiasts that focuses on endemic land birds and specialty seabirds. While on Kauai, birders will visit Kokee State Park, Alakai Wilderness Preserve, and Kilauea Point. The trip costs about $4,950 per person and includes accommodations, meals, ground transportation, interisland air, an eight-hour pelagic boat trip, and guided bird-watching excursions. Travelers must purchase their own airfare to and from their gateway city. Field Guides has been offering worldwide birding tours since 1984.

Victor Emanuel Nature Tours, the largest company in the world specializing in birding tours, has two nine-day trips that include Kauai. *Spring Hawaii* is the theme of the late February/early March birding trip, when seabird diversity on the island is at its peak. Birders will see the *koloa* (Hawaiian duck), one of Hawaii's most endangered wetland birds, as well as Laysan albatrosses, red- and white-tailed tropic birds, red-footed boobies, wedge-tailed shearwaters, great frigate birds, brown boobies, and possibly even red-billed tropic birds. Participants in the *Fall Hawaii* birding trip will visit Oahu, Kauai, and the Big Island in October. Birders will see Kauai honeycreepers and Hawaiian short-eared owls at Kokee State Park and Alakai Swamp and seabirds at the National Wildlife Refuges at Kilauea and Hanalei. Both the *Spring Hawaii* and *Fall*

Hawaii tours cost about $5,295 per person. Both trips include accommodations, meals, interisland air, ground transportation, and guided excursions. Travelers must purchase their own airline ticket to and from their gateway city. Tours begin in Honolulu and end up in Hilo.

CULTURE

Road Scholar (formerly Elderhostel), a nonprofit educational travel organization, offers several guided tours for older adults that focus on Hawaiian culture. With all the tours listed, travelers must purchase their own airline tickets to Hawaii. We've chosen a few of our favorite tours here, but more information on tour subjects can be found on the organization's website.

The Best of Oahu and Kauai is a nine-night tour that focuses on the history of the islands with visits to *heiau* (sacred temples) and museums along with a visit to a royal palace. The tour includes the Kilauea Lighthouse and Waimea Canyon on the Garden Island. The cost of this tour starts at $3,099 per person and includes accommodations, meals, ground transportation, admission fees, as well as tipping charges and a travel assistance plan.

The Best of Hawaii, Maui, Oahu, and Kauai is a more adventurous 21-day tour, split up by 8 nights on the Big Island of Hawaii, 4 nights on Maui, 4 nights on Kauai, and 4 nights on Oahu. Exploring the natural beauty of these islands, you'll visit Volcanoes National Park and the Hamakua Coast on Hawaii, Haleakala National Park on Maui, the Kilauea Point National Wildlife Refuge and the National Tropical Botanical Gardens on Kauai, and Pearl Harbor and Iolani Palace on Oahu, learning about these islands' diverse birdlife, marine life, forests, volcanoes, and more. Prices start at $8,499 per person and include accommodations, meals, ground transportation, admission fees, and interisland air travel between Kauai and the Big Island.

HIKING

Timberline Adventures offers periodic trips to the Garden Island, including its *Kauai: Waimea Canyon and the NaPali Coast,* a six-day journey into the rain forests of Kokee State Park and Waimea Canyon. With miles of hiking trails, it's an opportunity to explore Kauai's inner beauty, including rare birds, waterfalls, and spectacular scenery. Other day trips have you hiking Sleeping Giant and kayaking the Wailua River. Perhaps the best hike is along the Kalalau Trail up into Hanakapiai Falls, with a payoff of tropical tranquility. Approximate cost is $3,495 per person for a double booking or $4,395 for a single.

Travelers must purchase their own tickets to and from their gateway city.

 ## Visa

Except for citizens of Canada and Bermuda, most visitors to the United States must have a visa. If you are from one of the 38 designated members of the Visa Waiver Program, then you only require an ESTA (Electronic System for Travel Authorization) as long as you are staying for 90 days or less. However, some changes were made in the Visa Waiver Program in 2015, and nationals of Visa-Waiver nations who have traveled to Iran, Iraq, Libya, Somalia, Sudan, Syria, or Yemen no longer qualify for ESTA. Also, if you have been denied a visa to visit the United States, your application for the ESTA program most likely will be denied.

 ## When to Go

Kauai is beautiful in every season, but if you must have good beach weather, you should plan to visit between June and October. The rainy season runs from November through February, with the windward or east and north areas of the island receiving most of the rainfall. Nights can be chilly from November through March. Rain is possible throughout the year, of course, but it rarely rains everywhere on the island at once. If it's raining where you are, the best thing to do is head to another side of the island, usually south or west.

If you're a beach lover, keep in mind that big surf can make many North Shore beaches unswimmable during winter months, while the South Shore gets its large swells in summer. If you want to see the humpback whales, February is the best month, though they arrive as early as October and a few may still be around in early April. In winter, Napali Coast boat tours can be rerouted due to high seas, the Kalalau Trail can become very wet and muddy or, at times, impassable, and sea kayaking is not an option. If you have your heart set on visiting Kauai's famed coast, you may want to visit in the drier, warmer months (May–September).

Hawaiian Vocabulary

Although an understanding of Hawaiian is by no means required on a trip to the Aloha State, a *malihini*, or newcomer, will find plenty of opportunities to pick up a few of the local words and phrases. Traditional names and expressions are widely used in the Islands. You're likely to read or hear at least a few words each day of your stay.

Simplifying the learning process is the fact that the Hawaiian language contains only seven consonants—*H, K, L, M, N, P, W,* and the silent *'okina,* or glottal stop, written '—plus one or more of the five vowels. All syllables, and therefore all words, end in a vowel. Each vowel, with the exception of a few diphthongized double vowels such as *au* (pronounced "ow") or *ai* (pronounced "eye"), is pronounced separately. Thus *'Iolani* is four syllables (ee-oh-la-nee), not three (yo-la-nee). Although some Hawaiian words have only vowels, most also contain some consonants, but consonants are never doubled.

Pronunciation is simple. Pronounce *A* "ah" as in *father; E* "ay" as in *weigh; I* "ee" as in *marine; O* "oh" as in *no; U* "oo" as in *true.*

Consonants mirror their English equivalents, with the exception of *W.* When the letter begins any syllable other than the first one in a word, it is usually pronounced as a *V. 'Awa,* the Polynesian drink, is pronounced "ava," *'ewa* is pronounced "eva."

Almost all long Hawaiian words are combinations of shorter words; they are not difficult to pronounce if you segment them. *Kalaniana'ole,* the highway running east from Honolulu, is easily understood as *Kalani ana 'ole.* Apply the standard pronunciation rules—the stress falls on the next-to-last syllable of most two- or three-syllable Hawaiian words—and

Kalaniana'ole Highway is as easy to say as Main Street.

Now about that fish. Try *humu-humu nuku-nuku āpu a'a.*

The other unusual element in Hawaiian language is the *kahakō,* or macron, written as a short line (ˉ) placed over a vowel. Like the accent (´) in Spanish, the kahakō puts emphasis on a syllable that would normally not be stressed. The most familiar example is probably *Waikīkī.* With no macrons, the stress would fall on the middle syllable; with only one macron, on the last syllable, the stress would fall on the first and last syllables. Some words become plural with the addition of a macron, often on a syllable that would have been stressed anyway. No Hawaiian word becomes plural with the addition of an *S,* since that letter does not exist in the language.

The Hawaiian diacritical marks are not printed in this guide.

PIDGIN
You may hear pidgin, the unofficial language of Hawai'i. It is a Creole language, with its own grammar, evolved from the mixture of English, Hawaiian, Japanese, Portuguese, and other languages spoken in 19th-century Hawai'i, and it is heard everywhere.

GLOSSARY
What follows is a glossary of some of the most commonly used Hawaiian words. Hawaiian residents appreciate visitors who at least try to pick up the local language.

'a'ā: rough, crumbling lava, contrasting with *pāhoehoe,* which is smooth.

'ae: yes.

aikane: friend.

āina: land.

akamai: smart, clever, possessing savoir faire.

akua: god.

ala: a road, path, or trail.

ali'i: a Hawaiian chief, a member of the chiefly class.

aloha: love, affection, kindness; also a salutation meaning both greetings and farewell.

'ānuenue: rainbow.

'a'ole: no.

'apōpō: tomorrow.

'auwai: a ditch.

auwē: alas, woe is me!

'ehu: a red-haired Hawaiian.

'ewa: in the direction of 'Ewa plantation, west of Honolulu.

hala: the pandanus tree, whose leaves (*lau hala*) are used to make baskets and plaited mats.

hālau: school.

hale: a house.

hale pule: church, house of worship.

hana: to work.

haole: foreigner. Since the first foreigners were Caucasian, *haole* now means a Caucasian person.

hapa: a part, sometimes a half; often used as a short form of *hapa haole,* to mean a person who is part-Caucasian.

hau'oli: to rejoice. *Hau'oli Makahiki Hou* means Happy New Year. *Hau'oli lā hānau* means Happy Birthday.

heiau: an outdoor stone platform; an ancient Hawaiian place of worship.

he mea iki or **he mea 'ole:** you're welcome.

holo: to run.

holoholo: to go for a walk, ride, or sail.

holokū: a long Hawaiian dress, somewhat fitted, with a yoke and a train. It was worn at court, and at least one local translates the word as "expensive mu'umu'u."

holomū: a post–World War II cross between a *holokū* and a mu'umu'u, less fitted than the former but less voluminous than the latter, and having no train.

honi: to kiss; a kiss. A phrase that some tourists may find useful, quoted from a popular hula, is *Honi Ka'ua Wikiwiki:* Kiss me quick!

honu: turtle.

ho'omalimali: flattery, a deceptive "line," bunk, baloney, hooey.

huhū: angry.

hui: a group, club, or assembly. A church may refer to its congregation as a *hui* and a social club may be called a *hui.*

hukilau: a seine; a communal fishing party in which everyone helps to drive the fish into a huge net, pull it in, and divide the catch.

hula: the dance of Hawai'i.

iki: little.

ipo: sweetheart. Commonly seen as "ku'uipo," or "my sweetheart."

ka: the. This is the definite article for most singular words; for plural nouns, the definite article is usually *nā.* Since there is no *S* in Hawaiian, the article may be your only clue that a noun is plural.

kahuna: a priest, doctor, or other trained person of old Hawai'i, endowed with special professional skills that often included prophecy or other supernatural powers.

Hawaiian Vocabulary

kai: the sea, saltwater.

kalo: the taro plant from whose root *poi* (paste) is made.

kamā'aina: literally, a child of the soil; it refers to people who were born in the Islands or have lived there for a long time.

kanaka: originally a man or humanity, it is now used to denote a male Hawaiian or part-Hawaiian, but is occasionally taken as a slur when used by non-Hawaiians. *Kanaka maoli* is used by some Native Hawaiian rights activists to embrace part-Hawaiians as well.

kāne: a man, a husband. If you see this word (or kane) on a door, it's the men's room.

kapa: also called by its Tahitian name, *tapa,* a cloth made of beaten bark and usually dyed and stamped with a repeat design.

kapakahi: crooked, cockeyed, uneven. You've got your hat on *kapakahi.*

kapu: keep out, prohibited. This is the Hawaiian version of the more widely known Tongan word *tabu* (taboo).

kēia lā: today.

keiki: a child; *keikikāne* is a boy, *keikiwahine* a girl.

kōkua: to help, assist. Often seen in signs like "Please *kōkua* and throw away your trash."

kona: the leeward side of the Islands, the direction (south) from which the *kona* wind and *kona* rain come.

kula: upland.

kuleana: a homestead or small plot of ground on which a family has been installed for some generations without necessarily owning it. By extension, *kuleana* is used to denote any area or department in which one has a special interest or prerogative. You'll hear it used this way: "If you want to hire a surfboard, see Moki; that's his *kuleana.*"

kupuna: grandparent; elder.

lā: sun.

lamalama: to fish with a torch.

lānai: a porch, a balcony, an outdoor living room.

lani: heaven, the sky.

lau hala: the leaf of the *hala,* or pandanus tree, widely used in handicrafts.

lei: a garland of flowers.

lōlō: feeble-minded, crazy.

luna: a plantation overseer or foreman.

mahalo: thank you.

mahina: moon.

makai: toward the ocean.

mālama: to take care of, preserve, protect

malihini: a newcomer to the Islands.

mana: the spiritual power that the Hawaiians believe inhabits all things and creatures.

manō: shark.

manuahi: free, gratis.

mauka: toward the mountains.

mauna: mountain.

mele: a Hawaiian song or chant, often of epic proportions.

Mele Kalikimaka: Merry Christmas (a transliteration from the English phrase).

Menehune: a Hawaiian pixie. The *Menehune* were a legendary race of little people who accomplished prodigious work, such as building fishponds and temples in the course of a single night.

moana: the ocean.

mu'umu'u: the voluminous dress in which the missionaries enveloped Hawaiian women. Culturally sensitive locals have embraced the Hawaiian spelling but often shorten the spoken word to "mu'u." Most English dictionaries include the spelling "muumuu."

nani: beautiful.

nui: big.

'ohana: family.

'ono: delicious.

pāhoehoe: smooth, unbroken, satiny lava.

palapala: document, printed matter.

pali: a cliff, precipice.

pānini: prickly pear cactus.

paniolo: a Hawaiian cowboy, a rough transliteration of *español,* the language of the Islands' earliest cowboys.

pau: finished, done.

pilikia: trouble. The Hawaiian word is much more widely used here than its English equivalent.

pū: large conch shell used as trumpet before start of luau and other special events.

puka: a hole.

pule: prayer, blessing. Often performed before a meal or event.

pupule: crazy, like the celebrated Princess Pupule. This word has replaced its English equivalent in local usage.

pu'u: volcanic cinder cone.

tūtū: grandmother

waha: mouth.

wahine: a female, a woman, a wife, and a sign on the ladies' room door; the plural form is *wāhine.*

wai: freshwater, as opposed to saltwater, which is *kai.*

wailele: waterfall.

wikiwiki: to hurry, hurry up (since this is a reduplication of *wiki,* quick, neither *W* is pronounced as a *V*).

Great Itineraries

Road Trip: The Best of Kauai in 8 Days

Kauai is small, but its major byways generally circumnavigate the island with no through-roads, so it can take more time than you expect to get around. Hiking Kalalau Trail, kayaking Wailua River, showering in a waterfall, watching whales at Kilauea Lighthouse, shopping for gifts at Koloa Town shops, etc.: there's so much to see and do. Rather than trying to check everything off your list in one fell swoop, choose your favorites and devote a full day to the experiences.

DAY 1: SETTLE IN ON THE EAST SIDE

The East Side of the island is a convenient area to make a home base. Stay here and you'll have the easiest access to most of the island's top attractions. Fresh off a long flight, you'll likely just want to relax by the pool at your hotel/condo or hit **Kealia Beach** just north of funky Kapaa Town. The far end near the rock jetty is for safe swimming and easy bodysurfing. There are plenty of welcoming dining options around Kapaa, such as the **Lemongrass Grill** or **Hukilau Lanai,** for a fantastic first meal.

Logistics: Wailua/Kapaa traffic can be a nightmare, so avoid rush and midday times. It's 10 miles from the airport to Kapaa, but drive times can vary from 15 to 35 minutes. Kealia Beach is three minutes outside Kapaa and has plenty of parking.

DAY 2: TAKE IT ALL IN

For an incredible, and literal, overview of Kauai's beaches, forests, canyons, waterfalls, and ocean, take a morning helicopter trip with **Blue Hawaiian Helicopters** or **Jack Harter** out of Lihue. Images of the rolling verdant carpet far below will linger long in your memory. Afternoon is free for beach time or laid-back shopping in Kapaa Town. Or have lunch in Lihue and lounge on **Kalapaki Beach.**

Logistics: Lihue Airport to Kalapaki Bay is five minutes south of Lihue.

DAY 3: EAST SIDE OFFERINGS

Check out the Kapaa/Wailua area, which has a little something for everyone. Rent a bike at **Kauai Cycle** and coast along the Kauai Path (Ke Ala Hele Makalae), enjoying the ocean views and invigorating fresh air. Or take a moderate, 2-mile hike on the **Sleeping Giant Trail** for panoramic vistas of the entire East Side. Then get back on the main road for a few-minutes' drive up to **Opaekaa Falls,** one of the Wailua River's mightiest displays.

Logistics: From mid-Kapaa to the starting point of the Sleeping Giant Trail is 3 miles; just avoid rush hours.

DAY 4: SOUTH SIDE SIGHTS

Start with a hike on the **Mahaulepu Heritage Trail** for wondrous ocean-side views of pristine beaches and craggy ledges. A quick dip at **Poipu Beach Park** will refresh your limbs after your hike. Drive down Lawai Road to spot the **Spouting Horn,** Kauai's version of Old Faithful. Right next door is the **National Tropical Botanical Garden,** where you can tour beautiful grounds of exotic flora and learn about the biodiversity in Hawaii and the Pacific.

Logistics: The Mahaulepu Trail is about 10 minutes from Koloa Town. From there to Spouting Horn is about another 10-minute drive.

DAY 5: AT SEA ON NAPALI COAST

Choose your preferred watercraft (Zodiac for adventure rafting or catamaran for pleasure cruising) and depart from the boat harbor in Eleele for an unforgettable journey up breathtakingly scenic Napali Coast. Most trips are about four hours and usually include a light snack; some include drinks. Don't schedule anything too demanding afterwards, as you'll likely be tired, and you'll want to savor the memories of the sights you just beheld.

DAY 6: EXPLORE THE OTHER KAUAI

In the mountains of Kokee on the West Side, you'll enjoy the splendor of the mountains, the ocean, the sunlight, and the crisper air. Stop along the way at the scenic overlooks of **Waimea Canyon** and be dazzled by the interplay of light and shadow as the sun moves across this spectacular landscape. Hike the relatively short Canyon Trail to a divine waterfall. Have lunch at the **Kokee Lodge**, check out the **Kokee Museum** next door, and continue another 5 miles or so to the Kalalau Lookout.

Logistics: Drive up from Waimea and come down on the Kekaha side, which is more gradual. It's about 30 minutes straight up to the lodge, but scenic spots stretch it out.

DAY 7: NORTH SHORE PLAYGROUND

The North Shore's plentiful sights and activities include swimming, surfing, golf, tennis, botanical gardens, zip-lining, hiking, and horseback riding. Visit **Limahuli Garden** in Hanalei, which features an ancient Hawaiian layout of a typical self-sufficient community, or **Na Aina Kai** with its artistic and working-farm focus. At the **Kilauea Lighthouse** behold the cliffs, exotic birds, and magnificent coastal view. Spend the rest of your day at **Hanalei Bay** swimming, taking a surf lesson, or just walking the 2-mile jewel of a crescent-shape beach. For the family, a round of golf at **Kauai Mini-Golf** in Kilauea can be joyful and instructive as the 18-hole layout reveals Hawaii's story through its landscaping.

Logistics: Limahuli is about a 10-minute drive past Hanalei. From there back to Kilauea is about a 20-minute drive on the main road.

DAY 8: HIKE THE KALALAU TRAIL

You've taken in magnificent Napali Coast from the sea; now experience it from land. This moderate trek offers incredible views peering straight down over the deep blue sea, a visit to a lovely beach, and a hike up a stream to a 300-foot waterfall. You won't be taking the arduous 11-mile journey of the entire coastal Kalalau Trail, so take your time and enjoy Kauai's scenery. Be sure to secure a parking permit before hitting the trail.

Logistics: It's 2 miles in to Hanakapiai Beach. Allow an hour. The hike up the valley is also 2 miles—but plan on 90 minutes each way, as the trail cuts through jungle.

Contacts

Air

AIRPORTS Honolulu International Airport (HNL). ☎ 808/836–6413 ⊕ www.hawaii.gov/dot/airports. **Lihue Airport (LIH).** ☎ 808/246–1448 ⊕ www.hawaii.gov/dot/airports.

AIRPORT GREETINGS Kamaaina Leis, Flowers & Greeters. ☎ 808/836–3246 ⊕ aliigreetingservice.com.

GROUND TRANSPORTATION Kauai Luxury Transportation and Tours. ☎ 808/634–7260 ⊕ kauailuxurytransportation.com. **SpeediShuttle.** ☎ 877/242–5777 ⊕ www.speedishuttle.com.

Bus

Kauai Bus. ☎ 808/246–8110 ⊕ www.kauai.com/kauai-bus.

Car

State of Hawaii Department of Transportation. ☎ 808/241-3000 Report a highway problem or check traffic and roadwork ⊕ hidot.hawaii.gov/highways/roadwork/kauai.

Health

Kauai Veterans Memorial Hospital. ⊠ 4643 Waimea Canyon Dr., Waimea (Kauai County) ☎ 808/338-9431 ⊕ kauai.hhsc.org. **Wilcox Memorial Hospital.** ⊠ 3-3420 Kuhio Hwy., Lihue ☎ 808/245-1100 ⊕ www.hawaiipacifichealth.org/wilcox.

Lodging

Airbnb. ⊕ www.airbnb.com/s/Kauai-County–HI. **County of Kauai Camping.** ☎ 808/241-4463 for permits ⊕ www.kauai.gov/Camping.

Tours

RECOMMENDED COMPANIES Atlas Cruises & Tours. ☎ 800/942–3301 ⊕ www.atlastravelweb.com. **Globus.** ☎ 866/755–8581 ⊕ www.globusjourneys.com. **Tauck Travel.** ☎ 800/788–7885 ⊕ www.tauck.com.

BIRD-WATCHING Field Guides. ☎ 800/728–4953 ⊕ www.fieldguides.com. **Victor Emanuel Nature Tours.** ☎ 800/328–8368 ⊕ www.ventbird.com.

CULTURE Road Scholar. ☎ 800/454–5768 ⊕ www.roadscholar.org.

HIKING Sierra Club Outings. ☎ 415/977–5500 ⊕ sierraclubkauai.org. **Timberline Adventures.** ☎ 800/417–2453 ⊕ www.timberlineadventures.com.

Visitor Information

Hawaii Beach Safety. ⊕ hawaiibeachsafety.com. **Hawaii Department of Land and Natural Resources.** ⊕ dlnr.hawaii.gov. **Kauai Vacation Explorer.** ⊕ www.kauaiexplorer.com . **Kauai Visitors Bureau.** ⊠ 4334 Rice St # 101, Lihue ☎ 808/245-3971 ⊕ www.gohawaii.com/kauai.

Chapter 3

THE NORTH SHORE

WITH THE NAPALI COAST

Updated by
Charles E. Roessler

👁 Sights	🍴 Restaurants	🛏 Hotels	🛍 Shopping	🍸 Nightlife
★★★★★	★★☆☆☆	★★☆☆☆	★★★☆☆	★☆☆☆☆

WELCOME TO THE NORTH SHORE

TOP REASONS TO GO

★ **Napali Coast.** Whether you choose to hike the iconic Napali Coast or take a boat, the views will stay with you forever.

★ **Surfing Paradise.** Beautiful Hanalei Bay has spawned some of the greatest surfers in the world. Lay on the fine sand or walk the beach, stopping to picnic at the iconic Hanalei Pier.

★ **Kilauea Lighthouse.** More than just a light-house, the area is also home to numerous exotic bird colonies, includ-ing albatross and nene (Hawaiian goose).

★ **Beaches and Trails.** End-of-the-road Kee Beach is also the begin-ning of the Kalalau Trail. The beach is safe for novices in the summer and snorkeling is good.

★ **Lush Gardens.** In one of the most biodiverse valleys of Hawaii, the Limahuli Garden is home to an impressive array of native Hawaiian plants and birds.

1 Hanalei. With magical waterfalls and a classic bay, Hanalei is a top draw on Kauai even if the town center has become overcrowded.

2 Haena. Deep blue surf and a refurbished visitor area makes Haena a great choice for nature walks. In summer, bring your snorkel.

3 Princeville. This upscale community is the place to golf, play tennis, surf, and access isolated beaches. There's also a small shopping center.

4 Kilauea. The former plantation town has grown into more than a bedroom community. The standout Kilauea Light-house attracts endan-gered birds.

5 Napali Coast. To the northwest, Kauai's unfor-gettable coastline can be seen by hiking, boat, or helicopter ride. It's isolated the first 2 miles toward Kalalau Valley.

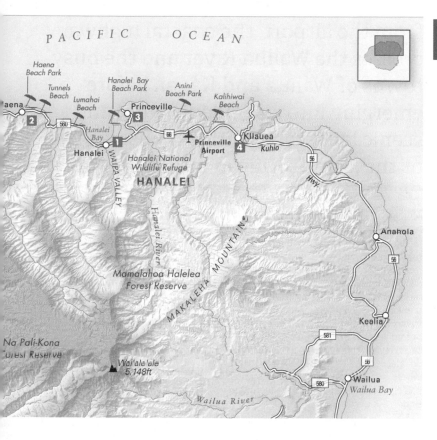

The North Shore of Kauai includes the environs of Kilauea, Princeville, Hanalei, and Haena. Traveling north on Route 56 from the airport, the coastal highway crosses the Wailua River and the busy towns of Wailua and Kapaa before emerging into a decidedly rural and scenic landscape, with expansive views of the island's rugged interior mountains.

As the two-lane highway turns west and narrows, it winds through spectacular scenery and passes the posh resort community of Princeville before dropping down into Hanalei Valley. Here it narrows further and becomes a federally recognized scenic roadway, replete with one-lane bridges (the local etiquette is for six or seven cars to cross at a time, before yielding to those on the other side), hairpin turns, and heart-stopping coastal vistas. The road ends at Kee, where the ethereal rain forests and fluted sea cliffs of the Napali Coast Wilderness State Park begin.

Floods in 2018 caused major physical changes to the North Shore, including landslide areas, stream diversions, downed power lines, and general infrastructure chaos. One major result is a newly instituted permitting system for visitors to Haena State Park, which begins with a check-in system at the park itself. New rules limit the number of vehicles to 900 per day, as opposed to the previous average of 2,000 per day. The result is a less crowded, better maintained, and way calmer atmosphere at Kee Beach.

And as long as you've come this far, you might as well take the 2-mile hike into Hanakapiai Valley. Along the way you'll see mind-blowing scenes of coastal beauty. Another 2 miles up the valley is a towering 300-foot waterfall.

In winter Kauai's North Shore receives more rainfall than other areas of the island. Don't let this deter you from visiting. The clouds drift over the mountains of Namolokama creating a mysterious mood and then, in a blink, disappear, rewarding you with mountains laced with a dozen waterfalls or more. The views of the mountain—as well as the sunsets over the ocean—from Hanalei Bay and Kee Beach are fantastic.

The North Shore attracts all kinds—from celebrities to surfers. In fact, the late Andy Irons, three-time world surfing champion, along with his brother Bruce and legend Laird Hamilton grew up riding waves along the North Shore.

Planning

Getting Here and Around

There is only one road leading beyond Princeville to Kee Beach at the western end of the North Shore: Route 560. Hanalei's commercial stretch fronts this route, and you'll find parking at the shopping compounds on each side of the road. After Hanalei, parking is restricted to two main areas, Haena Beach Park and a new lot at Haena State Park, and there are few pullover areas along Route 560. Traffic and especially parking have become major concerns as the North Shore has gained popularity, so be prepared to be patient.

AIR

Travelers to Kauai fly into Lihue (LIH) on the East Side. A more expensive, less common option is to heli into Princeville Airport, where Makani Kai Air flies in and out once a day.

CAR

Having a car is the best way to see it all on the North Shore, though the highway can be busy and driving is a challenge past Hanalei Town, with twisty roads and one-lane bridges. However, the new North Shore Shuttle ($15 r/t) can take you from Princeville to the end of the road at Kee Beach. With 7 stops along the way, you can pick and choose attractions including Limahuli Garden and Kee Beach.

Beaches

If you've ever dreamed of Hawaii—and who hasn't—you've dreamed of Kauai's North Shore. Lush, tropical, and abundant are just a few words to describe this rugged and dramatic area. And the views to the sea aren't the only attraction—the inland views of velvety-green valley folds and carved mountain peaks will take your breath away. Rain is the reason for all the greenery on the North Shore, and winter is the rainy season. Flooding in 2018 resulted in repairs to areas of Haena and Haena Beach Park. Not to worry, though; it rarely rains *everywhere* on the island at one time. ■TIP→ **The rule of thumb is to head south or west when it rains in the north.**

The waves on the North Shore can be big—and we mean huge—in winter, drawing crowds to witness nature's spectacle. By contrast, in summer the waters can be completely serene.

Hotels

The North Shore is mountainous and wet, which accounts for its rugged, lush landscape. Posh resorts and condominiums await you at Princeville, a community with dreamy views, an excellent golf course, and lovely sunsets. It maintains the lion's share of North Shore accommodations—primarily luxury hotel rooms and condos built on a plateau overlooking the sea. The St. Regis Princeville Resort here was sold to 1 Hotels, and after extensive remodeling, it will reopen in 2022. Hanalei, a bayside town in a broad valley, has a smattering of hotel rooms and numerous vacation rentals, many within walking distance of the beach. Prices tend to be high in this resort area. If you want to do extensive sightseeing on other parts of the island, be prepared for a long drive—one that's very dark at night.

Restaurants

Because of the North Shore's isolation, restaurants have enjoyed a captive audience of visitors who don't want to make the long, dark trek into Kapaa Town for dinner. As a result, dining in this region has been characterized by expensive fare that isn't especially memorable. Fortunately, the situation is slowly improving as new restaurants open and others change hands or menus.

Still, dining on the North Shore can be pricier than on other parts of the island, and not especially family friendly. Most of the restaurants are found either in Hanalei Town or the Princeville resorts. Consequently, you'll encounter delightful mountain and ocean views, but just one restaurant with oceanfront dining.

HOTEL AND RESTAURANT PRICES

Hotel prices in the reviews are the lowest cost of a standard double room in high season. Restaurant prices in the reviews are the average cost of a main course at dinner, or if dinner is not served, at lunch.

WHAT IT COSTS in U.S. Dollars			
$	$$	$$$	$$$$
RESTAURANTS			
under $18	$18-$26	$27-$35	over $35
HOTELS			
under $180	$180-$260	$261-$340	over $340

Hanalei, Haena, and West

Haena is 40 miles northwest of Lihue; Hanalei is 5 miles southeast of Haena.

Crossing the historic one-lane bridge into Hanalei reveals old-world Hawaii, including working taro farms, poi making, and evenings of throwing horseshoes at Black Pot Beach Park—found unmarked (as many places are on Kauai) at the east end of Hanalei Bay Beach Park. Although the current real-estate boom on Kauai has attracted mainland millionaires to build estate homes on the few remaining parcels of land in Hanalei, there's still plenty to see and do. It's *the* gathering place on the North Shore. Restaurants, shops, and people-watching here are among the best on the island, and you won't find a single brand name, chain, or big-box store around—unless you count surf brands like Quiksilver and Billabong.

The beach and river at Hanalei offer swimming, snorkeling, body boarding, surfing, and kayaking. Those hanging around at sunset often congregate at the Hanalei Pavilion, where a husband-and-wife slack-key-guitar-playing combo makes impromptu appearances. There's an old rumor, since quashed by the local newspaper, the *Garden Island*, that says Hanalei was the inspiration for the song "Puff the Magic Dragon," performed by the 1960s singing sensation Peter, Paul and Mary. Even with the newspaper's clarification, some tours still point out the shape of the dragon carved into the mountains encircling the town.

Once you pass through Hanalei Town, the road shrinks even more as you skirt the coast and pass through Haena. Blind corners, quick turns, and one-lane bridges force slow driving along this scenic stretch across the Lumahai and Wainiha Valleys. Extensive flooding ravaged Haena and its state park in 2018, but they've since been repaired.

Sights

Hanalei Pier

MARINA | Built in 1892, the historic Hanalei Pier can be seen from miles across the bay. It came to fame when it was featured in the award-winning 1957 movie *South Pacific*. Kids use it as a diving board, fishers fish, and picnickers picnic. Refurbished after flooding in 2018, it's a great spot for photos or taking a leisurely stroll, and it attracts a gathering every sunset. ⊠ *Weke Rd., Princeville.*

★ Hanalei Valley Overlook

VIEWPOINT | Dramatic mountains and a patchwork of neat taro farms bisected by the wide Hanalei River make this one of

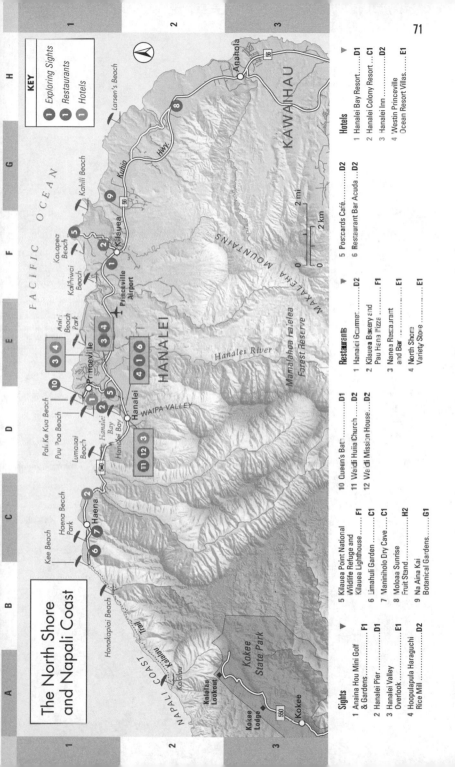

The North Shore and Napali Coast

FACIFIC OCEAN

KAWAIHAU

HANALEI

WAIPA VALLEY

MAKALEHA MOUNTAINS

Mamalahoa Halelea Forest Reserve

Hanalei River

NAPALI COAST

Kokee State Park

KEY

1 Exploring Sights

1 Restaurants

1 Hotels

0   2 mi

0   2 km

Sights ▶

1 Anaina Hou Mini Golf
  & Gardens............... F1
2 Hanalei Pier D1
3 Hanalei Valley
  Overlook E1
4 Hoopulapula Haraguchi
  Rice Mill D2

5 Kilauea Point National
  Wildlife Refuge and
  Kilauea Lighthouse....... F1
6 Limahuli Garden C1
7 Maniniholo Dry Cave....... C1
8 Moloaa Sunrise
  Fruit Stand H2
9 Na Aina Kai
  Botanical Gardens........ G1

10 Queen's Bath............... D1
11 Waioli Huiia Church....... D2
12 Waioli Mission House....D2

Restaurants ▶

1 Hanalei Gourmet............ D2
2 Kilauea Bakery and
  Pau Hana Pizza F1
3 Nanea Restaurant
  and Bar E1
4 North Shore
  Variety Store E1

5 Postcards Café............. D2
6 Restaurant Bar Acuda ...D2

Hotels ▶

1 Hanalei Bay Resort........ D1
2 Hanalei Colony Resort.... C1
3 Hanalei Inn D2
4 Westin Princeville
  Ocean Resort Villas....... E1

Did You Know?

From the Hanalei Valley Overlook, you can spot green fields of kalo (taro), the plant used to make traditional Hawaiian poi.

Hawaii's loveliest sights, even with the flood damage it sustained in 2018. The fertile Hanalei Valley has been planted with taro since perhaps AD 700, save for an 80-year-long foray into rice that ended in 1960. (The historic Haraguchi Rice Mill is all that remains of that era.) Many taro farmers lease land within the 900-acre Hanalei National Wildlife Refuge, helping to provide wetland habitat for four species of endangered Hawaiian water-birds. ⊠ *Rte. 56, across from Foodland, Princeville.*

Hoopulapula Haraguchi Rice Mill

FARM/RANCH | Rice grew in the taro fields of Hanalei Valley for almost 80 years—beginning in the 1880s and ending in the early 1960s. Today, this history is embodied in the Haraguchi family, whose ancestors threshed, hulled, polished, separated, graded, and bagged rice in their 3,500-square-foot rice mill, which was demolished once by fire, twice by hurricanes, and was seriously damaged by flooding in 2018. Rebuilt to the exacting standards of the National Register of Historic Places, the mill—and neighboring taro fields—is open for tours on a very limited schedule mainly due to endangered bird-nesting areas. The family still farms taro on the onetime rice paddies and also operates the Hanalei Taro & Juice kiosk in Hanalei Town. Reservations are required for the flood-recovery ecotour, which currently runs on Wednesday at 10 am. All proceeds go to nonprofit education programs. ⊠ *5-5070 Kuhio Hwy., next to Kayak Kauai, Hanalei* ☎ *808/651–3399* ⊕ *haraguchiricemill.org* ⌑ *$70.*

Limahuli Garden

GARDEN | Narrow Limahuli Valley, with its fluted mountain peaks and ancient stone taro terraces, creates an unparalleled setting for this botanical garden and nature preserve. Dedicated to protecting native plants and unusual varieties of taro, it represents the principles of conservation and stewardship held by its founder,

Charles "Chipper" Wichman. Limahuli's primordial beauty and strong *mana* (spiritual power) eclipse the extensive botanical collection. It's one of the most gorgeous spots on Kauai and the crown jewel of the National Tropical Botanical Garden, which Wichman now heads. Call ahead to reserve a guided tour, or tour on your own. A reservation is now required to park here, though North Shore Shuttle riders are exempt. Be sure to check out the quality gift shop and revolutionary compost toilet, and be prepared to walk a somewhat steep hillside. ⊠ *5-8291 Kuhio Hwy., Hanalei* ☎ *808/826–1053* ⊕ *www.ntbg.org* ⌑ *Self-guided tour $20, guided tour $40 (reservations required).*

Maniniholo Dry Cave

CAVE | Kauai's North Shore caves echo an enchanting, almost haunting, alternative to sunny skies and deep blue seas. Steeped in legend, Maniniholo Dry Cave darkens and becomes more claustrophobic as you glide across its sandy floor, hearing the drips down the walls and wondering at its past. Legend has it that Maniniholo was the head fisherman of the Menehune—Kauai's quasimythical first inhabitants. After gathering too much food to carry, Maniniholo's men stored the excess in the dry cave overnight. When he returned in the morning, the food had vanished, and he blamed the imps living in the cracks of the cave. He and his men dug into the cliff to find and destroy the imps, leaving behind the cave. Across the highway from Maniniholo Dry Cave is Haena State Park. ⊠ *Rte. 560, Haena.*

Waioli Huiia Church

RELIGIOUS SITE | Designated a National Historic Landmark, this little church—affiliated with the United Church of Christ—doesn't go unnoticed right alongside Route 560 in downtown Hanalei, and its doors are often wide open (from 10 am to 2 pm, give or take) inviting inquisitive visitors in for a look around. Like the Waioli Mission House behind it, it's an exquisite representation of New England architecture crossed with Hawaiian thatched buildings. During Hurricane Iniki's visit in 1992, which brought sustained winds of 160 mph and wind gusts up to 220 mph, this little church was lifted off its foundation but, thankfully, lovingly restored. Services are held at 10 am on Sunday with many hymns sung in Hawaiian and often accompanied by piano, ukulele, and hula. ⊠ *5-5363A Kuhio Hwy., Hanalei* ☎ *808/826–6253* ⊕ *www.hanaleichurch.org.*

Waioli Mission House

BUILDING | This 1837 home was built by missionaries William and Mary Alexander. Its tidy New England architecture and formal koa-wood furnishings epitomize the prim and proper missionary influence, while the informative guided tours offer a fascinating peek into the private lives of Kauai's early white residents. Half-hour guided tours are available for a $10 requested donation on Tuesday, Thursday, and Saturday from 9 am to 3 pm. ■TIP→ **If no one is there when you arrive, don't despair; just ring the bell by the chimney.** ⊠ *Kuhio Hwy., Hanalei* ☎ *808/245–3202* ⊕ *grovefarm.org/waioli-missionhouse* 🎟 *$10.*

⏱ Beaches

★ Haena Beach Park

BEACH—SIGHT | This is a drive-up beach park popular with campers year-round. The wide bay here —named Makua—is bordered by two large reef systems creating favorable waves for skilled surfers during peak winter conditions. In July and August, waters at this same beach usually are as calm as a lake. Entering the water can be dangerous in winter when the big swells roll in. ■TIP→ **During the summer months only, this is a premier snorkeling site on Kauai.** It's not unusual to find a food vendor parked here selling sandwiches and drinks out of a converted bread van. **Amenities:** food and drink; lifeguards; parking; showers; toilets. **Best for:** snorkeling; surfing; walking. ⊠ *Near end of Rte. 560, across from "Dry Cave," Haena.*

Hanakapiai Beach

BEACH—SIGHT | If you're not up for the full 11-mile haul to Kalalau Beach, you can explore Napali Coast via a 2-mile hike to Hanakapiai Beach, which fronts a tropical valley. It'll take about two hours, and you'll have plenty of company on the trail. This is no longer a secluded beach, although it is still wilderness, and you'll find no amenities except pit toilets. The ocean here is what locals like to call "confused," and Hanakapiai Bay has been the site of numerous drownings. In the winter, surf often eats up the beach, exposing lava rock boulders backing the sand. Be cautious when crossing the stream that runs through the valley, as it can quickly flood, stranding hikers on the wrong side. This has resulted in helicopter rescues and even deaths, as people are swept out to sea while attempting to cross. ■TIP→ **A new bridge makes the passage easier, but don't attempt to cross during heavy rain. Amenities:** toilets. **Best for:** sunset. ⊠ *Kalalau Trail, End of Rte. 560, 7 miles west of Hanalei, Hanalei* ⊕ *www.hawaiistateparks.org.*

★ Hanalei Bay

BEACH—SIGHT | FAMILY | This 2-mile crescent beach cradles a wide bay in a setting that is quintessential Hawaii. The sea is on one side, and behind you are the mountains, often ribboned with waterfalls and changing color in the shifting light. In winter, Hanalei Bay boasts some of the biggest onshore surf breaks in the state, attracting world-class surfers, and the beach is plenty wide enough for sunbathing and strolling. In summer, the bay is transformed—calm waters lap the beach, sailboats moor in the bay, and outrigger-canoe paddlers ply the sea. Pack the cooler, haul out the beach umbrellas, and don't forget the beach toys, because Hanalei Bay is worth scheduling for an entire day, maybe two. Several county beach parks, some with pavilions, can be found along the bay. **Amenities:** lifeguards; parking; showers; toilets. **Best for:** sunset; surfing; swimming; walking. ⊠ *Weke Rd., Hanalei.*

★ Kalalau

BEACH—SIGHT | Located at the end of the trail with the same name, Kalalau is a remote beach in spectacular Napali Coast State Wilderness Park. Reaching it requires an arduous 11-mile hike along sea cliff faces, through steaming tropical valleys, and across sometimes-raging streams. Another option is to paddle a kayak to the beach—summer only, though, or else the surf is way too big. The beach is anchored by a *heiau* (a stone platform used as a place of worship) on one end and a waterfall on the other. The safest time to come is summer, when the trail is dry and the beach is wide, cupped by low, vegetated sand dunes and a large walk-in cave on the western edge. Day hikes into the valley offer waterfalls, freshwater swimming pools, and wild, tropical fruits. Though state camping permits are required, the valley often has a significant illegal crowd, which has strained park facilities and degraded much of its former peaceful solitude. Helicopter overflights are near-constant in good weather. **Amenities:** none. **Best for:** sunset; walking; solitude. ⊠ *Trailhead starts at end of Rte. 560, 7 miles west of Hanalei* ⊕ *www.hawaiistateparks.org.*

★ Kee Beach

BEACH—SIGHT | Highway 560 on the North Shore literally dead-ends at this beach, pronounced "kay-eh." This is also the start of the famous Kalalau Trail and a culturally significant area to Native Hawaiians, who still use an ancient *heiau* dedicated to hula. (It's not appropriate to h-- out on the grass platform or rings there.) The setting is with Makana (a prominent Hollywood dubbed "Bali Hai" kbuster musical *South Pacific*)

dramatically imposing itself on the lovely coastline and lots of lush tropical vegetation. The small beach is protected by a reef—except during high surf—creating a small sandy-bottom lagoon that's a popular snorkeling spot. There can be a strong current in winter. Beach-area amenities were greatly improved after repairs from flooding in 2018. There is now a mandatory permit system that limits guests and prevents overcrowding. The new parking area is 1/3 of a mile from the beach on a path partially on a boardwalk so be prepared to lug your beach gear. It's a great place to watch the sunset lighting up Napali Coast. **Amenities:** lifeguards; parking; showers; toilets. **Best for:** snorkeling; sunset; swimming; walking. ⊠ *End of Rte. 560, 7 miles west of Hanalei.*

Lumahai Beach

BEACH—SIGHT | Famous as the beach where Nurse Nellie washed that man right out of her hair in *South Pacific,* Lumahai's setting is picturesque, with a river and ironwood grove on the western end and stands of hala (pandanus) trees and black lava rock on the eastern side. In between is a long stretch of thick olivine-flecked sand that can be wide or narrow, depending on surf. It can be accessed in two places from the highway; one involves a steep hike from the road. The ocean can be very dangerous here, with a snapping shore break year-round and monster swells in the winter. The current can be strong near the river. Parking is very limited, along the road or in a rough dirt lot near the river. **Amenities:** none. **Best for:** solitude; sunset; walking. ⊠ *On winding section of Rte. 560, near mile marker 5, Hanalei.*

🍴 Restaurants

Hanalei Gourmet

$$ | **AMERICAN** | This spot in Hanalei's restored old schoolhouse offers dolphin-safe tuna, low-sodium meats, fresh-baked breads, and homemade desserts as well as a casual atmosphere where

Hanalei Bay attracts big-wave surfers in the winter and then becomes a calm haven for swimmers in the summer.

both families and the sports-watching crowd can feel equally comfortable. Lunch and dinner menus feature sandwiches, burgers, hearty salads, a variety of pupus, and nightly specials of fresh local fish. **Known for:** friendly bar; consistently good food; fresh bread. $ *Average main: $25* ✉ *Hanalei Center, 5-5161 Kuhio Hwy., Hanalei* ☎ *808/826–2524* ⊕ *www.hanaleigourmet.com.*

Postcards Café

$$$ | AMERICAN | This plantation-cottage restaurant has a menu full of seafood but also offers additive-free vegetarian and vegan options. Top menu picks include taro fritters, scallops over squid-ink linguini, and Wagyu strip steak. **Known for:** meat-free menu; cozy dining room; historic setting. $ *Average main: $35* ✉ *5-5075A Kuhio Hwy., Hanalei* ☎ *808/826–1191* ⊕ *postcardscafe.com* ⊙ *No lunch.*

★ Restaurant Bar Acuda

$$$$ | TAPAS | This hip and pricey tapas bar is a top place in Hanalei in terms of flavor and creativity, with food that's often organic and consistently remarkable. The dining room is supercasual but chic, with a welcoming bar and a nice porch for outdoor dining. **Known for:** sophisticated cuisine; innovative specials; eclectic menu. $ *Average main: $40* ✉ *Hanalei Center, 5-5161 Kuhio Hwy., Hanalei* ☎ *808/826–7081* ⊕ *www.restaurantbaracuda.com.*

Hotels

Hanalei Colony Resort

$$$$ | RESORT | The only true beachfront resort on Kauai's North Shore, Hanalei Colony is a laid-back, go-barefoot kind of resort sandwiched between towering mountains and the sea. **Pros:** ocean-front setting; private, quiet property; well-maintained units with Hawaiian-style furnishings. **Cons:** weak cell-phone reception; damp in winter; isolated location. $ *Rooms from: $375* ✉ *5-7130 Kuhio Hwy., Haena* ☎ *808/826–6235, 800/628–3004* ⊕ *www.hcr.com* ⬦ *48 units* ⊙ *No meals.*

Hanalei Inn

$ | RENTAL | If you're looking for lodgings that won't break the bank a block from gorgeous Hanalei Bay, look no further, as this is literally the only choice among the town's pricey vacation rentals. **Pros:** quick walk to beach, bus stop, and shops; full kitchen; coin-operated laundry on-site. **Cons:** strict cancellation policy; daytime traffic noise; older property. $ *Rooms from: $179* ✉ *5 5468 Kuhio Hwy., Hanalei* ☎ *808/826–9333, 888/773–4730* ⊕ *www.hanaleiinn.net* ⇆ *4 studios* ⦿ *No meals.*

Nightlife

Hanalei Gourmet

BARS/PUBS | The sleepy North Shore stays awake—until 10:30, that is—each evening in this small, convivial deli and bar inside Hanalei's restored old school building. There's local live Hawaiian, jazz, rock, and folk music on Saturday and Sunday evening. ✉ *Hanalei Center, 5-5161 Kuhio Hwy., Hanalei* ☎ *808/826–2524* ⊕ *www.hanaleigourmet.com.*

Tahiti Nui

BARS/PUBS | This venerable and funky institution in sleepy Hanalei still offers its famous luau at 5 on Wednesday evenings, although the bar is the big attraction. Spirits are always high at this popular hangout for locals and visitors alike, which houses live nightly entertainment and Hawaiian slack-key guitar music on Friday evenings. Open until 1 am on weekends. ✉ *5-5134 Kuhio Hwy., Hanalei* ☎ *808/826–6277* ⊕ *www.thenui.com.*

Performing Arts

Hanalei Slack-Key Concerts

MUSIC | Relax to the instrumental music form created by Hawaiian *paniolo* (cowboys) in the early 1800s. Shows are Wednesday in Kapaa at All Saints Church and Tuesday at the Princeville Community Center. If you're looking for a scenic setting, head to Hale Halawai Ohana

Mai Tais

Hard to believe, but the cocktail known around the world as the mai tai has been around since 1944. While the recipe has changed slightly over the years, the original formula, created by bar owner Victor J. "Trader Vic" Bergeron, included 2 ounces of 17-year-old J. Wray & Nephew rum over shaved ice, ½ ounce Holland Dekuyper orange curaçao, ¼ ounce Trader Vic's rock candy syrup, ½ ounce French Garnier orgeat syrup, and the juice of one fresh lime. Done the right way, this tropical drink still lives up to the name "mai tai!" meaning, "out of this world!"

O Hanalei, on Friday and Sunday; it's *mauka* (toward the mountains) down a dirt access road across from St. William's Catholic Church (Malolo Road) and then left down another dirt road. ✉ *5-5299 Kuhio Hwy., Hanalei* ☎ *808/826–1469* ⊕ *www.hawaiianslackkeyguitar.com* ⦿ *From $10.*

Shopping

Hanalei has two shopping centers directly across from each other, which offer more than you would expect in a remote, relaxed town.

Ching Young Village

SHOPPING CENTERS/MALLS | This popular shopping center has its roots in the Chinese immigrants who came to Hawaii in the early 19th century. Hanalei's only full-service grocery store is here along with a number of other shops useful to locals and visitors, such as a music shop selling ukulele and CDs, jewelry stores, art galleries, a surf shop, variety store, and several smallish restaurants. ✉ *5-5190 Kuhio Hwy., near mile marker 2, Hanalei* ⊕ *chingyoungvillage.com.*

Crystal & Gems Gallery

JEWELRY/ACCESSORIES | Sparkling crystals of every shape, size, type, and color, as well as jewelry and paintings, are sold in this small, amply stocked boutique. The knowledgeable staff can help you choose crystals for specific healing purposes. ✉ *4489 Aku Rd., Hanalei* ☎ *808/826–9304* ⊕ *www.crystals-gems.com.*

Hanalei Center

SHOPPING CENTERS/MALLS | Once an old Hanalei schoolhouse, the Hanalei Center is now a bevy of boutiques and restaurants. You can dig through '40s and '50s vintage memorabilia, find Polynesian artifacts, or search for that unusual gift. Buy beach gear as well as island wear and women's clothing. Find a range of fine jewelry and paper art jewelry. There are a full-service salon and a yoga studio in the two-story modern addition to the center, which also houses a small natural foods grocery. ✉ *5-5161 Kuhio Hwy., near mile marker 2, Hanalei* ☎ *808/826–7677.*

Princeville and Kilauea

Princeville is 4 miles northeast of Hanalei; Kilauea is 5 miles east of Princeville.

Built on a bluff offering gorgeous sea and mountain vistas, including Hanalei Bay, Princeville is the creation of a 1970s resort development. The area is anchored by a few large hotels, world-class golf courses, and lots of condos and time-shares.

Five miles down Route 56, Kilauea, a former plantation town, maintains its rural flavor in the midst of unrelenting gentrification encroaching all around it. Especially noteworthy are its historic lava-rock buildings, including **Christ Memorial Episcopal Church** on Kolo Road and, on Keneke and Kilauea Road (commonly known as Lighthouse Road), the Kong Lung Company, which is now an expensive shop.

GETTING HERE AND AROUND

There is only one main road through the Princeville resort area, so maneuvering a car here can be a nightmare. If you're trying to find a smaller lodging unit, be sure to get specific driving directions. Parking is available at the Princeville Shopping Center at the entrance to the resort. Kilauea is about 5 miles east on Route 56. There's a public parking lot in the town center as well as parking at the end of Kilauea Road for access to the lighthouse.

Sights

Anaina Hou Mini Golf & Gardens

GOLF | The island's first miniature-golf course also has a small botanical garden and a new 300-seat theater/arts center. The 18-hole course was designed to be challenging, beautiful, and family-friendly. Replacing the typical clown's nose and spinning wheels are some water features and tropical tunnels. Surrounding each hole is plant life that walks players through different eras of Hawaiian history. The new Porter Pavillion hosts special events such as concerts, plays, private parties, and community meetings. There is also a children's playground made from recycled materials on-site. A gift shop with local products and a concessions counter make it a fun activity for any time of day. On Saturday morning and Monday afternoon, a farmers' market is adjacent to the course with fresh Kauai produce and local goods. ✉ *5-273 Kuhio Hwy., Kilauea* ☎ *808/828–2118* ⊕ *www. anainahou.org* ✉ *$18.*

★ Kilauea Point National Wildlife Refuge and Kilauea Lighthouse

LIGHTHOUSE | A beacon for sea traffic since it was built in 1913, this National Historic Landmark celebrated its centennial in 2013 and has the largest clamshell lens of any lighthouse in the world. It's within a national wildlife refuge, where thousands of seabirds soar on the trade winds and nest on the steep ocean cliffs.

Kilauea Point Lighthouse is located in the Kilauea Point National Wildlife Refuge, a sanctuary for seabirds.

Seeing endangered nene geese, white- and red-tailed tropic birds, and more (all identifiable by educational signboards) as well as native plants, dolphins, humpback whales, huge winter surf, and gorgeous views of the North Shore are well worth the modest entry fee. The gift shop has a great selection of books about the island's natural history and an array of unique merchandise, with all proceeds benefiting education and preservation efforts. ⊠ *Kilauea Lighthouse Rd., Kilauea* ☎ *808/828–0384* ⊕ *www.kilaueapoint. org, www.fws.gov/kilaueapoint* ⊠ *$10, under 15 free.*

Moloaa Sunrise Fruit Stand
FOOD/CANDY | Don't let the name fool you; they don't open at sunrise (more like 7:30 am, so come here after you watch the sunrise elsewhere). And it's not just a fruit stand. Breakfast is light and includes bagels, granola, smoothies, coffee, espresso, cappuccino, latte, and, of course, tropical-style fresh juices (pine-apple, carrot, watermelon, guava, even sugarcane, in season). This is also a great spot to get out and stretch, take in the mountain view, and pick up sandwiches to go. Select local produce is available, although the variety is often not as good as at the island's farmers' markets. What makes this fruit stand different is the fresh, natural ingredients like multigrain breads and cold, homemade salads like potato or chicken curry that are perfect for a picnic. ⊠ *6011 Koolau Rd., at Kuhio Hwy., Kilauea* ☎ *808/822–1441.*

★ Na Aina Kai Botanical Gardens
GARDEN | Joyce and Ed Doty's love for plants and art spans 240 acres and includes many different gardens, a hardwood plantation, an *ahupuaa* (a Hawaiian land division), a re-created Navaho compound and an Athabascan village, a Japanese teahouse, a hedge maze, a waterfall, and access to a sandy beach. Throughout are more than 200 bronze sculptures, one of the nation's largest collections. One popular feature is a children's garden with a 16-foot-tall Jack and the Beanstalk bronze sculpture, gecko maze, tree house, kid-size train,

and, of course, a tropical jungle. Located in a residential neighborhood and hoping to maintain good neighborly relations, the Gardens, a nonprofit organization, limits tours (guided only). Tour lengths vary widely, from 1½ to 5 hours. Reservations are required. ⊠ *4101 Wailapa Rd., Kilauea* ☎ *808/828–0525* ⊕ *www.naainakai.org* ⌂ *From $35.*

Queen's Bath

HOT SPRINGS | A tropical path tucked away in a North Shore neighborhood winds its way down to the oceanfront, where a large tide pool has been carved into the dark lava rock creating nature's version of an infinity pool. It's a pretty sight to see when the surf is calm, but we do not recommend descending all the way down (it takes some dexterity and reef shoes to get there, and the path can be muddy and slippery) nor diving into this pool, as big surf can be dangerous. ⚠ **Be careful: October through May brings big surf, and people have been swept off the rocks and have drowned. If you choose to go, always heed warning signs.** ⊠ *Kapiolani Rd., Princeville.*

Beaches

Anini Beach Park

BEACH—SIGHT | **FAMILY** | A great family park, Anini features one of the longest and widest fringing reefs in all Hawaii, creating a shallow lagoon that is good for snorkeling and kids splashing about. It is safe except when surf is raging outside the reef and strong currents are created. A rip current exists between the two reefs where the boats enter and exit the beach ramp, so avoid swimming there. The entire reef follows the shoreline for some 2 miles and extends 1,600 feet offshore at its widest point. There's a narrow ribbon of sandy beach and lots of grass and shade, as well as a county campground at the western end and a small boat ramp. **Amenities:** lifeguard; parking; showers; toilets. **Best for:**

---

sunrise; swimming; walking. ⊠ *Anini Rd., off Rte. 56, Princeville.*

Kahili Beach (*Rock Quarry*)

BEACH—SIGHT | You wouldn't know it today, but this beach on Kilauea Bay was once an interisland steamer landing and a rock quarry. Today, it's a fairly quiet beach, although when the surf closes out many other North Shore surf spots, the break directly offshore from Kilauea Stream near the abandoned quarry is still rideable. For the regular ocean goer, summer's your best bet, although the quickly sloping ocean bottom makes for generally treacherous swimming. The stream estuary is quite beautiful, and the ironwood trees and false kamani growing in the generous sand dunes at the rear of the beach provide protection from the sun. It's a wonderful place to observe seabirds. **Amenities:** none. **Best for:** solitude; surfing; walking. ⊠ *Off Wailapa Rd., turn left on dirt road and follow to the end, Kilauea.*

Kalihiwai Beach

BEACH—SIGHT | A winding road leads down a cliff face to picture-perfect Kalihiwai Beach, which fronts a bay of the same name. It's another one of those drive-up beaches, so it's very accessible. Most people park under the grove of ironwood trees, near the stream, where young kids like to splash and older kids like to body board. Though do beware: the stream carries leptospirosis, a potentially lethal bacteria that can enter through open cuts. In winter months, beware of a treacherous shore break. Summer is the only truly safe time to swim. There's a local-favorite winter surf spot off the eastern edge of the beach, for advanced surfers only. The toilets here are the portable kind, and there are no showers. **Amenities:** parking; toilets. **Best for:** surfing; swimming; walking; solitude. ⌧ *Kalihiwai Rd., on Kilauea side of Kalihiwai Bridge, Kilauea.*

Kauapea Beach (*Secret Beach*)

BEACH—SIGHT | This beach went relatively unknown—except by local fishermen, of course—for a long time, hence the common reference to it as "Secret Beach." You'll understand why once you stand on the coarse white sands of Kauapea and see the solid wall of rock that runs the length of the beach, making it fairly inaccessible. For the hardy, there is a steep hike down the western end. From there, you can walk for a long way in either direction in summer. During winter, big swells cut off access to sections of the beach. You may witness dolphins just offshore, and it's a great place to see seabirds, as the Kilauea Point National Wildlife Refuge and its historic lighthouse lie at the eastern end. Nudity is not uncommon, though it is illegal in Hawaii. A consistent onshore break makes swimming here typically very dangerous. On big-surf days, don't go near the shoreline. **Amenities:** parking. **Best for:** solitude; sunrise; walking. ⌧ *Kalihiwai Rd., just past turnoff for Kilauea, Kilauea.*

Larsen's Beach

BEACH—SIGHT | The long, wide fringing reef here is this beach's trademark. The waters near shore are generally too shallow for swimming; if you go in, wear a rash guard to protect against prickly sea urchins and sharp coral on the bottom. This area is known for its tricky currents, especially during periods of high surf, and has been the site of numerous drownings. It can be dangerous to snorkel here. There's some nudity at the western end. Accessing this long strand of coarse, white sand requires hiking down a steep, rocky trail. Slippery when wet. **Amenities:** parking. **Best for:** solitude; sunrise; walking. ⌧ *Off Koolau Rd., look for dirt road and "beach access" sign, Kilauea.*

Pali Ke Kua Beach (*Hideaways Beach*)

BEACH—SIGHT | This is actually two very small pocket beaches separated by a narrow rocky point. The beach area itself is narrow and can all but disappear in wintertime. However, in summer, the steep, rocky trail (don't trust the rusty handrails and rotting ropes) that provides access reduces the number of beachgoers, at times creating a deserted beach feel. Winter's high surf creates dangerous conditions. ■**TIP**→ **Don't attempt the trail after a heavy rain—it turns into a mudslide.** **Amenities:** parking. **Best for:** sunset; surfing. ⌧ *End of Ka Haku Rd., on dirt trail between parking lot and condominium complex, Princeville.*

Puu Poa Beach

BEACH—SIGHT | The coastline along the community of Princeville is primarily made up of sea cliffs with a couple of pocket beaches. The sea cliffs end with a long, narrow stretch of beach just east of the Hanalei River. Public access is via 100-plus steps around the back of the hotel; hotel guests can simply take the elevator down to sea level. The beach itself is subject to the hazards of winter's surf, narrowing and widening with the surf height. On calm days, snorkeling is good thanks to a shallow reef system

Beach Safety on Kauai

Hawaii's world-renowned, beautiful beaches can be extremely dangerous at times due to large waves, wind, and strong currents—so much so that the state rates wave hazards using three signs: a yellow square (caution), a red stop sign (high hazard), and a black diamond (extreme hazard). Signs are posted and updated three times daily or as conditions change.

Visiting beaches with lifeguards is strongly recommended, and you should swim only when there's a normal caution rating. Never swim alone or dive into unknown water or shallow breaking waves. If you're unable to swim out of a rip current, tread water and wave your arms in the air to signal for help.

Even in calm conditions, there are other dangerous things in the water to be aware of, including razor-sharp coral, jellyfish, eels, and sharks, to name a few.

Jellyfish cause the most ocean injuries, and signs are sometimes posted along beaches when they're present. Reactions to a sting are usually mild (burning sensation, redness, welts); however, in some cases they can be severe (breathing difficulties). If you're stung, pick off the tentacles, rinse the affected area with water, and apply ice.

The chances of getting bitten by a shark in Hawaiian waters are very low; sharks attack swimmers or surfers three or four times per year. Of the 40 species of shark found near Hawaii, tiger sharks are considered the most dangerous because of their size and indiscriminate feeding behavior. They're easily recognized by their blunt snouts and vertical bars on their sides.

Here are a few tips to reduce your shark-attack risk:

■ Swim, surf, or dive with others at beaches patrolled by lifeguards.

■ Avoid swimming at dawn, dusk, and night, when some shark species may move inshore to feed.

■ Don't enter the water if you have open wounds or are bleeding.

■ Avoid murky waters, harbor entrances, areas near stream mouths (especially after heavy rains), channels, or steep drop-offs.

■ Don't wear high-contrast swimwear or shiny jewelry.

■ Don't swim near dolphins, which are often prey for large sharks.

The website ⊕ *oceansafety.ancl. hawaii.edu* provides beach hazard maps as well as weather and surf advisories.

---

pocked with sand. Sometimes a shallow sandbar extends across the river to Black Pot Beach Park, part of the Hanalei Beach system, making it easy to cross the river. On high-surf days, the outer edge of the reef near the river draws internationally ranked surfers. The resort's pool is off-limits to nonguests, but the restaurants and bars are not. **Amenities:** food and drink; parking. **Best for:** snorkeling; sunset; surfing. ⊠ *End of Ka Haku Rd., off Rte. 560, Princeville.*

 **Restaurants**

A rough couple of years have diminished the restaurant selection in the Princeville and Kilauea areas, starting in 2018

Budget-Friendly Eats: North Shore

It's not easy to find cheap food on the North Shore, but these little eateries serve up dinner for two for under $20.

Foodland. In a pinch, you can pick up pretty good sushi, ready-to-eat hot entrées, deli items, bakery goods, and panini sandwiches at the Foodland grocery store. ⊠ *Princeville Shopping Center, 5-4280 Kuhio Hwy., Princeville* ☎ *808/826–9880.*

Harvest Market. Health foods, such as rice dishes, soups, and salads, are served in the back of this natural-foods store at the Hanalei Center;

takeout only. ⊠ *5-5161 Kuhio Hwy., Hanalei* ☎ *808/826–0089.*

North Shore Variety Store. Yes, it's in a gas station. But it's a local favorite for hamburgers. For lunch, try the popular chili pepper chicken plate lunch. ⊠ *5-4280 Kuhio Hwy., Princeville* ☎ *808/826–7992.*

Tropical Taco. This place is a safe choice for very basic Mexican food, though the prices are high for the cuisine. Takeout or limited outdoor seating. ⊠ *5-5088 Kuhio Hwy., Hanalei* ☎ *808/827–8226* ⊕ *www.tropicaltaco. com.*

---

with massive flooding and continuing through 2020 with widespread closures due to the coronavirus. Restaurants at the former St. Regis, under renovation to become a 1 Hotel, have also closed. Though it may not offer what it once did, this area still has a number of good spots—after all, people need to eat no matter what. You'll find everything from inexpensive holes in the wall to relatively sophisticated and expensive establishments.

Kilauea Bakery and Pau Hana Pizza

$$ | **AMERICAN** | **FAMILY** | Open from 6:30 am, the bakery serves coffee drinks, delicious fresh pastries, bagels, and breads in the morning. Late risers beware: breads and pastries sell out quickly. **Known for:** its starter of Hawaiian sourdough made with guava; specialty pizzas topped with eclectic ingredients; fresh chocolate chip cookies made in-house daily. ⑤ *Average main: $20* ⊠ *Kong Lung Center, 2484 Keneke St., Kilauea* ☎ *808/828–2020* ⊕ *www.kilaueabakery. com.*

Nanea Restaurant and Bar

$$$ | **HAWAIIAN** | **FAMILY** | This is the signature restaurant of the Westin Princeville Ocean Resort Villas, and its casual, open-air seating is the perfect compliment to an island-style menu that is sure to please a wide range of diners. The grilled rib eye is served with bacon and sour cream mashed potatoes, while the half-chicken — smoked kalua style — is accompanied by Molokai sweet potatoes. **Known for:** kids eat free; inventive cocktails; local ingredients. ⑤ *Average main: $35* ⊠ *Westin Princeville Ocean Resort Villas, 3838 Wyllie Rd., Princeville* ☎ *808/827–8808* ⊕ *www.westinprinceville.com.*

North Shore Variety Store

$ | **AMERICAN** | Attached to a gas station and small items store, this classic hole-in-the-wall has the best deals for pick-up lunch on the North Shore. Darron's local-beef burgers have a loyal following, and you may have to get in line for his lunchtime favorite, chili-pepper chicken. **Known for:** chili-pepper chicken; burgers; food truck at Anini Beach on weekdays. ⑤ *Average main: $8* ⊠ *Princeville Shopping Center, 5-4280 Kuhio Hwy., Princeville* ☎ *808/826–7992.*

The upscale community of Princeville is home to golf courses and isolated beaches.

Hotels

Hanalei Bay Resort

$$ | RESORT | FAMILY | The nicest feature of this condominium resort overlooking Hanalei Bay and Napali Coast is its upper-level pool, with authentic lava-rock waterfalls, an open-air hot tub, and a kid-friendly sand "beach." Three-story buildings angle down the cliffs, making for some steep walking paths. **Pros:** beautiful views; pool, tennis courts, and fitness center on property; lively lounge. **Cons:** steep walkways; long walk to beach. ⑤ *Rooms from: $215* ✉ *5380 Honoiki Rd., Princeville* ☎ *808/826–6522, 877/507–1428* ⊕ *www.hanaleibayresort. com* 🛏 *134 units* ❙❍❙ *No meals.*

★ Westin Princeville Ocean Resort Villas

$$$$ | RESORT | FAMILY | Spread out over 18½ acres on a bluff above Anini Beach, this Westin property marries the comforts of spacious condominium living with the top-notch service and amenities of a luxurious hotel resort. **Pros:** on-site

minimarket; ocean views; kids' program. **Cons:** path to the nearby beach is a steep six- to seven-minute walk; whirlpool tub is small; units can be far from parking. ⑤ *Rooms from: $356* ✉ *3838 Wyllie Rd., Princeville* ☎ *808/827–8700* ⊕ *www. westinprinceville.com* 🛏 *366 units* ❙❍❙ *No meals.*

Nightlife

★ Happy Talk Lounge

BARS/PUBS | Want to sip an umbrella cocktail while you gaze at the original Bali Hai? Open on two sides, Happy Talk Lounge offers breezy views across Hanalei Bay to plush emerald mountains. If you think the scene looks familiar, maybe you've seen the film classic *South Pacific,* filmed here. The film version of Bali Hai is actually Kauai's Mount Makana. Order a tropical cocktail and *pupu* (Hawaiian hors d'oeuvres) and enjoy a truly enchanting evening as the sun sets over the sparkling waters. ■ **TIP→ Nearby Tunnels Beach (aka Haena Beach and Makua) is**

often called Nurses' Beach, where Mitzi Gaynor sang about washing that man right outta her hair; Hanalei Bay is where Bloody Mary sang "Bali Hai." ⊠ *Hanalei Bay Resort, 5380 Honoiki Rd., Princeville* ☎ *808/431–4084* ⊕ *www.happytalk-lounge.com.*

Shopping

Princeville Shopping Center is a bustling little mix of businesses, necessities, and some unique, often pricey, shops. Kilauea is a bit more sprawled out and offers a charming, laid-back shopping scene with a neighborhood feel.

Kong Lung Co

GIFTS/SOUVENIRS | Sometimes called the Gump's of Kauai, this gift store sells elegant clothing, glassware, books, gifts, and artwork—all very lovely and expensive. The shop is housed in a beautiful 1892 stone building in the heart of Kilauea. It's the showpiece of the pretty little Kong Lung Center, where everything from handmade soaps to hammocks can be found. A great bakery and pizzeria round out the offerings, along with an exhibit of historical photos. ⊠ *2484 Keneke St., Kilauea* ☎ *808/828–1822* ⊕ *www.konglungkauai.com*

Princeville Shopping Center

SHOPPING CENTERS/MALLS | The big draws at this small center are a full-service grocery store and a hardware store, but there's also a fun toy store, a bar, a mailing service, a very nice sandal boutique, women's clothing, and an ice-cream shop. This is also the last stop for gas and banking when you're heading to the North Shore. ⊠ *5-4280 Kuhio Hwy., near mile marker 28, Princeville* ☎ *808/826–9497* ⊕ *www.princevillecenter.com.*

Napali Coast

Napali Coast is considered the jewel of Kauai, and for all its greenery, it would surely be an emerald. After seeing the coast, many are at a loss for words, because its beauty is so overwhelming. Others resort to poetry. Pulitzer Prize–winning poet W. S. Merwin wrote a book-length poem, *The Folding Cliffs,* based on a true story set in Napali. *Napali* means "the cliffs," and while it sounds like a simple name, it's quite an apt description. The coastline is cut by a series of small valleys, like fault lines, running to the interior, with the resulting cliffs seeming to bend back on themselves like an accordion-folded fan made of green velvet. More than 5 million years old, these sea cliffs rise thousands of feet above the Pacific, and every shade of green is represented in the vegetation that blankets their lush peaks and folds. At their base there are caves, secluded beaches, and waterfalls to explore.

Let's put this in perspective: even if you had only one day on Kauai, we'd still recommend heading to Napali Coast on Kauai's northwest side. Once you're there, you'll understand why no road traverses this series of folding-fan cliffs. That leaves three ways to experience the coastline—by air, by water, or on foot. We recommend all three, in that order—each one gets progressively more sensory.(⇨ *See the Napali feature in this chapter.*) A helicopter tour is your best bet if you're strapped for time; we recommend Jack Harter Helicopters (⇨ *see Aerial Tours in the Activities chapter for more information*). Boat tours are great for family fun, and hiking, of course, is the most budget-friendly option.

Whatever way you choose to visit Napali, you might want to keep this awe-inspiring fact in mind: at one time, thousands of Hawaiians lived self-sufficiently in these valleys.

Continued on page 96

NAPALI COAST: EMERALD QUEEN OF KAUAI

If you're coming to
Kauai, Napali ("the cliffs"
in Hawaiian) is a major must see.
More than 5 million years old, these
sea cliffs rise thousands of feet above the
Pacific, and every shade of green is represented in the vegetation that blankets their
lush peaks and folds. At their base, there are
caves, secluded beaches, and waterfalls to explore.

The big question is how to explore this gorgeous
stretch of coastline. You can't drive to it, through it, or
around it. You can't see Napali from a scenic lookout.
You can't even take a mule ride to it. The only way to
experience its magic is from the sky, the ocean, or the trail.

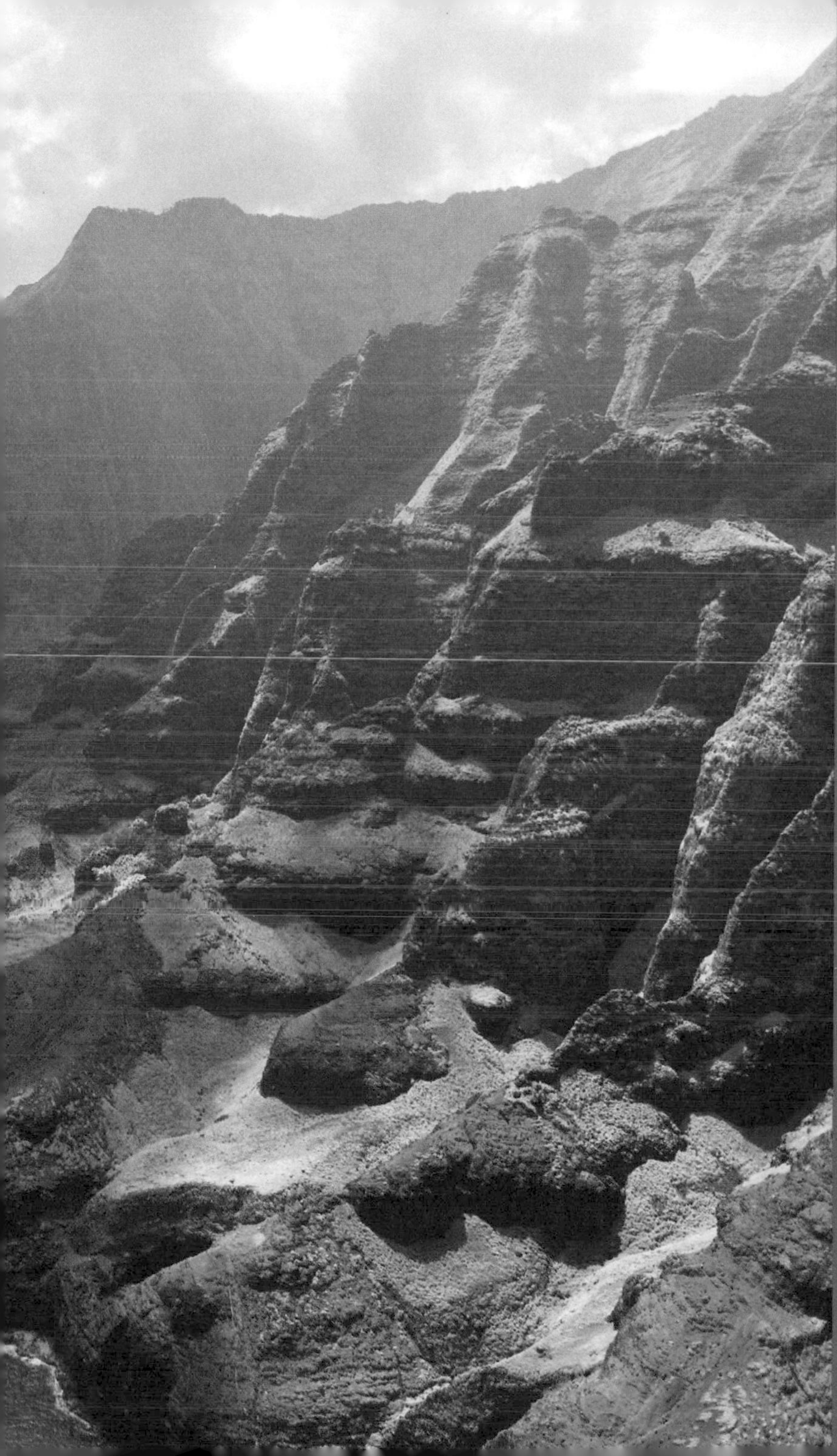

FROM THE SKY

If you've booked a helicopter tour of Napali, you might start wondering what you've gotten yourself into on the way to the airport. Will it feel like being on a small airplane? Will there be turbulence? Will it be worth all the money you just plunked down?

Your concerns will be assuaged on the helipad, once you see the faces of those who have just returned from their journey: Everyone looks totally blissed out. And now it's your turn.

Climb on board, strap on your headphones, and the next thing you know the helicopter gently lifts up, hovers for a moment, and floats away like a spider on the wind—no roaring engines, no rumbling down a runway. If you've chosen a flight with music, you'll feel as if you're inside your very own IMAX movie.

Pinch yourself if you must, because this is the real thing. Your pilot shares history, legend, and lore. If you miss something, speak up: pilots love to show off their island knowledge. You may snap a few pictures (not too many or you'll miss the eyes-on experience!), nudge a friend or spouse, and point at a whale breeching in the ocean, but mostly you stare, mouth agape. There is simply no other way to take in the immensity and greatness of Napali but from the air.

(left) The Napali Coast is a breathtaking stretch of Kauai coastline lined by sea cliffs rising thousands of feet into the sky. (bottom) Helicopter tour over Napali Coast

GOOD TO KNOW

Helicopter companies depart from the north, east, and west sides of the island. Most are based in Lihue, near the airport.

If you want more adventure—and air—choose one of the helicopter companies that flies with the doors off.

Some companies offer flights without music. Know the experience you want ahead of time. Some even sell a DVD of your flight, so you don't have to worry about taking pictures.

Wintertime rain grounds some flights; plan your trip early in your stay in case the flight gets rescheduled.

IS THIS FOR ME?

Taking a helicopter trip is the most expensive way to see Napali—as much as $300 for an hour-long tour.

Claustrophobic? Choose a boat tour or hike. It's a tight squeeze in the helicopter, especially in one of the middle seats.

Short on time? Taking a helicopter tour is a great way to see the island.

WHAT YOU MIGHT SEE

■ Nualolo Kai (an ancient Hawaiian fishing village) with its fringed reef

■ The 300-foot Hanakapiai Falls

■ A massive sea arch formed in the rock by erosion

■ The 11-mile Kalalau Trail threading its way along the coast

■ The amazing striations of aa and pahoehoe lava flows that helped push Kauai above the sea

FROM THE OCEAN

Napali from the ocean is two treats in one: spend a good part of the day on (or in) the water, and gaze up at majestic green sea cliffs rising thousands of feet above your head.

There are three ways to see it: a mellow pleasure-cruise catamaran allows you to kick back and sip a mai tai; an adventurous raft (Zodiac) tour will take you inside sea caves under waterfalls, and give you the option of snorkeling; and a daylong outing in a kayak is possible in the summer.

Any way you travel, you'll breathe ocean air, feel spray on your face, and see pods of spinner dolphins, green sea turtles, flying fish, and, if you're lucky, a rare Hawaiian monk seal.

Napali stretches from Kee Beach in the north to Polihale beach on the West Side. You'll be heading towards the lush Hanakapiai Valley, where within a few minutes, you'll see caves and waterfalls galore. About halfway down the coast just after the Kalalau Trail ends, you'll come to an immense arch—formed where the sea eroded the less dense basaltic rock—and a thundering 50-foot waterfall. And as the island curves near Nualolo State Park, you'll begin to notice less vegetation and more rocky outcroppings.

(left and top right) Kayaking on Napali Coast
(bottom right) Dolphin on Napali Coast

GOOD TO KNOW

If you want to snorkel, choose a morning rather than an afternoon tour—preferably during a summer visit—when seas are calmer.

If you're on a budget, choose a non-snorkeling tour.

If you want to see whales, take any tour, but be sure to plan your vacation for December through March.

You can only embark from the North Shore in summer. If you're staying on the South Shore, it might not be worth your time to drive to the north, so head to the West Side.

IS THIS FOR ME?

Boat tours are several hours long, so if you have only a short time on Kauai, a helicopter tour is a better alternative.

Even on a small boat, you won't get the individual attention and exclusivity of a helicopter tour.

Prone to seasickness? A large boat can be surprisingly rocky, so be prepared. Afternoon trips are rougher because the winds pick up.

WHAT YOU MIGHT SEE

■ Hawaii's state fish—the humuhumunukunukuapuaa otherwise known as the reef triggerfish

■ Waiahuakua Sea Cave, with a waterfall coming through its roof

■ Tons of marine life, including dolphins, green sea turtles, flying fish, and humpback whales, especially in February and March

■ Waterfalls—especially if your trip is after a heavy rain

FROM THE TRAIL

If you want to be one with Napali—feeling the soft red earth beneath your feet, picnicking on the beaches, and touching the lush vegetation—hiking the Kalalau Trail is the way to do it.

Most people hike only the first 2 miles of the 11-mile trail and turn around at Hanakapiai. This 4-mile round-trip hike takes three to four hours. It starts at sea level and doesn't waste any time gaining elevation. (Take heart—the uphill lasts only a mile and tops out at 400 feet; then it's downhill all the way.) At the half-mile point, the trail curves west and the folds of Napali Coast unfurl.

Along the way you might share the trail with feral goats and wild pigs. Some of the vegetation is native; much is introduced.

After the 1-mile mark the trail begins its drop into Hanakapiai. You'll pass a couple of streams of water trickling across the trail, and maybe some banana, ginger, the native uluhe fern, and the Hawaiian ti plant. Finally the trail swings around the eastern ridge of Hanakapiai for your first glimpse of the valley and then switchbacks down the mountain. You'll have to boulder-hop across the stream to reach the beach. If you like, you can take a 4-mile, round-trip fairly strenuous side trip from this point to the gorgeous Hanakapiai Falls.

(left) Awaawapuhi mountain biker on razor-edge ridge
(top right) Feral goats in Kalalau Valley
(bottom right) Napali Coast

GOOD TO KNOW

Wear comfortable, amphibious shoes. Unless your feet require extra support, wear a self-bailing sort of shoe (for stream crossings) that doesn't mind mud. Don't wear heavy, waterproof hiking boots.

During winter the trail is often muddy, so be extra careful; sometimes it's completely inaccessible.

Don't hike after heavy rain—flash floods are common.

If you plan to hike the entire 11-mile trail (most people do the shorter hike described at left) you'll need a permit to go past Hanakapiai.

IS THIS FOR ME?

Of all the ways to see Napali (with the exception of kayaking the coast), this is the most active. You need to be in decent shape to hit the trail.

If you're vacationing in winter, this hike might not be an option due to flooding—whereas you can take a helicopter year-round.

WHAT YOU MIGHT SEE

■ Big dramatic surf right below your feet

■ Amazing vistas of the cool blue Pacific

■ The spectacular Hanakaplai Falls; if you have a permit don't miss Hanakoa Falls, less than 1/2 mile off the trail

■ Wildlife, including goats and pigs

■ Zany-looking hala trees, with aerial roots and long, skinny serrated leaves known as lau hala. Early Hawaiians used them to make mats, baskets, and canoe sails.

GETTING HERE AND AROUND

Napali Coast runs 15 miles from Kee Beach (one of Kauai's more popular snorkeling spots) on the island's North Shore, to Polihale State Park (the longest stretch of beach in the state) on the West Side of the island.

How do you explore this gorgeous stretch of coastline? You can't drive to it, through it, or around it. You can't see Napali from a scenic lookout. You can't even take a mule ride to it. The only way to experience its magic is from the sky, the ocean, or the trail. The Kalalau Trail can be hiked from the "end of the road" at Kee Beach, where the trailhead begins in Haena State Park at the northwest end of Kuhio Highway (Route 56). There's no need to hike the entire 11 miles to get a full experience, especially if you just hike the first 2 miles into Hanakapiai Beach and another 2 miles up that valley. ⇨ *For information on Napali Coast tour operators, see the Boat Tours section and Aerial Tours section in the Activities chapter.*

 Beaches

Hanakapiai Beach

BEACH—SIGHT | Hanakapiai Beach is a small jewel you'll discover after the first 2 miles of Napali Trail and crossing the stream. It's a beauty, with fine sand, a feeling of isolation, and a tropical stream valley to explore. Unfortunately, the beach is only swimmable in summer under the right conditions, as there is often a dangerous shore break. And, at all times of the year, it's a sweep-away beach, since it is not protected as a bay would be. For relaxation, sunning, and as a solid refresher on your hiking journey, Hanakapiai offers a welcome and stunning respite. **Best for:** sunset; solitude. **Amenities:** toilets. ⊠ *Hanalei* ✛ *Trailhead is at end of Rte. 560, 7 miles west of Hanalei.*

Kee Beach State Park

BEACH—SIGHT | This stunning beach marks the start of majestic Napali Coast. The 11-mile **Kalalau Trail** begins near the parking lot, drawing day hikers and backpackers. Permits are required to take the entire trek, but day-trippers can head 2 miles into Hanakapiai Beach for a dollar. Another path leads from the sand to a stone hula platform dedicated to **Laka**, the goddess of hula, which has been in use since ancient times. This is a sacred site that should be approached with respect; it's inappropriate for visitors to leave offerings at the altar, which is tended by students in a local hula *halau* (school). Local etiquette suggests observing from a distance. Most folks head straight for the sandy beach and its dreamy lagoon, which is great for snorkeling when the sea is calm. ⊠ *Western end of Rte. 560, Haena.*

Chapter 4

THE EAST SIDE

4

Updated by
Charles E. Roessler

⊙ Sights	🍴 Restaurants	🛏 Hotels	🛍 Shopping	🍸 Nightlife
★★★★☆	★★★☆☆	★★★☆☆	★★★★☆	★★☆☆☆

WELCOME TO THE EAST SIDE

TOP REASONS TO GO

★ **Golden Beaches.** With open fields and a large pool for snorkeling, Lydgate State Park is great for picnics and safe swimming. A beautiful seaside pathway, Ke Ala Hele Makalae Path, starts here.

★ **Mountain Hikes.** Trek up to the Sleeping Giant for a great view of the island from high up in the Nounou mountains. Variations in terrain make the East Side suitable for hikers of all abilities.

★ **Hidden Waterfalls.** You can watch water tumble hundreds of feet down from mighty Opaekaa Falls and get great views of the Wailua River Valley here.

★ **Location, Location.** Reasonably priced restaurants, affordable lodging prices, and central location close to Kauai's airport make the East Side a practical place to stay. It's also a great place to meet the locals.

★ **Kapaa Town.** Kapaa's old plantation-style buildings now house boutiques and eateries as well as art shops. Sidestreets offer a reminder of Kauai before commercialization.

1 Kapaa. This colorful former plantation town recalls an earlier era. Its small shops, eateries, and art shops make for a lively stroll around town.

2 Wailua. This area of the Coconut Coast has great places to stay, eat, and shop on an affordable budget, and its central location is hard to beat.

3 Lihue. The island's "capital," as well as its business and commercial center, is where you'll fly into Kauai. Busy during the work day, it's quiet in the evening except for a few nightspots.

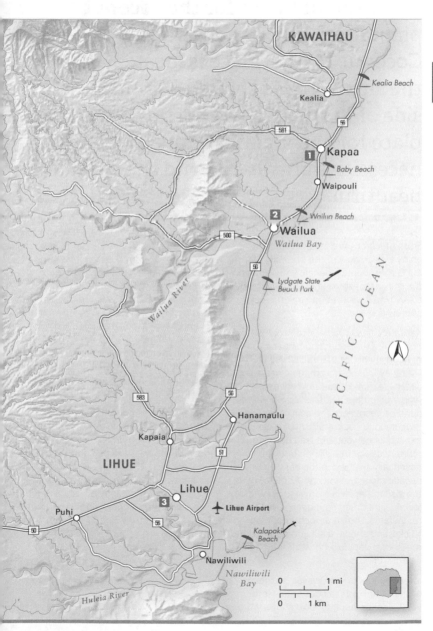

The East Side encompasses Lihue, Wailua, and Kapaa. It's also known as the Coconut Coast for the coconut plantation where today's aptly named Coconut Marketplace is located and the small groves that still sit on each side of Kuhio Highway. It's a convenient place for the practical traveler, as all the necessities are nearby and the coast is beautiful.

From much of the East Side you can enjoy a clear view of the eternally Sleeping Giant mountain behind you. While on the *makai* (ocean) side of the highway, a short walk takes you to a semi-rocky shoreline.

Kapaa Town was Kauai's commercial hub during the sugar and pineapple eras. Many descendants still live on the land they inherited from their Hawaiian, Japanese, and Portuguese ancestors who worked the fields as immigrants a hundred years ago. The past few decades have seen Kapaa's residential areas expand as newcomers lead demand for more housing. The island population has essentially doubled in the past three decades to a present-day 72,000. For the visitor, Kapaa is a small town with jewelry and dress boutiques, smaller restaurants, tourist emporiums, food trucks, and shops. It's a good area to meet local people who work the smaller establishments.

Kapaa connects with Wailua by means of the ill-defined Waipouli area. Here you'll find restaurants, bike shops, a chiropractor, a bikini shop, and a general assortment of small businesses. The Wailua area, now marked with the shell of the former Coco Palms Hotel across from Wailua Beach, was the traditional home of Kauai's famous *alii*, rulers of the commoners. Much of Kauai's Hawaiian history can be traced to the Wailua River area. More recently, Sinatra and Presley graced the coast while filming movies and enjoying the laid-back scene of old Kauai.

Lihue is the county seat, and the whole East Side is the island's center of commerce, so early-morning and late-afternoon drive times (or rush hour) can get very congested in what's known locally as Kapaa Krawl. If you're driving, take advantage of the Kapaa bypass, which can take you from northern Kapaa Town all the way past Wailua, avoiding most of the traffic.

Planning

Getting Here and Around

The island's major airport is in Lihue, making the East Side a practical base for travelers to Kauai. Turn to the right out of the airport at Lihue for the road to Wailua. Careful, though—the zone between Lihue and Wailua has been the site of many car accidents. Two bridges—under which the very culturally significant Wailua River gently flows—mark the beginning of Wailua. It quickly blends into Kapaa via Waipouli; there's no real demarcation. Pay attention and drive carefully, always knowing where you are going and when to turn off.

Route 56 leads into Lihue from the north, and Route 50 comes here from the south and west. The road from the airport (where Kauai's car rental agencies are) leads to the middle of Lihue. Many of the area's stores and restaurants are on and around Rice Street, which also leads to Kalapaki Bay and Nawiliwili Harbor.

Beaches

The East Side of the island is considered the "windward" side, a term you'll often hear in weather forecasts. It simply means the side of the island receiving most of the onshore winds. The wind helps break down rock into sand, so there are plenty of beaches here. Unfortunately, only a few of those beaches are protected, so many are not ideal for beginning ocean goers, though they are perfect for long sunrise ambles. On superwindy days, kiteboarders sail along the east shore, sometimes jumping waves and performing acrobatic maneuvers in the air.

Hotels

Location, location, location. The East Side, or Coconut Coast, is a good centralized home base if you want to see and do it all. This is one of the few resort areas on Kauai where you can actually walk to the beach, restaurants, and stores from your condo, hotel, or vacation-rental unit. It's not only convenient, but comparatively cheap. You pay less for lodging, meals, services, merchandise, and gas here—mainly because much of the coral-reef coastline isn't as ideal as the sandy bottom bays that front the fancy resorts. We think the shoreline is just fine. There are pockets in the reef to swim in, and the coast is uncrowded and boasts spectacular views. ■TIP➜ Traffic on the main highway can be bumper-to-bumper in the afternoon. All in all, it's a good choice for families because the prices are right and there's plenty to keep everyone happy and occupied.

Restaurants

Because the East Side is the island's largest population center, it makes sense that it should boast a wide selection of restaurants. It's also a good place to get both cheaper meals and the local-style cuisine that residents favor.

Most of the eateries are found along Kuhio Highway between Kapaa and Wailua; a few are tucked into shopping centers and resorts. In Lihue, it's easier to find lunch than dinner because many restaurants cater to the business crowd.

You'll find all the usual fast-food joints in both Kapaa and Lihue, as well as virtually every ethnic cuisine available on Kauai. Although fancy gourmet restaurants are less abundant in this part of the island, there's plenty of good, solid food, and a few stellar attractions. But unless you're staying on the East Side, or passing through, it's probably not worth the long drive from the North Shore or Poipu resorts to eat here.

HOTEL AND RESTAURANT PRICES

Hotel prices in the reviews are the lowest cost of a standard double room in high season. Restaurant prices in the reviews are the average cost of a main course at dinner, or if dinner is not served, at lunch.

WHAT IT COSTS in U.S. Dollars			
$	$$	$$$	$$$$
RESTAURANTS			
under $18	$18–$26	$27–$35	over $35
HOTELS			
under $180	$180–$260	$261–$340	over $340

Tours

Roberts Hawaii Tours

BUS TOURS | The *Round-the-Island Tour* , sometimes called the *Waimea Canyon–Fern Grotto Tour,* gives a good overview of half the island, including Fort Elizabeth and Opaekaa Falls. Guests are transported in air-conditioned, 25-passenger minibuses. The $110 trip includes a boat ride up the Wailua River to the Fern Grotto and a visit to the lookouts above Waimea Canyon. They also offer a *Kauai Movie Tour* for $109. ⊠ *3-4567 Kuhio Hwy., Hanamaulu* ☎ *808/245–9101, 800/831–5541* ⊕ *www.robertshawaii. com/kauai/* 🖘 *From $110.*

Kapaa and Wailua

Kapaa is 16 miles southeast of Kilauea; Wailua is 3 miles southwest of Kapaa.

Old Town Kapaa was once a sugar and pineapple plantation town, which is no surprise—most of the larger towns on Kauai once were. Old Town Kapaa is made up of a collection of wooden-front shops, some built by plantation workers and still run by their progeny today. Kapaa houses two of the biggest grocery stores on the island, side by side: Foodland and Safeway. It also offers plenty of dining options for breakfast, lunch, and dinner, and gift shopping. If the timing is right, plan to cruise the town on the first Saturday evening of each month when the bands are playing and the town's wares are on display. To the south, Wailua comprises a few restaurants and shops, a few mid-range resorts along the coastline, and a local housing community *mauka* (toward the mountains).

Sights

Fern Grotto

NATURE SITE | The Fern Grotto has a long history on Kauai, and though it's really not much to look at, visitors seem to like it. Perhaps it's the serenity of just cruising up and down the river accompanied by Hawaiian music to see it. The grotto itself is nothing more than a yawning lava tube swathed in lush fishtail ferns 3 miles up the Wailua River. Though it was significantly damaged after Hurricane Iniki in 1992 and again after heavy rains in 2006, the greenery has completely recovered. The Smith's Kauai tour group is the only way to legally see the grotto. You can access the entrance with a kayak, but if boats are there, you may not be allowed to land. ⊠ *Rte. 56, just south of Wailua River, Kapaa* ☎ *808/821–6893* ⊕ *smithskauai.com* 🖘 *$25.*

Kamokila Hawaiian Village

TOWN | **FAMILY** | The village is dramatically ensconced at the base of a steep, long, winding road right down to the Wailua River. In the days of King Kaumualii, it made the perfect hideout to tuck away his war canoes in this crook of the river. Today, there's a replica Hawaiian village in place of war canoes—numerous thatched-roof structures and abundant plant life along with traditional Hawaiian games. Yet, the lack of human activity here makes it seem abandoned, which may be why Hollywood found it an appealing location for the movie *Outbreak*. Visitors can rent canoes for the day and paddle up to the Fern Grotto or Secret Falls. ☒ *5443 Kuamoo Rd., Kapaa* ☎ *808/823–0559* ⊕ *www.villagekauai. com* ☒ *$5.*

Keahua Forestry Arboretum

GARDEN | Tree-lined and grassy, this is a perfect spot for a picnic—and there are lots of picnic tables scattered throughout the parklike setting. A shallow, cascading stream makes for a fun spot for kids to splash, although the water's a bit chilly. After crossing the stream on the brand-new bridge, the 1-mile walking trail meanders through mango, monkeypod, and exquisite rainbow eucalyptus trees. This is an exceptionally peaceful place—good for yoga and meditation—that is, unless the resident roosters decide to crow. ☒ *Kuamoo Rd., Wailua (Kauai County).*

★ Ke Ala Hele Makalae Path

TRAIL | Running from the southern end of Lydgate Park to Donkey Beach, between Kealia and Anahola, this seaside path is a favorite of visitors and locals alike. Sea breezes, gorgeous ocean views, smooth pavement, and friendly smiles from everyone as they bike, walk, skate, and run can be seen on the trail. The path has many entry points, and you'll have your choice of bike shops just off the trail. ☒ *1121 Moanakai Rd., Kapaa* ⊕ *www. kauaipath.org/kauaicoastalpath.*

Kealia Scenic Viewpoint

VIEWPOINT | This ocean overlook is perfect for spotting whales during their winter migration. In fact, on three Saturdays in winter, the Hawaiian Islands Humpback Whale National Marine Sanctuary conducts its annual whale count from this spot. The lookout was rebuilt and doubled in size a few years ago, and it's now easy to hop on the cement bike-and-walking path just below for a coastal stroll or ride. Most days you can see clear to Lihue and

beyond. If you packed them, bring your binoculars. ☒ *Rte. 56, Kapaa* ⊹ *Between mile markers 9 and 10.*

Lydgate Farms

FARM/RANCH | Hawaii is the only state in the country where *theobroma cacao* grows, the tree whose seeds become chocolate. The Lydgates are on a mission to grow enough cacao on their family farm that one day they will produce an identifiable Kauai homegrown chocolate. For now, you can tour this organic farm (in addition to cacao, they grow vanilla, timber trees, bamboo, and many tropical fruits) and learn how chocolate is made, "from branch to bar," as they put it. The three-hour tour includes, of course, plenty of chocolate tastings. Reservations are required for the morning tour, which runs weekdays at 9 am. Children 12 and under are free. ☒ *5730 Olohena Rd., Kapaa* ☎ *808/821–1857* ⊕ *www.steelgrass.org* ☒ *$95.*

Opaekaa Falls

BODY OF WATER | **FAMILY** | The mighty Wailua River produces many dramatic waterfalls, and Opaekaa (pronounced "oh-pie-kah-ah") is one of the best. It plunges hundreds of feet to the pool below and can be easily viewed from a scenic overlook with ample parking. Opaekaa means "rolling shrimp," which refers to tasty native crustaceans that were once so abundant they could be seen tumbling in the falls. Do not attempt to hike down to the pool. ■TIP➔ **Just before reaching the parking area for the waterfall, turn left into a scenic pullout for great views of the Wailua River Valley and its march to the sea.** ☒ *Kuamoo Rd., Wailua (Kauai County)* ⊹ *From Rte. 56, turn mauka onto Kuamoo Rd. and drive 1½ miles.*

★ Poliahu Heiau

ARCHAEOLOGICAL SITE | Storyboards near this ancient *heiau* (sacred site) recount the significance of the many sacred structures found along the Wailua River. It's unknown exactly how the ancient Hawaiians used Poliahu Heiau—one

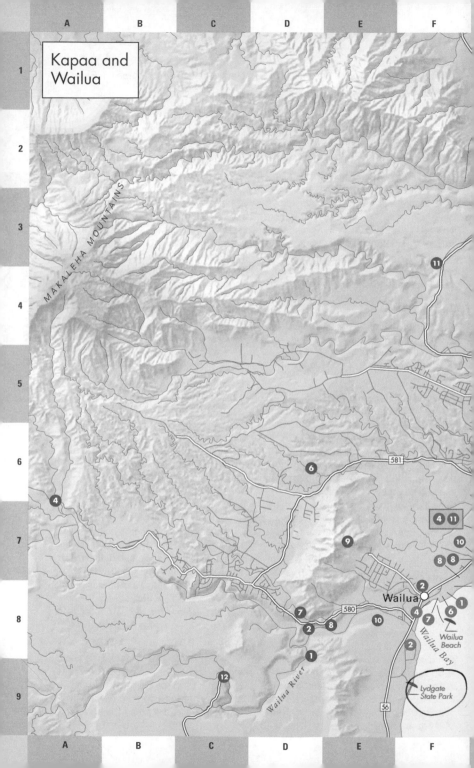

Kapaa and Wailua

MAKALEHA MOUNTAINS

Wailua

Wailua River

Wailua Beach

Wailua Bay

Lydgate State Park

KEY

1 Exploring Sights
1 Restaurants
1 Hotels

0 ___ 1 mi
0 ___ 1 km

of the largest pre-Christian temples on the island—but legend says it was built by the Menehune because of the unusual stonework found in its walled enclosures. From this site, drive downhill toward the ocean to *pohaku hanau,* a two-piece birthing stone said to confer special blessings on all children born there, and *pohaku piko,* whose crevices were a repository for umbilical cords left by parents seeking a clue to their child's destiny, which reportedly was foretold by how the cord fared in the rock. Some Hawaiians feel these sacred stones shouldn't be viewed as tourist attractions, so always treat them with respect. Never stand or sit on the rocks or leave any offerings. ⊠ *Rte. 580, Kuamoo Rd., Wailua (Kauai County).*

Sleeping Giant

MOUNTAIN—SIGHT | Although its true name is Nounou, this landmark mountain ridge is better known as the Sleeping Giant because of its resemblance to a very large man sleeping on his back. Legends differ on whether the giant is Puni, who was accidentally killed by rocks launched at invading canoes by the Menehune, or Nunui, a gentle creature who has not yet awakened from the nap he took centuries ago after building a massive temple and enjoying a big feast. ⊠ *Rte. 56, Kapaa* ✛ *About 1 mile north of Wailua River.*

Smith's Tropical Paradise

GARDEN | **FAMILY** | Nestled next to Wailua Marina along the mighty Wailua River, this 30-acre botanical and cultural garden offers a glimpse of exotic foliage, including fruit orchards, a bamboo rain forest, and tropical lagoons. Take the tram and enjoy a narrated tour or stroll along the mile-long pathways during the luau. It's a popular spot for wedding receptions and other large events, and its luau is one of the island's oldest and best. ⊠ *3-5971 Kuhio Hwy., just south of Wailua River, Kapaa* ☎ *808/821–6895* ⊕ *smithskauai. com.*

Roadside Vendors

Lei. Tropical flowers. Fresh fish. Rambutan. Avocados. *Huli huli* chicken. Kalua pig. It's not uncommon to run across individuals selling flowers, produce, and food on the side of the road. Some are local farmers trying to make a living; others are people fundraising for the local canoe club. Don't be afraid to stop and buy. Most are friendly and enjoy chatting.

Spalding Monument

VIEWPOINT | The Colonel Zephaniah Spalding monument commemorates the Civil War veteran who purchased this splendid property overlooking an area from Anahola to Kapaa in 1876 and soon established what became the Kealia Sugar Plantation. Turn onto Kealia Road just after mile marker 10 for an off-the-beaten-track scenic detour. Immediately on your right are a small post office and a food truck and, on your left, rodeo grounds often in use on summer weekends. The road ascends, and 2½ miles later you'll reach a grassy area with the concrete remains of a monument. It's a nice place to picnic or to simply gaze at the nearby grazing horses. If you're an early riser, this is a great spot to watch the sun rise; if not, check the local newspaper for the next full moon and bring a bottle of wine. It's possible to continue on for another very bumpy 2 miles, where you'll reconnect with Highway 56 near the town of Anahola, but your bike or car will not thank you for it. You're better off doubling back. ⊠ *Kealia Rd., Kapaa.*

★ Wailua Falls

BODY OF WATER | **FAMILY** | You may recognize this impressive cascade from the opening sequences of the *Fantasy Island* television series. Kauai has plenty

of noteworthy waterfalls, but this one is especially gorgeous, easy to find, and easy to photograph. To reach it, drive north from Lihue following Maalo Road in Hanamaulu, then travel uphill for 3 miles. ⊠ *Maalo Rd., off Rte. 580, Lihue.*

Beaches

Aliomanu Beach

BEACH—SIGHT | This narrow beach is lined with homes, most of them set back a bit and screened with vegetation that blocks access along the sand in a number of places when the surf is up or tide is high. The waters off Aliomanu Beach are protected by the fringing reef 100 yards or so out to sea, and there are pockets for swimming. However, currents can be tricky, especially near the stream tucked in the beach's elbow toward the northern end, and at the river mouth on the southern end that demarcates neighboring Anahola Beach. This beach is in Hawaiian Homelands, an area held in trust for Native Hawaiians by the State of Hawaii, and is frequently used by fishermen and local families for camping. **Amenities:** parking. **Best for:** solitude; sunrise. ⊠ *Aliomanu Rd., north of mile marker 14, Anahola.*

Anahola Beach Park

BEACH—SIGHT | Anahola is part of the Hawaiian Homelands on Kauai, so Anahola Beach Park is definitely a locals' hangout, especially for families with small children. The shallow and calm water at the beach road's end is tucked behind a curving finger of land and perfect for young ones. As the beach winds closer to the river mouth, there's less protection and a shore break favorable for body boarders if the trades are light or *kona* (south) winds are present. The long, sandy beach is nice for a morning or evening stroll, but the campground often makes this beach busier in summer. **Amenities:** lifeguards; parking; showers; toilets. **Best for:** surfing; swimming;

walking. ⊠ *Anahola Rd., south of mile marker 14, Anahola.*

Baby Beach

BEACH—SIGHT | **FAMILY** | There aren't many safe swimming beaches on Kauai's East Side; however, this one usually ranks highly with parents because there's a narrow, lagoonlike area between the beach and the near-shore reef perfect for small children. In winter, watch for east and northeast swells that would make this not such a safe option. There are no beach facilities—no lifeguards—so watch your babies. There is an old-time shower spigot (cold water only) along the roadside available to rinse off the salt water. **Amenities:** parking; showers. **Best for:** sunrise; swimming. ⊠ *Moanakai Rd., Kapaa.*

Donkey Beach (*Paliku Beach*)

BEACH—SIGHT | This beach gets its unusual name from the former Lihue Plantation Company, which once kept a herd of mules and donkeys in the pasture adjacent to the beach. If the waves are right, body boarders and surfers might be spotted offshore. However, the waters here are usually rough and not recommended for swimming and snorkeling. Instead, we suggest a morning walk along the easy trail that overlooks the coast, starting at the northern end of Kealia Beach. It's not uncommon to see nude sunbathers here. **Amenities:** none. **Best for:** solitude; sunrise; surfing. ⊠ *Rte. 56, north of Kealia Kai subdivision, Kealia.*

Kealia Beach

BEACH—SIGHT | A half mile long and adjacent to the highway heading north out of Kapaa, Kealia Beach attracts body boarders and surfers year-round. It's a favorite with locals and visitors alike. Kealia is not generally a great beach for swimming, but it's a place to sunbathe and enjoy the beach scene. The safest area to swim is at the far north end of the beach, protected by a lava rock sea wall. The waters are often rough and the waves crumbly due to an onshore break (no protecting reef) and northeasterly trade winds. A scenic lookout on the southern end, accessed off the highway, is a superb location for saluting the morning sunrise or spotting whales during winter. A level, paved section of the Ke Maka Hele Makalae bike path with small, covered pavilions runs along the coastline here, and is very popular for walking and biking. **Amenities:** lifeguard; parking; showers; toilets. **Best for:** sunrise; surfing; swimming; walking. ⊠ *Rte. 56, at mile marker 10, Kealia.*

Lydgate State Park

BEACH—SIGHT | FAMILY | This is by far the best family beach park on Kauai. The waters off the beach are protected by a hand-built breakwater, creating two boulder-enclosed saltwater pools for safe swimming and snorkeling most of the year. Heavy rains upriver do occasionally deposit driftwood, clogging the pools. The smaller of the two pools is perfect for *keiki* (children). Behind the beach is Kamalani Playground; children of all ages—that includes you—enjoy the swings, lava-tube slides, tree house, and open field. Picnic tables abound in the park, and pavilions for day use and overnight camping are available by permit. The Kamalani Kai Bridge is a second playground, south of the original. (The two are united by the Ke Ala Hele Makalae bike and pedestrian coastal path.) ■ TIP→ **This park system is perennially popular; the quietest times to visit are early mornings and weekdays. Amenities:** lifeguards; parking; showers; toilets. **Best for:** partiers; sunrise; swimming; walking. ⊠ *Leho Dr., just south of Wailua River, Wailua (Kauai County).*

Wailua Beach

BEACH—SIGHT | At the mouth of Hawaii's only navigable river, Wailua Beach has considerable cultural significance. At the river's mouth, petroglyphs carved on boulders are sometimes visible during low surf and tide conditions. Surfers and stand-up paddlers enjoy this beach, and many families spend the weekend days under the Wailua Bridge at the river mouth, even hauling out their portable grills and tables to go with their beach chairs. The great news about Wailua Beach is that it's almost impossible to miss; however, parking can be a challenge. The best parking for the north end of the beach is on Papaloa Road behind the Shell station. For the southern end of the beach, park at Wailua River State Park. **Amenities:** parking; showers; toilets. **Best for:** surfing; swimming; walking; windsurfing. ⊠ *Kuhio Hwy., Wailua (Kauai County).*

🍴 Restaurants

In recent years, the most affordable, hip new eateries on the island have opened in Kapaa. Unlike the resort-dominated South and North Shores, Kapaa is local, fun, and eclectic, with food trucks on the side of the road, vegetarian venues, and bars serving up artful appetizers. Diversity is the key to this area; there is something for everyone, especially those on a budget.

Bull Shed

$$$ | STEAKHOUSE | The A-frame structure makes this popular restaurant look distinctly rustic from the outside, but inside, light colors and a full wall of glass highlight an ocean view that is one of the best on Kauai. The food is simple, but they know how to do surf and turf. **Known for:** views of the surf crashing on the rocks; unlimited salad bar; quiet bar. Ⓢ *Average main: $35* ⊠ *796 Kuhio Hwy.* 🕾 *808/822–3791* ⊕ *www.bullshedrestaurant.com* ☾ *No lunch.*

Eat Healthy Kauai

$$ | VEGETARIAN | A restored plantation cottage surrounded by tropical foliage is the casual setting for this island café. The menu emphasizes local and organic products, with many vegan, vegetarian, and gluten-free options including nori wraps and tofu-based entrées. **Known for:** outdoor seating in the vine-covered garden;

Best Beaches

He says "to-mah-toe," and she says "to-may-toe." When it comes to beaches on Kauai, the meaning behind that axiom holds true: people are different. What rocks one person's world wreaks havoc for another's. Here are some additional tips on how to choose a beach that's right for you.

Best for Families

Lydgate State Park, East Side. The kid-designed playground, the protected swimming pools, and Kamalani Bridge guarantee you will not hear these words from your child: "Mom, I'm bored."

Poipu Beach Park, South Shore. The *keiki* (children's) pool and lifeguards make this a safe spot for kids. The near-perpetual sun isn't so bad, either.

Best Stand-Up Paddling

Anini Beach Park, North Shore. The reef and long stretch of beach give beginners to stand-up paddling a calm place to give this new sport a try. You won't get pummeled by waves here.

Wailua Beach, East Side. On the East Side, the Wailua River bisects the beach and heads inland 2 miles, providing stand-up paddlers with a long and scenic stretch of water before they have to figure out how to turn around.

Best Surfing

Hanalei Bay Beach Park, North Shore. In winter, Hanalei Bay offers a range of breaks, from beginner to advanced. Surfing legends Laird Hamilton and the Irons Brothers grew up surfing the waters of Hanalei.

Waiohai Beach, South Shore. Surf instructors flock to this spot with their students for its gentle, near-shore break. Then, as students advance, they can paddle out a little farther to an intermediate break—if they dare.

Best Sunsets

Kee Beach, North Shore. Even in winter, when the sun sets in the south and out of view, you won't be disappointed here, because the "golden hour," as photographers call the time around sunset, paints Napali Coast with a warm gold light. Plan ahead and have your visitor permit at hand when you arrive. ⊕ *www.gohaena.com*

Polihale State Park, West Side. This due-west-facing beach may be tricky to get to, but it does offer the most unobstructed sunset views on the island. The fact that it's so remote means you won't have strangers in your photos, but you will have Niihau, the Forbidden Island. Also, you will want to depart right after sunset or risk getting spooked in the dark.

Best for Celeb Spotting

Haena Beach Park, North Shore. Behind those gated driveways and heavily foliaged yards that line this beach live—at least, part-time—some of the world's most celebrated music and movie moguls.

Hanalei Bay Beach Park, North Shore. We know we tout this beach often, but it deserves the praise. It's a mecca for everyone—regular joes, surfers, fishers, young people, old folks, locals, visitors, and, especially, the famous. You may also recognize Hanalei Bay from the movie *The Descendants*.

delicious food with healthy ingredients; smoothies like Chocolate Coffee Kiss and I Heart Blueberries. ⑤ *Average main: $24* ✉ *4-369 Kuhio Hwy., Wailua (Kauai County)* ☎ *808/822–7990* ⊕ *eathealthykauai. com* ⊗ *No dinner Sun. and Mon.*

★ Hukilau Lanai

$$ | AMERICAN | Relying heavily on superfresh island fish and local meats and produce, this restaurant offers quality food that is competently and creatively prepared. The nightly fish specials—served grilled, steamed, or sautéed with succulent sauces—shine here. **Known for:** nightly fish specials; gluten-free options; delicious desserts. ⑤ *Average main: $25* ✉ *Kauai Coast Resort, Coconut Marketplace, 520 Aleka Loop, Wailua (Kauai County)* ☎ *808/822–0600* ⊕ *www. hukilaukauai.com* ⊗ *Closed Mon.*

★ JO2 Restaurant

$$$ | ECLECTIC | The creation of Jean-Marie Josselin, the renowned chef who brought Hawaii regional cuisine to Kauai in 1990, reflects his growth as a chef. The food is very imaginative, with its French, Japanese, and Islands influences, and it's served with flair in a chic yet casual dining room that's tucked away in a nondescript strip mall. **Known for:** the $35 prix fixe 5–6 pm; inventive cuisine; excellent service. ⑤ *Average main: $35* ✉ *4-971 Kuhio Hwy., Kapaa* ☎ *808/212–1627* ⊕ *www.jotwo.com.*

Kountry Kitchen

$ | AMERICAN | FAMILY | If you like a hearty breakfast, try this family-friendly restaurant with its cozy, greasy-spoon atmosphere and friendly service; it's a great spot for omelets, banana pancakes, waffles, and eggs Benedict in two sizes. Lunch selections include sandwiches, burgers, and *loco mocos* (a popular local rice, beef, gravy, and eggs concoction). **Known for:** all day breakfast; take-out options; hearty portions. ⑤ *Average main: $14* ✉ *1485 Kuhio Hwy., Kapaa* ☎ *808/822–3511* ⊕ *www.kountrystyle-kitchen.com* ⊗ *No dinner.*

Lemongrass Grill

$$ | ASIAN FUSION | The inside of Kapaa's Lemongrass Grill may remind you of a Pacific Rim–theme rustic tavern, with its stained wood interior, numerous paintings and carvings, and eclectic Asian-influenced menu. There's something for everybody here: salads, poultry, steaks and ribs, vegetarian fare, and, of course, a wide selection of seafood, all with an island flair. **Known for:** curries and satays; live acoustic music; fresh fish. ⑤ *Average main: $25* ✉ *4-871 Kuhio Hwy., Kapaa* ☎ *808/821–2888* ⊕ *www.lemongrasshawaii.com* ⊗ *No lunch.*

Mermaid's Café

$ | ECLECTIC | Located right on the main drag of Kapaa, the exterior is a bit grimy and noisy, but it's worth it to order takeout and walk to the beach instead. The ahi nori wrap made of fresh seared tuna, rice, cucumber, and wasabi cream sauce with pickled ginger and soy sauce is the best pick here. **Known for:** ahi nori wrap; hearty fresh salads; chicken or tofu satay. ⑤ *Average main: $12* ✉ *1384 Kuhio Hwy., Kapaa* ☎ *808/821–2026* ⊕ *www. mermaidskauai.com* ⊟ *No credit cards.*

Monico's Taqueria

$ | MEXICAN | Monico's Taqueria, now moved to the other side of the highway from Kinipopo Plaza, still offers its signature authentic Mexican cuisine. They're open for lunch Tuesday through Saturday from 11 am to 3 pm, and dinner runs from 5 pm until 9 pm. **Known for:** ahi fish tacos; margaritas; nachos. ⑤ *Average main: $12* ✉ *4-733 Kuhio Hwy., Kapaa* ✛ *on Kuhio Hwy.* ☎ *808/822–4300* ⊕ *www.monicostaqueria.net.*

Papaya's

$ | AMERICAN | Kauai's largest natural-foods market contains a limited, buffet-style café with decent vegan and vegetarian food at low prices. Food items change daily, but there's always a salad bar, and favorites like wraps, taro burgers, and fish tacos for lunch and dinner, as well as smoothies, a juice bar, coffee, and muffins. **Known for:** vegan and vegetarian food at good prices; fresh, organic produce; tasty tempeh dishes. ⑤ *Average main: $9* ✉ *4-901 Kuhio Hwy., Kapaa* ☎ *808/823–0190* ⊕ *www.papayasnaturalfoods.com.*

Shivalik Indian Cuisine

$ | **INDIAN** | This eatery provides a refreshing alternative to the typical surf and turf offerings at most of Kauai's restaurants. Boasting no particular Indian regional style, this small-plaza hideaway turns out delectable biryani and tandoori, light and flavorful naan, many vegetarian items, as well as curries and chicken and lamb dishes. **Known for:** Wednesday and Friday night all-you-can-eat buffet; tandoor oven; extensive menu. ⑤ *Average main: $17* ✉ *4-771 Kuhio Hwy., Wailua (Kauai County)* ☎ *808/821–2333* ⊕ *www.shivalikindiancuisines.com* ⊘ *Closed Tues.*

Tiki Tacos

$ | **MEXICAN** | Tiki Tacos is a notch above most Kauai taco joints, with excellent authentic Mexican food at reasonable prices. The meals are made from quality ingredients, many of them organic and locally sourced. **Known for:** large portions; good value; friendly service. ⑤ *Average main: $8* ✉ *4-971 Kuhio Hwy., Kapaa* ☎ *808/823–8226.*

🛏 Hotels

Since Kapaa is the island's major population center, this area, including Waipouli and Wailua, has a lived-in, real-world feel. This is where you'll find some of the best deals on accommodations and a wider choice of inexpensive restaurants and shops than in the resort areas. The beaches here are so-so for swimming but nice for sunbathing, walking, and watching the sun- and moonrise.

The Wailua area is rather compact and much of it can be accessed from a coastal walking and biking path. The resorts here are attractive to middle-class travelers seeking a good bang for their buck.

Budget-Friendly Eats

At these small, local-style eateries, two people can generally eat dinner for less than $20.

Garden Island BBQ and Chinese Restaurant ✉ 4252-A Rice St., Lihue ☎ 808/245–8868.

Hamura Saimin ✉ 2956 Kress St., Lihue ☎ 808/245–3271.

Papaya's ✉ 4-831 Kuhio Hwy., Kapaa ⊕ www.papayasnaturalfoods.com ☎ 808/823–0190.

Waipouli Restaurant ✉ Waipouli Town Center, 4-771 Kuhio Hwy., Kapaa ☎ 808/822–9311.

Wailua had a rich cultural significance for the ancient Hawaiians. Their royalty lived here, and ancient sacred grounds, called *heiau,* are clearly marked.

Aston Islander on the Beach

$$ | **HOTEL** | A low-rise, Hawaii-plantation-style design gives this 6-acre beachfront property a pleasant, relaxed feeling. **Pros:** convenient location; free airport shuttle; online rate deals. **Cons:** smallish pool; no restaurant on the property; no resort amenities. ⑤ *Rooms from: $189* ✉ *440 Aleka Pl., Wailua (Kauai County)* ☎ *808/822–7417, 866/774–2924* ⊕ *www.aquaaston.com* ⇗ *200 rooms* ⦿ *No meals.*

Hilton Garden Inn Kauai Wailua Bay

$$$ | **RESORT** | **FAMILY** | Nestled alongside Wailua Bay and the Wailua River, this low-key, low-rise hotel is a convenient place to stay as it's within walking distance of Lydgate Beach Park, with its lifeguard and lawns, and also close to shops and low-cost restaurants. **Pros:** close to ocean; convenient locale; oceanfront walking path near property. **Cons:** prices

are high for modest facilities; restaurant meals are average; traffic is busy fronting hotel. $ *Rooms from: $340* ✉ *3-5920 Kuhio Hwy., Kapaa* ☎ *808/823–6000, 888/823–5111* ⊕ *hiltongardeninn3.hilton. com* ⌂ *250 units* ⦿ *Free Breakfast.*

Hotel Coral Reef

$$ | **HOTEL** | **FAMILY** | In business since 1956, this small hotel is something of a Kauai beachfront landmark, with clean, comfortable rooms, some with great ocean views, and a large pool that overlooks the water; expect great sunrises. **Pros:** free parking; oceanfront setting; convenient location. **Cons:** located in a busy section of Kapaa; ocean swimming is marginal; traffic noise. $ *Rooms from: $219* ✉ *4-1516 Kuhio Hwy., Kapaa* ☎ *808/822–4481, 800/843–1659* ⊕ *www. hotelcoralreefresort.com* ⌂ *27 rooms* ⦿ *Free Breakfast.*

Kapaa Sands

$ | **RENTAL** | An old rock etched with *kanji* (Japanese characters) reminds you that the site of this condominium gem was once occupied by a Shinto temple. **Pros:** discounts for extended stays; walking distance to shops, restaurants, and beach; turtle and monk seal sightings common. **Cons:** no-frills lodging; small bathrooms; traffic noise in rear units. $ *Rooms from: $179* ✉ *380 Papaloa Rd., Wailua (Kauai County)* ☎ *808/822–4901, 800/222–4901* ⊕ *www.kapaasands.com* ⌂ *24 units* ⦿ *No meals.*

★ Kauai Coast Resort at the Beachboy

$$ | **RENTAL** | **FAMILY** | Fronting an uncrowded stretch of beach, this three-story primarily time-share resort is convenient and a bit more upscale than nearby properties. **Pros:** central location; nice sunrises; free parking. **Cons:** beach is narrow; ocean not ideal for swimming; daily housekeeping fee. $ *Rooms from: $215* ✉ *520 Aleka Loop, Wailua (Kauai County)* ☎ *808/822–3441, 866/729–7182* ⊕ *www.shellhospitality.com* ⌂ *108 units* ⦿ *No meals.*

Kauai Shores

$ | **HOTEL** | This oceanfront inn has been transformed into an affordable boutique hotel, thanks to a much-needed renovation of its guest rooms and public spaces. **Pros:** convenient location; free Wi-Fi; great sunrises; discount for LGBTQ+ travelers. **Cons:** coral reef makes ocean swimming marginal; modest property; minimal amenities; daily hospitality fee. $ *Rooms from: $158* ✉ *420 Papaloa Rd., Wailua (Kauai County)* ☎ *808/822–4951, 800/560–5553* ⊕ *www.kauaishoreshotel. com* ⌂ *202 rooms* ⦿ *No meals.*

Outrigger at Lae Nani

$$$ | **RENTAL** | Ruling Hawaiian chiefs once returned from ocean voyages to this spot, now host to comfortable condominiums. **Pros:** nice beach; walking distance to playground; attractively furnished. **Cons:** third floor is walk up; no Wi-Fi; cleaning fee. $ *Rooms from: $339* ✉ *410 Papaloa Rd., Wailua (Kauai County)* ☎ *808/823–1401, 866/956–4262* ⊕ *www. outrigger.com* ⌂ *84 units* ⦿ *No meals.*

Plantation Hale Suites

$$ | **RENTAL** | These older, plantation-style one-bedroom units have well equipped kitchenettes and garden lanai and clean, comfortable rooms, some of which have been recently renovated. **Pros:** friendly staff; three pools; walking distance to shops, restaurant, beach. **Cons:** traffic noise in mountain-view units; coral reef makes ocean swimming challenging; older units. $ *Rooms from: $199* ✉ *525 Aleka Loop, Wailua (Kauai County)* ☎ *808/822–4941, 800/775–4253* ⊕ *www. plantation-hale.com* ⌂ *104 units* ⦿ *No meals.*

Sheraton Kauai Coconut Beach Resort

$$ | **RESORT** | This popular hotel, one of the few true oceanfront properties on Kauai, sits on a ribbon of sand in Kapaa with bright, spacious rooms that face the ocean or pool. **Pros:** convenient location; close to ocean; pleasant grounds. **Cons:** coastline not conducive to swimming; small pool; high daily parking fee.

4

The East Side KAPAA AND WAILUA

⑤ *Rooms from: $224* ⊠ *650 Aleka Loop, Wailua (Kauai County)* ☎ *808/822–3455, 800/760–8555* ⊕ *www.marriott.com* ⤳ *311 rooms* ⑪ *No meals.*

Nightlife

★ Hukilau Lanai

BARS/PUBS | This open-air bar and restaurant is on the property of the Kauai Coast Resort but operates independently. Trade winds waft through the modest little bar, which looks out onto a coconut grove. If the mood takes you, go on a short walk to the sea, or recline in big, comfortable chairs in Wally's Bar in the lobby while listening to mellow jazz or Hawaiian slack-key guitar. Live music plays from 6 to 9 every night, but the restaurant and bar are closed on Monday. Poolside happy hour runs from 3 to 5. Freshly infused tropical martinis—perhaps locally grown lychee and pineapple or a Big Island vanilla bean infusion—are house favorites. ⊠ *520 Aleka Loop, Wailua (Kauai County)* ☎ *808/822–0600* ⊕ *www.hukilaukauai. com* ⌖ *Closed Mon.*

Trees Lounge

BARS/PUBS | This cool bar and restaurant hosts live music nightly that gets people out on the tiny dance floor. It's behind the Coconut Marketplace and next to the Kauai Coast Resort in Kapaa. ⊠ *440 Aleka Pl., Kapaa* ☎ *808/823–0600* ⊕ *www. treesloungekauai.com* ⌖ *Closed Sun.*

🎭 Performing Arts

Although the commercial luau experience is a far cry from the backyard luau thrown by local residents to celebrate a wedding, graduation, or baby's first birthday, they're nonetheless entertaining and a good introduction to the Hawaiian food that isn't widely sold in restaurants. With many, you can watch a roasted pig being carried out of its *imu,* a hole in the ground used for cooking meat with heated stones. Besides the feast and free mai tais, there's often an exciting

dinner show with Polynesian-style music and dancing. It all makes for a fun evening that's suitable for couples, families, and groups, and the informal setting is conducive to meeting other people. Every luau is different, reflecting the cuisine and tenor of the host facility, so compare prices, menus, and entertainment before making your reservation. Most luau on Kauai are offered only on a limited number of nights each week, so plan ahead to get the luau you want. We tend to prefer those *not* held on resort properties, because they feel a bit more authentic.

★ Smith's Tropical Paradise Luau

THEMED ENTERTAINMENT | A 30-acre tropical garden on the Wailua River provides the lovely setting for this popular luau, which begins with the traditional blowing of the conch shell and *imu* (pig roast) ceremony, followed by cocktails, an island feast, great music, and an international show in the amphitheater overlooking a torch-lighted lagoon. It's fairly authentic and a better deal than the pricier resort events. ⊠ *174 Wailua Rd., Kapaa* ☎ *808/821–6895* ⊕ *www.smithskauai. com* ⤳ *$108.*

👜 Shopping

Kapaa is the most heavily populated area on Kauai, so it's not surprising that it has the most diverse shopping opportunities on the island. Unlike the North Shore's retail scene, shops here are not neatly situated in centers; they are spread out along a long stretch of road, with many local retail gems tucked away that you may not find if you're in a rush.

AREAS AND SHOPPING CENTERS

Kauai Village Shopping Center

SHOPPING CENTERS/MALLS | The buildings of this Kapaa shopping village are in the style of a 19th-century plantation town. **ABC Discount Store** sells sundries; **Safeway** carries groceries and alcoholic beverages; **Papaya's** has health foods and a

Kauai: Undercover Movie Star

Though Kauai has played itself in the movies, starring in *The Descendants* (2011), much of its screen time has been as a stunt double for a number of tropical paradises. The island's remote valleys portrayed Venezuelan jungle in Kevin Costner's *Dragonfly* (2002) and a Costa Rican dinosaur preserve in Steven Spielberg's *Jurassic Park* (1993). Spielberg was no stranger to Kauai, having filmed Harrison Ford's escape via seaplane from Menehune Fishpond in *Raiders of the Lost Ark* (1981).

The fluted cliffs and gorges of Kauai's rugged Napali Coast play the misunderstood beast's island home in *King Kong* (1976), and a jungle dweller of another sort, in *George of the Jungle* (1997), also frolicked on Kauai. Harrison Ford returned to the island for 10 weeks during the filming of *Six Days, Seven Nights* (1998), a romantic adventure set in French Polynesia. Part-time Kauai resident Ben Stiller used the island as a stand-in for the jungles of Vietnam in *Tropic Thunder* (2008) and Johnny Depp came here to film some of *Pirates of the Caribbean: On Stranger Tides* (2011). But these are all relatively contemporary movies. What's truly remarkable is that Hollywood discovered Kauai in 1933 with the making of *White Heat*, which was set on a sugar plantation and—like *South Pacific* (also filmed on Kauai)—dealt with an interracial love story.

Then, it was off to the races, as Kauai saw no fewer than a dozen movies filmed on the island in the 1950s, though not all of them were Oscar contenders. Rita Hayworth starred in *Miss Sadie Thompson* (1953) and no one you'd recognize starred in the tantalizing *She Gods of Shark Reef* (1956).

The movie that is still immortalized on the island in the names of restaurants, real estate offices, a hotel, and even a sushi item is *South Pacific* (1957). (You guessed it, right?) That mythical place called Bali Hai is never far away on Kauai.

In the 1960s Elvis Presley filmed *Blue Hawaii* (1961) and *Girls! Girls! Girls!* (1962) on the island. A local movie tour likes to point out the stain on a hotel carpet where Elvis's jelly doughnut fell.

Kauai has welcomed a long list of Hollywood's A-List: John Wayne in *Donovan's Reef* (1963); Jack Lemmon in *The Wackiest Ship in the Army* (1961); Richard Chamberlain in *The Thorn Birds* (1983); Gene Hackman in *Uncommon Valor* (1983); Danny DeVito and Billy Crystal in *Throw Momma from the Train* (1987); and Dustin Hoffman, Morgan Freeman, Renee Russo, and Cuba Gooding Jr. in *Outbreak* (1995).

Kauai has also appeared on a long list of TV shows and made-for-TV movies, including *Gilligan's Island, Fantasy Island, Starsky & Hutch, Baywatch Hawaii*—even reality TV shows *The Bachelor* and *The Amazing Race 3.*

For the record, just because a movie did some filming here doesn't mean the entire movie was filmed on Kauai. *Honeymoon in Vegas* filmed just one scene here, while the murder mystery *A Perfect Getaway* (2009) was set on the famous Kalalau Trail and featured beautiful Kauaian backdrops, but was shot mostly in Puerto Rico.

The Independent Island

Kauai's residents have had a reputation for independence since ancient times. Called "The Separate Kingdom," Kauai alone resisted King Kamehameha's charge to unite the Hawaiian Islands. In fact, it was only by kidnapping Kauai's king, Kaumualii, and forcing him to marry Kamehameha's widow that the Garden Isle was joined to the rest of Hawaii. That spirit lives on today as Kauai residents try to resist the lure of tourism dollars captivating the rest of the Islands. Local building tradition maintains that no structure be taller than a coconut tree, and Kauai's capital, Lihue, is still more small town than city.

minimalist café. There's also a small bakery, **Ross Dress for Less,** and a **UPS store.** Other shops sell jewelry, art, and home decor. Restaurants include Chinese and Vietnamese options, and there's also a **Starbucks** and a bar. ✉ *4-831 Kuhio Hwy., Kapaa* ☎ *808/822–3777.*

Kinipopo Shopping Village

SHOPPING CENTERS/MALLS | Kinipopo is a tiny little center on Kuhio Highway. **Korean Barbeque** fronts the highway, as does **Goldsmith's Kauai Gallery,** which sells handcrafted Hawaiian-style gold jewelry. There's also a clothing shop, beauty salon, bakery, cake shop, and a healing-arts center. ✉ *4-356 Kuhio Hwy., Kapaa* ⊕ *www.kinipopovillage.com.*

Waipouli Town Center

SHOPPING CENTERS/MALLS | **Foodland** is the focus of this small retail plaza, one of three shopping centers anchored by grocery stores in Kapaa. You can also find an Indian restaurant, **McDonald's, Auto Zone,** and **The Coffee Bean,** along with a local-style restaurant. ✉ *4-771 Kuhio Hwy., Kapaa.*

CLOTHING

A.Ell Atelier

CLOTHING | Clothing designer Angelique Ell sells everything from custom wedding gowns to men's aloha shirts to children's clothing, using all-natural fabrics. Home linens are also sold in this distinctive boutique, as are soaps, jewelry, candles, handbags, and artwork by local artists.

✉ *4-1320 Kuhio Hwy., Kapaa* ☎ *808/212–7550* ⊕ *www.aellatelier.com.*

Deja Vu Surf Hawaii: Kapaa

CLOTHING | This family operation has a great assortment of surf wear and clothes for outdoors fanatics, including tank tops, visors, swimwear, and Kauai-style T-shirts. They also carry body boards and water-sports accessories. Good deals can be found at sidewalk sales. ✉ *4-1419 Kuhio Hwy., Kapaa* ☎ *808/320–7108* ⊕ *www.dejavusurf.com.*

Marta's Boat

CLOTHING | This charming boutique sells handmade, one-of-a-kind clothing by husband-and-wife team Ambrose and Marta Curry. He creates silk-screen art with nontoxic paint on fabric in his studio next door, then she cuts and sews the fabric into bags and clothing for men, women, and children. ✉ *4-770 Kuhio Hwy., Kapaa* ☎ *808/822–3926.*

GALLERIES

ALOHA Images

ART GALLERIES | ALOHA stands for "Affordable Location of Original Hawaiian Art." A self-proclaimed "candy store for art lovers," it has a large selection of Hawaiian-themed art, ranging from $75 up to the rare $25,000, and owner Ray offers layaway plans to those who request one. ✉ *4504 Kukui St., Kapaa* ☎ *808/631–8026* ⊕ *www.alohaimages.com.*

One of the best places for a luau is here at Smith's Tropical Paradise.

Kela's Glass Gallery

ART GALLERIES | The colorful vases, bowls, and other fragile items sold in this distinctive gallery, now expanded into a new, larger space, are definitely worth viewing if you appreciate quality handmade glass art. It's expensive, but if something catches your eye, they'll happily pack it for safe transport home. They also ship worldwide. ⊠ *4-1400 Kuhio Hwy., Kapaa* ☎ *808/822–4527* ⊕ *www. glass-art.com.*

GIFTS

Kalani Tropicals

FLOWERS | Kauai-based Kalani Tropicals will take your order online or by phone and ship heliconia, anthurium, ginger, and other tropicals as cut flowers or fashioned into distinctive arrangements. ⊠ *6242 Olohena Rd., Kapaa* ☎ *808/823–6547* ⊕ *kalanitropicals.com* ⊙ *Closed Sun.*

Pagoda

ANTIQUES/COLLECTIBLES | Pagoda is a tiny shop big on exceptional antiques, Hawaiiana, and gifts. The owner, Liane, has

been collecting rare finds most of her life and now has a place to showcase them. ⊠ *4-369 Kuhio Hwy., Kapaa* ☎ *808/821–2172* ⊕ *www.pagodakauai.com* ⊙ *Closed Sun. and Mon.*

Vicky's Fabric Shop

GIFTS/SOUVENIRS | This small store is packed full of tropical and Hawaiian prints, silks, slinky rayons, soft cottons, and other fine fabrics. A variety of sewing patterns and notions are featured as well, making it a must-stop for any seamstress and a great place to buy unique island-made gifts. Check out the one-of-a-kind selection of purses, aloha wear, and other quality hand-sewn items. ⊠ *4-1326 Kuhio Hwy., Kapaa* ☎ *808/822–1746* ⊕ *www.vickysfabrics.com* ⊙ *Closed Sun.*

HOME DECOR

Otsuka's

HOUSEHOLD ITEMS/FURNITURE | Family-owned Otsuka's has a large clientele of visitors who appreciate the wide selection of unique furniture, artwork, candles, tropical-print pillows, accessories, and knickknacks that can be found here. ✉ *4-1624 Kuhio Hwy., Kapaa* ☎ *808/822–7766* ⊕ *www.otsukas.com* ⊘ *Closed Sun. and Mon.*

JEWELRY
Jim Saylor Jewelers
JEWELRY/ACCESSORIES | Jim Saylor and his team of jewelers have been designing beautiful keepsakes on Kauai since 1976. Gems from around the world, including black pearls, diamonds, and more, appear in his unusual settings. ✉ *4-1318 Kuhio Hwy., Kapaa* ☎ *808/822–3591* ⊕ *www. jimsaylorjewelers.com* ⊘ *Closed Sun.*

MARKET
Kauai Products Fair
OUTDOOR/FLEA/GREEN MARKETS | Open daily, the Kauai Products Fair outdoor market features an assortment of stalls selling fresh produce, tropical plants and flowers, clothing, aloha wear, jewelry, and gifts. ✉ *4-1613 Kuhio Hwy., Kapaa* ☎ *808/246–0988.*

Lihue

7 miles southwest of Wailua.

The commercial and political center of Kauai County, which includes the islands of Kauai and Niihau, Lihue is home to the island's major airport, harbor, and hospital. This is where you can find the state and county offices that issue camping and hiking permits and the same fast-food eateries and big-box stores that blight the mainland. The county is seeking help in reviving the downtown by sprucing up Rice Street; for now, once your business is done, there's little reason to linger in lackluster Lihue.

⊙ Sights

★ Alekoko (Menehune) Fishpond
ARCHAEOLOGICAL SITE | No one knows just who built this intricate aquaculture structure in the Huleia River. Legend attributes it to the Menehune, a mythical—or real, depending on whom you ask—ancient race of people known for their small stature, industrious nature, and superb stoneworking skills. Volcanic rock was cut and fit together into massive walls 4 feet thick and 5 feet high, forming an enclosure for raising mullet and other freshwater fish that has endured for centuries. ✉ *Hulemalu Rd., Niumalu.*

Grove Farm Homestead
FARM/RANCH | Guided tours of this carefully restored 80-acre country estate offer a fascinating and authentic look at how upper-class Caucasians experienced plantation life in the mid-19th century. The tour focuses on the original home, built by the Wilcox family in 1860 and filled with a quirky collection of classic Hawaiiana. You can also see the workers' quarters, farm animals, orchards, and gardens that reflect the practical, self-sufficient lifestyle of the island's earliest Western inhabitants. Tours of the homestead are conducted twice a day, three days a week. To protect the historic building and its furnishings, tours may be canceled on very wet days. ■TIP→ **With a six-person limit per tour, reservations are essential.** ✉ *4050 Nawiliwili Rd., Lihue* ☎ *808/245–3202* ⊕ *www.grovefarm.org* ⌨ *$20 requested donation.*

★ Kauai Museum
MUSEUM | Maintaining a stately presence on Rice Street, the historic museum building is easy to find. It features a permanent display, "The Story of Kauai," which provides a competent overview of the Garden Island and Niihau, tracing the Islands' geology, mythology, and cultural history. Local artists are represented in changing exhibits in the second-floor Mezzanine Gallery. The expanded gift shop alone is worth a visit, with a fine collection of authentic Niihau shell lei, feather hatband lei, hand-turned wooden bowls, reference books, and other quality arts, crafts, and gifts—many of them locally made. ✉ *4428 Rice St., Lihue* ☎ *808/245–6931* ⊕ *www.kauaimuseum. org* ⌨ *$15.*

Kilohana Plantation

FARM/RANCH | FAMILY | This estate dates back to 1850, shortly after the "Great Mahele"—the division of land by the Hawaiian people. Plantation manager Albert Spencer Wilcox developed it as a working cattle ranch, and his nephew, Gaylord Parke Wilcox, took over in 1936, building Kauai's first mansion. Today the 16,000-square-foot, Tudor-style home houses specialty shops, art galleries, the Koloa Rum Co., and Gaylord's, a pretty restaurant with courtyard seating. Nearly half the original furnishings remain, and the gardens and orchards were replanted according to the original plans. You can tour the grounds for free, or take a 40-minute train ride and learn the agricultural story of Kauai while viewing a working farm. The Luau Kalamaku completes a day at Kilohana. ⌂ 3-2007 Kaumualii Hwy., Lihue ☎ 808/245-5608 ⊕ www.kilohanakauai.com ☞ Train tours $19.50.

Beaches

Kalapaki Beach

BEACH—SIGHT | FAMILY | Five minutes south of the airport in Lihue, you'll find this wide, sandy-bottom beach fronting the Kauai Marriott. This beach is almost always safe from rip currents and undertows because it's around the back side of a peninsula, in its own cove. There are tons of activities here, including all the usual water sports—beginning and intermediate surfing, body boarding, bodysurfing, and swimming—plus, there are two outrigger canoe clubs paddling in the bay and the Nawiliwili Yacht Club's boats sailing around the harbor. **Kalapaki** is the only place on Kauai where double-hulled canoes are available for rent (at Kauai Beach Boys, which fronts the beach next to Duke's Canoe Club restaurant). Visitors can also rent snorkel gear, surfboards, body boards, and kayaks from Kauai Beach Boys. A volleyball court on the beach is often used by a loosely organized group of local players; visitors are always welcome. ■**TIP→ Avoid the stream on the south side of the beach; it often has high bacteria counts.** Duke's Canoe Club restaurant is one of only a couple of restaurants on the island actually on a beach; the restaurant's lower level is casual, even welcoming beach attire and sandy feet, perfect for lunch or an afternoon cocktail. **Amenities:** food and drink; lifeguard; parking; showers; toilets; water sports. **Best for:** partiers; surfing; swimming; walking. ⌂ Off Rice St., Lihue ⊕ www.kauai.com/kalapaki-beach.

🍴 Restaurants

You will probably find yourself in Lihue at least a few times during your stay. When it comes to restaurants, Lihue isn't especially outstanding. There are some decent restaurants and some good low-cost eateries that feed locals and the business-lunch crowd—but nothing really stellar. If you are in town for lunch, don't pass up some of the authentic local spots.

Café Portofino

$$$ | ITALIAN | The lengthy menu at this mostly authentic northern Italian restaurant is as impressive as the views of Kalapaki Bay and the Haupu range, and it's packed with many pasta, veal, chicken, and fresh fish selections, as well as vegetarian entrées. Linger over coffee and ice cream–filled profiteroles or traditional tiramisu while enjoying classical music. **Known for:** roasted rack of lamb; romantic ambience; open-air dining. ⑤ Average main: $30 ⊠ Kauai Marriott Resort & Beach Club, 3481 Hoolaulea Way, Kalapaki Beach, Lihue ⊕ www.cafeportofino. com ☽ No lunch.

Dani's Restaurant

$ | HAWAIIAN | FAMILY | Kauai residents frequent this eatery near the Lihue Fire Station for hearty, local-style food at breakfast and lunch; it's a good place to try traditional luau cuisine

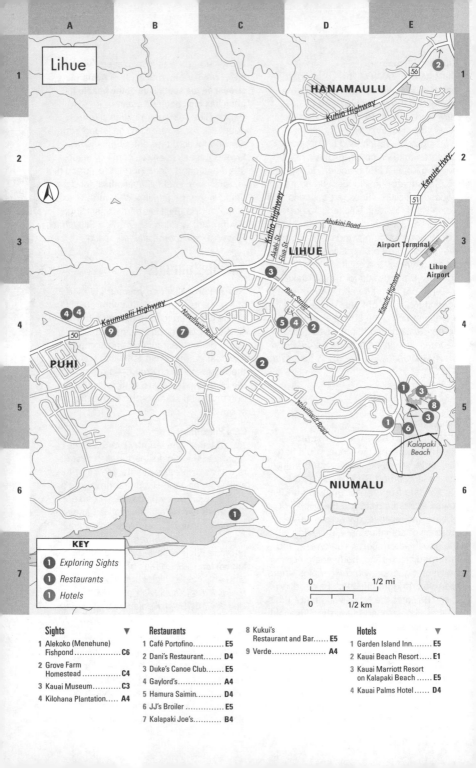

Lihue

Sights ▼

1 Alekoko (Menehune) Fishpond **C6**

2 Grove Farm Homestead **C4**

3 Kauai Museum **C3**

4 Kilohana Plantation..... **A4**

Restaurants ▼

1 Café Portofino............ **E5**

2 Dani's Restaurant....... **D4**

3 Duke's Canoe Club....... **E5**

4 Gaylord's.................. **A4**

5 Hamura Saimin........... **D4**

6 JJ's Broiler **E5**

7 Kalapaki Joe's........... **B4**

8 Kukui's Restaurant and Bar...... **E5**

9 Verde..................... **A4**

Hotels ▼

1 Garden Island Inn........ **E5**

2 Kauai Beach Resort..... **E1**

3 Kauai Marriott Resort on Kalapaki Beach **E5**

4 Kauai Palms Hotel...... **D4**

KEY

- ① Exploring Sights
- ① Restaurants
- ① Hotels

without commercial luau prices. You can order Hawaiian-style *laulau* (pork and taro leaves wrapped in ti leaves and steamed) or kalua pig, slow roasted in an underground oven. **Known for:** local-style dining; low prices; casual setting. Ⓢ *Average main: $8 ⊠ 4201 Rice St., Lihue ☎ 808/245–4991 ⊘ Closed Sun. No dinner.*

Duke's Canoe Club

$$$ | SEAFOOD | Surfing legend Duke Kahanamoku is immortalized at this casual bi-level restaurant and bar on Kalapaki Beach where surfboards, photos, and other memorabilia marking Duke's long tenure as a waterman adorn the walls. Downstairs, you'll find simple fare ranging from fish tacos to stir-fried cashew chicken to hamburgers, served 11 am to 10:30 pm, while upstairs, at dinner, fresh fish prepared in a variety of styles is the best choice, though the prime rib is a favorite among locals. **Known for:** live music; lively bar; hula pie ice-cream dessert. Ⓢ *Average main: $30 ⊠ Kauai Marriott Resort & Beach Club, 3610 Rice St., Kalapaki Beach, Lihue ☎ 808/246–9599 ⊕ www.dukeskauai.com.*

Gaylord's

$$$ | ECLECTIC | Located in what was once Kauai's most expensive plantation estate, Gaylord's pays tribute to the elegant dining rooms of 1930s high society—candlelit tables sit on a cobblestone patio that surrounds a fountain and overlooks a wide lawn. The menu is eclectic, ranging from tender seared scallops served in a fennel cream to grilled filet mignon. **Known for:** lavish Sunday brunch buffet; quiet dining; delightful outdoor seating. Ⓢ *Average main: $30 ⊠ Kilohana Plantation, 3-2087 Kaumualii Hwy., Puhi ☎ 808/245–9593 ⊕ www.gaylordskauai.com.*

★ Hamura Saimin

$ | ASIAN | Folks just love this old plantation-style diner—locals and tourists stream in and out all day long, and neighbor islanders stop in on their way to the airport to pick up take-out orders to bring home. Their famous *saimin* soup is the big draw, and each day the Hiraoka family dishes up about 1,000 bowls of the steaming broth and homemade noodles, topped with a variety of garnishes. **Known for:** classic Kauai experience; grilled chicken and beef sticks; counter-style dining. Ⓢ *Average main: $7 ⊠ 2956 Kress St., Lihue ☎ 808/245–3271 ▭ No credit cards.*

JJ's Broiler

$$$ | AMERICAN | This spacious, low-key restaurant has a great ocean view and serves hearty fare, with dinner specials such as lobster and Slavonic steak, a broiled sliced tenderloin dipped in buttery wine sauce, and local-style kalua pig and cabbage; you can save money by ordering from the lunch menu at dinner time. On sunny afternoons, ask for a table on the lanai overlooking Kalapaki Bay and try one of the generous salads or appetizers and a drink. **Known for:** one of the best ocean views in Lihue; great place for a drink; friendly service. Ⓢ *Average main: $30 ⊠ Anchor Cove, 3416 Rice St., Nawiliwili ☎ 808/246–4422 ⊕ www.jjsbroiler.com.*

Kalapaki Joe's

$$ | AMERICAN | Both locations—in Lihue's Kukui Grove and in Poipu—appeal to sports fans who like a rip-roaring happy hour. The appetizer menu is extensive, and you can also choose from burgers, salads, sandwiches, fish tacos, steaks, ribs, and fresh fish specials. **Known for:** wide-ranging menu; boisterous bar; affordable, casual dining. Ⓢ *Average main: $20 ⊠ 3-2600 Kaumualii Hwy., Lihue ☎ 808/245–6366 ⊕ www.kalapakijoes.com.*

Kukui's Restaurant and Bar

$$ | ECLECTIC | FAMILY | The meals at Kukui's feature Hawaiian, Asian, and contemporary American influences, and the open-air setting makes it a pleasant place to dine. It's very spacious, and not as busy and noisy as the other eateries at the Marriott, making it well suited to

Did You Know?

According to legend, the
mythical Menehune built
the Alekoko Fishpond
more than 1,000 years ago,
in just one night.

families and those who want a relaxed setting. **Known for:** garden setting; lavish buffets; evening entertainment. $ *Average main: $25* ✉ *Kauai Marriott Resort & Beach Club, 3610 Rice St., Kalapaki Beach, Lihue* ☎ *808/245–5042* ⊕ *www. marriott.com.*

Verde

$ | **MEXICAN** | Combining classic Mexican food with chili-based sauces and creations from the chef's home state of New Mexico, Verde's menu includes tostadas, enchiladas, and tacos served with fresh fish, slow-cooked chicken, or local grass-fed beef. The seared tuna tacos with red chili aioli and the stacked enchilada, with chicken or beef short ribs smothered in red or green chili sauce, are favorites. **Known for:** super hot sauce; quality local ingredients; casual setting. $ *Average main: $13* ✉ *4454 Nuhou St., Ste. 501, Lihue* ☎ *808 /320–7088* ⊕ *www.verdehawaii.com.*

 Hotels

Lihue is not the most desirable place to stay on Kauai, in terms of scenic beauty, although it does have its advantages, including easy access to the airport. Restaurants and shops are plentiful, and there's lovely Kalapaki Bay for beachgoers. Aside from the Marriott and the Kauai Beach Resort, most of the limited lodging possibilities are smaller and aimed at the cost-conscious traveler.

Garden Island Inn

$$ | **HOTEL** | Budget travelers love this three-story inn near Kalapaki Bay and Anchor Cove shopping center as it's clean, offers free Wi-Fi, and the innkeepers are friendly, sharing fruit, flowers, and beach gear. **Pros:** walk to beach, restaurants, and shops; good for extended stays and budget travel; air-conditioning. **Cons:** some traffic noise; near a busy harbor; no pool. $ *Rooms from: $185* ✉ *3445 Wilcox Rd., Kalapaki Beach, Lihue*

☎ *808/245–7227, 800/648–0154* ⊕ *www. gardenislandinn.com* ⤴ *21 rooms* ⃝| *No meals.*

Kauai Beach Resort

$$$ | **RESORT** | This plantation-style hotel provides a relaxing, upscale experience close to the airport, but without the noise. **Pros:** unique sand-bottom pool with 12-foot waterfall; shuttle service to airport; resort amenities. **Cons:** not a good swimming beach; windy at times; no nearby restaurants or resorts. $ *Rooms from: $279* ✉ *4331 Kauai Beach Dr., Hanamaulu* ☎ *808/246–5576* ⊕ *www.kauaibeachresortandspa.com* ⤴ *350 rooms* ⃝| *No meals.*

Kauai Marriott Resort on Kalapaki Beach

$$$ | **RESORT** | **FAMILY** | An elaborate tropical garden, waterfalls right off the lobby, Greek statues and columns, and an enormous 26,000-square-foot swimming pool characterize the grand—and grandiose—scale of this resort on Kalapaki Beach, which looks out at the dramatic Haupu Ridge. **Pros:** oceanfront setting; numerous restaurants; convenient location; airport shuttle. **Cons:** airport noise; ocean water quality can be poor at times; located near an industrial area. $ *Rooms from: $339* ✉ *3610 Rice St., Kalapaki Beach, Lihue* ☎ *808/245–5050, 800/220–2925* ⊕ *www.kauaimarriott.com* ⤴ *367 rooms* ⃝| *Free Breakfast.*

Kauai Palms Hotel

$ | **HOTEL** | Not only is this low-cost alternative close to the airport, but it's also a great base for day trips to all sides of the island. **Pros:** friendly staff; inexpensive; centrally located. **Cons:** bare-bones amenities; smallish rooms; traffic noise. $ *Rooms from: $114* ✉ *2931 Kalena St., Lihue* ☎ *808/246–0908* ⊕ *www. kauaipalmshotel.com* ⤴ *33 rooms* ⃝| *No meals.*

Continued on page 128

HAWAII'S PLANTS 101

Tropical Hibiscus

Hawaii is a bounty of rainbow-colored flowers and plants. The evening air is scented with their fragrance. Just look at the front yard of almost any home, travel any road, or visit any local park and you'll see a spectacular array of colored blossoms and leaves. What most visitors don't know is that many of the plants they are seeing are not native to Hawaii; rather, they were introduced during the last two centuries as ornamental plants, or for timber, shade, or fruit.

Hawaii boasts nearly every climate on the planet, excluding the two most extreme: arctic tundra and arid desert. The Islands have wine-growing regions, cactus-speckled ranchlands, icy mountaintops, and the rainiest forests on earth.

Plants introduced from around the world thrive here. The lush lowland valleys along the windward coasts are predominantly populated by non-native trees including yellow- and red-fruited **guava**, silvery-leafed **kukui**, and orange-flowered **tulip trees.**

The colorful **plumeria flower**, very fragrant and commonly used in lei making, and the giant multicolored **hibiscus flower** are both used by many women as hair adornments, and are two of the most common plants found around homes and hotels. The umbrella-like **monkeypod tree** from Central America provides shade in many of Hawaii's parks including Kapiolani Park in Honolulu. Hawaii's largest tree, found in Lahaina, Maui, is a giant **banyan tree**. Its canopy and massive support roots cover about two-thirds of an acre. The native **ohia tree**, with its brilliant red brush-like flowers, and the **hapuu**, a giant tree fern, are common in Hawaii's forests and are also used ornamentally in gardens.

Naupaka, Limahuli Garden

Bougainvillea

Guava

Monkeypod

Banyan

Ohia Lehua*

Tulip Tree

Plumeria

Pandanus

Hibiscus

Anthurium

Kukui

Hapuu

*endemic to Hawaii

DID YOU KNOW?

More than 2,200 plant species are found in the Hawaiian Islands, but only about 1,000 are native. Of these, 320 are so rare, they are endangered. Hawaii's endemic plants evolved from ancestral seeds arriving in the Islands over thousands of years as baggage with birds, floating on ocean currents, or drifting on winds from continents thousands of miles away. Once here, these plants evolved in isolation, creating many new species known nowhere else in the world.

Shave Ice

Nothing goes down quite as nicely as shave ice on a hot day. This favorite island treat has been likened to a sno-cone, but that description doesn't do a good shave ice justice. Yes, it is ice served up in a cone-shaped cup and drenched with sweet syrup, but the similarities end there. As its name implies, the ice should be feathery light—the texture of snowflakes, not frozen slush. And alongside the standard cherry and grape, you'll find all sorts of exotic island flavorings, such as passion fruit, pineapple, coconut, mango, and, of course, a rainbow mix or snow topping of condensed milk.

Not all shave ice meets these high standards, and when you're hot, even the average ones taste great. But a few places are worth seeking out. On the East Side, the best is **Hawaiian Blizzard** (⊠ *Kapaa Shopping Center, 4-1105 Kuhio Hwy.*), a true shave-ice stand that opens up weekday afternoons next to the Big Save grocery store in Kapaa. In Lihue, try **Halo Halo Shave Ice** in the Harbor Mall Shopping Center (⊠ *3501 Rice St.*) or **Uncle's** (⊠ *4454 Nuhou St.*), which uses ice cream as a base. And on the hot, dry West Side, make a beeline for **Jo-Jo's Clubhouse** (⊠ *Mile marker 23, Kaumualii, Hwy. 50*), on the main drag in Waimea. All three places have benches where you can sit and slurp.

🍸 Nightlife

Duke's Barefoot Bar

BARS/PUBS | This is one of the liveliest bars in Nawiliwili. Contemporary Hawaiian music is usually performed at this beachside bar and restaurant every day but Tuesday during "Aloha Hours" from 4 to 6 pm. On Saturday nights, live music is held from 8:30 to 10:30 pm. ⊠ *Kalapaki Beach, 3610 Rice St., Lihue* ☎ *808/246–9599* ⊕ *www.dukeskauai.com.*

Rob's Good Times Grill

BARS/PUBS | Let loose at this popular restaurant and sports bar, which has live music Monday through Thursday from 4 to 6 pm. Tuesday offers swing dancing from 7:30 to 10 pm, Friday features live music until midnight, Saturday has late-night club dancing with DJ, while Sunday through Thursday go full-on karaoke until closing. Lunch is a good choice, too. ⊠ *4303 Rice St., Lihue* ☎ *808/246–0311* ⊕ *www.kauaisportsbarandgrill.com.*

🎭 Performing Arts

FESTIVALS
Bon Festival

DANCE | **FAMILY** | Traditional Japanese celebrations in honor of loved ones who have died are held from late June through August at various Buddhist temples all over the island. It sounds somber, but it's really a community festival of dance. To top it off, you're welcome to participate. Dance, eat, play carnival games, and hear Japanese *taiko* drumming at one of the Bon folk dances, which take place on temple lawns every Friday and Saturday night from dusk to midnight. Some dancers wear the traditional kimono; others wear board shorts and a tank top. The moves are easy to follow, the event is lively and wholesome, and it's free. A different temple hosts a dance each weekend. Watch the local paper for that week's locale.

Nothing beats shave ice (no, not "shaved" ice) on a hot Hawaiian day.

LUAU

Luau Kalamaku

THEMED ENTERTAINMENT | Set on historic sugar-plantation land, this luau bills itself as the only "theatrical" luau on Kauai. The luau feast is served buffet style, there's an open bar, and the performers aim to both entertain and educate about Hawaiian culture. Guests sit at tables around a circular stage; tables farther from the stage are elevated, providing unobstructed views. Additional packages offer visitors the opportunity to watch the show only, tour the 35-acre plantation via train, or enjoy special romantic perks like a lei greeting and champagne. ⊠ *Kilohana Plantation, 3-2087 Kaumualii St., Lihue* ☎ *877/622–1780* ⊕ *www.luaukalamaku. com* ✉ *From $57.*

MUSIC AND PLAYS

Kauai Community College Performing Arts Center

ARTS CENTERS | This is a main venue for island entertainment, hosting a concert music series, visiting musicians, dramatic productions, and special events such as educational forums. ⊠ *3-1901 Kaumualii Hwy., Lihue* ☎ *808/245–8311* ⊕ *www. kauai.hawaii.edu/pac.*

Kauai Community Players

THEATER | This talented local group presents plays throughout the year in its intimate theater. ⊠ *4411 Kikowaena St., across from Kauai Community College, Lihue* ☎ *808/245–7700* ⊕ *www.kauai-communityplayers.org* ✉ *From $10.*

Kauai Concert Association

MUSIC | This group offers a seasonal program at the Kauai Community College Performing Arts Center that features well-known classical musicians, including soloists and small ensembles. ⊠ *3-1901 Kaumualii Hwy., Lihue* ☎ *808/245–7464* ⊕ *www.kauai-concert.org* ✉ *From $30.*

Shopping

Lihue is the business area on Kauai, as well as home to all the big-box stores (Costco, Home Depot, and Walmart) and the only real mall. Do not mistake this town as lacking in rare finds, however.

Sunshine Markets

If you want to rub elbows with the locals and purchase fresh produce and flowers at (somewhat) reasonable prices, head for Sunshine Markets, also known as Kauai's farmers' markets. These busy markets are held throughout the week, usually in the afternoon, at locations all around the island—just ask any local person. They're good fun, and they support neighborhood farmers. Arrive a little early, bring dollar bills to speed up transactions and your own shopping bags to carry your produce, and be prepared for some pushy shoppers. Farmers are usually happy to educate visitors about unfamiliar fruits and veggies, especially when the crowd thins. For schedules and information on all of the Sunshine Markets, check out Kauai's government website at ⊕ www.kauai.gov.

East Side Sunshine Markets
⊠ *Vidinha Stadium, Lihue, ½ mile south of airport on Rte. 51*, Friday 3 pm. ⊠ *Kapaa, turn mauka on Rte. 581/Olohena Rd. for 1 block*, Wednesday 3 pm.

North Shore Sunshine Markets
⊠ *Waipa, mauka of Rte. 560 north of Hanalei after mile marker 3, Hanalei*, Tuesday 2 pm. ⊠ *Kilauea Neighborhood Center, on Keneke St., Kilauea*, Thursday 4:30 pm. ⊠ *Hanalei Community Center, 5299 Kuhio Hwy, Hanalei*, Saturday 9:30 am.

South Shore Sunshine Markets
⊠ *Ballpark, Koloa, north of intersection of Koloa Rd. and Rte. 520*, Monday noon.

West Side Sunshine Markets ⊠ *Kalaheo Community Center, on Papalina Rd. just off Kaumualii Hwy., Kalaheo*, Tuesday 3 pm. ⊠ *Hanapepe Park, Hanapepe*, Thursday 3 pm. ⊠ *Kekaha Neighborhood Center, Elepaio Rd., Kekaha*, Saturday 9 am.

Lihue is steeped in history and diversity while simultaneously welcoming new trends and establishments.

AREAS AND SHOPPING CENTERS
Hokulei Village
SHOPPING CENTERS/MALLS | Just down the highway between Kauai Community College and the Lihue town center, this retail plaza has a Safeway, Petco, Verde New Mexican restaurant, a bank, and Jack in the Box. It's got California vibes, and it is fresher and more inviting than some of Kauai's older malls. ⊠ *4454 Nuhou St.*

Kilohana Plantation
SHOPPING CENTERS/MALLS | This 16,000-square-foot Tudor mansion contains art galleries, a jewelry store, and the restaurant Gaylord's. Kilohana Plantation is filled with antiques from its original owner, and the restored outbuildings house a craft shop and a Hawaiian-style clothing shop. Train rides on a restored railroad are available, with knowledgeable guides reciting the history of sugar on Kauai. The site is also now the home of Luau Kalamaku and Koloa Rum Company. ⊠ *3-2087 Kaumualii Hwy., Lihue* ☎ *808/245–5608* ⊕ *www.kilohanakauai.com.*

Kukui Grove Center
SHOPPING CENTERS/MALLS | This is Kauai's only true mall. Anchor tenants are Longs Drugs, Macy's, Ross, Kukui Grove Cinemas, and Times Supermarket. The mall's stores offer women's clothing, surf wear, art, toys, athletic shoes, jewelry, a hair salon, and locally made crafts. Restaurants range from fast food and sandwiches to sushi and Korean, with a popular

The gift shop at the Kauai Museum is one of the best places on the island to find reasonably priced local crafts and books.

Starbucks and Jamba Juice. The center stage often has entertainment, especially on Friday night, and there is a farmers' market on Monday afternoon. ✉ 3-2600 Kaumualii Hwy., Lihue ☎ 808/245–7784 ⊕ www.kukuigrovecenter.com.

CLOTHING

Hilo Hattie, The Store of Hawaii

CLOTHING | This is the big name in aloha wear for tourists throughout the Islands, and Hilo Hattie has only one store on Kauai. Located a mile from Lihue Airport, come here for cool, comfortable aloha shirts and muumuu in bright floral prints, as well as other souvenirs. Also, be sure to check out the line of Hawaii-inspired home furnishings. ✉ 3252 Kuhio Hwy., Lihue ☎ 808/245–3404 ⊕ www.hilohattie.com.

FOOD SPECIALTIES

Kauai Fruit and Flower Company

FOOD/CANDY | At this shop near Lihue and five minutes away from the airport, you can buy fresh Hawaii Gold pineapple, sugarcane, ginger, tropical flowers, coconuts, local jams, jellies, and honey, plus papayas, bananas, and mangoes from Kauai. Some of the fruit at Kauai Fruit and Flower Company cannot be shipped out of state. ✉ 3-4684 Kuhio Hwy., Lihue ☎ 808/245–1814 ⊕ www. kauaifruit.com ⊗ Closed Sat. afternoon and Sun.

GIFTS

★ Kapaia Stitchery

GIFTS/SOUVENIRS | Hawaiian quilts made by hand and machine, a beautiful selection of fabrics, quilting kits, handmade aloha shirts, and unique fabric arts fill Kapaia Stitchery, a cute little red plantation-style building a mile outside of Lihue. There are also many locally made gifts and quilts for sale in this locally owned store. The staff is friendly and helpful, even though a steady stream of customers keeps them busy. ✉ 3-3551 Kuhio Hwy., Lihue ☎ 808/245–2281 ⊕ kapaiastitchery.com ⊗ Closed Sun.

★ Kauai Museum

GIFTS/SOUVENIRS | The gift shop at the museum sells some fascinating books, maps, and prints, as well as lovely authentic Niihau shell jewelry, handwoven *lau hala* hats, and koa wood bowls. Also featured at the Kauai Museum are tapa cloth, authentic *tikis* (hand-carved wooden figurines), as well as other good-quality local crafts and books at reasonable prices. ⊠ *4428 Rice St., Lihue* ☎ *808/245–6931* ⊕ *www.kauaimuseum. org* ☉ *Closed Sun.*

HOME DECOR

Two Frogs Hugging

HOUSEHOLD ITEMS/FURNITURE | At Two Frogs Hugging, you'll find lots of interesting housewares, accessories, knickknacks, and hand-carved collectibles, as well as baskets and furniture from Indonesia, the Philippines, and China. The shop occupies expansive quarters in the Lihue Industrial Park. ⊠ *3094 Aukele St., Lihue* ☎ *808/246–8777* ⊕ *www.twofrogshugging.com* ☉ *Closed Sun.*

MARKETS

★ Kauai Community Market

OUTDOOR/FLEA/GREEN MARKETS | **FAMILY** | This is the biggest and best farmers' market on Kauai, sponsored by the Kauai Farm Bureau at the community college in Lihue and held on Saturday mornings. You'll find fresh produce and flowers, as well as packaged products like breads, goat cheese, pasta, honey, coffee, soaps, lotions, and more, all made locally. Seating areas are available to grab a snack or lunch from the food booths, and lunch wagons set up here. ⊠ *3-1901 Kaumualii Hwy., Lihue* ☎ *808/855–5429* ⊕ *www. kauaicommunitymarket.com.*

Chapter 5

THE SOUTH SHORE

Updated by
Mary F. Williamson

◉ Sights	🍴 Restaurants	🛏 Hotels	🛍 Shopping	🍸 Nightlife
★★★★★	★★★★★	★★★★★	★★★★★	★★★☆☆

WELCOME TO THE SOUTH SHORE

TOP REASONS TO GO

★ **Natural Wonders.** Whether it's a stop at Spouting Horn blowhole, a hike along wild sea cliffs, or a stroll through lush tropical gardens, you'll have lots of opportunity to unplug and marvel at nature.

★ **Beautiful Beaches.** Sunny and swimmable much of the year, the beaches on the South Shore are perfect for snorkeling or taking a surf lesson. Poipu Beach is one of the best in Kauai.

★ **Farming Heritage.** Koloa is the birthplace of the sugar industry in Hawaii, and the monument at the center of town is worth a look. The crop shaped the demographics, food, and language of today.

★ **Active Adventure.** Besides the beach, you can try ziplining, ATV-ing, and exploring miles of paths by horseback or on foot.

★ **All the Food.** With everything from picnic fare to casual fine dining, you'll have a good selection of Hawaiian classics on this part of the island.

1 **Koloa.** Home to Hawaii's first sugar plantation, Koloa Town is the South Shore's commercial hub, with shops, eateries, a grocery store, post office, and bank.

2 **Poipu.** Resorts hug the sunny coast of Kauai's most popular yet low-key area. The beaches are well worth a day or two of sunbathing.

Kalaheo

0   2 mi

0   2 km

As you follow the main road south from Lihue, the landscape becomes lush and densely vegetated before giving way to drier conditions that characterize Poipu, the South Side's major resort area. Poipu owes much of its popularity to a steady supply of sunshine and a string of sandy beaches, although the beaches are smaller and more covelike than those on the West Side. With its extensive selection of accommodations, services, and activities, the South Shore attracts more visitors than any other area of Kauai.

It also attracted developers with big plans for the onetime sugarcane fields that are nestled in this region and enveloped by mountains. There are few roads in and out, and local residents are concerned about increased traffic as well as construction. If you're planning to stay on the South Side, be sure to ask if your hotel, condo, or vacation rental will be affected by development during your visit.

Both Poipu and nearby Koloa (site of Kauai's first sugar mill) can be reached via Route 520 (Maluhia Road) from the Lihue area. Route 520 is known locally as Tree Tunnel Road, due to the stand of eucalyptus trees lining the road that were planted at the turn of the 20th century by Walter Duncan McBryde, a Scotsman who began cattle ranching on Kauai's South Shore. The canopy of trees was ripped to literal shreds twice—in 1982 during Hurricane Iwa and again in 1992 during Hurricane Iniki. And, true to Kauai, both times the trees grew back into an impressive tunnel. It's a distinctive way to announce, "You are now on vacation," for there's a definite feel of leisure in the air here. There's still plenty to do—snorkel, bike, walk, horseback ride, take an ATV tour, surf, scuba dive, shop, and dine—everything you'd want on a tropical vacation. From the west, Route 530 (Koloa Road) slips into downtown Koloa, a string of fun shops and restaurants, at an intersection with the only gas station on the South Shore.

Planning

Getting Here and Around

Lihue Airport serves all areas of Kauai. It's roughly a half hour drive to the South Shore, depending on traffic. The South Shore's primary access road is Highway 520, a tree-lined, two-lane, windy road. As you drive along it, there's a sense of tunneling down a rabbit hole into another world, à la Alice. And the South Shore is certainly a wonderland. On average, it rains only 30 inches per year, so if you're looking for fun in the sun, this is a good place to start. Taxis and ride-sharing services are limited on this rural island.

Beaches

The South Shore's beaches, with their powdery-fine sand, are consistently good year-round, except during high surf, which, if it hits at all, will be in summer. If you want solitude, this isn't it; if you want excitement—well, as much excitement as quiet Kauai offers, this is the place for you. ■TIP→ Poipu's beaches are among the best on the island for families, with sandy shores, shallow waters, and grassy lawns down to the sand.

Hotels

Sunseekers usually head south to the condo-studded shores of Poipu, where three- and four-story complexes line the coast and the surf is generally ideal for swimming. As the island's primary resort community, Poipu has the bulk of the island's accommodations, and more condos than hotels, with prices in the moderate to expensive range. Although it accommodates many visitors, its extensive, colorful landscaping and low-rise buildings save it from feeling dense and overcrowded, and it has a delightful coastal promenade perfect for sunset strolls.

Restaurants

Most South Shore restaurants are more upscale and located within resorts and shopping centers. If you're looking for a gourmet meal in a classy setting, the South Shore is where you'll find it. Poipu has a number of excellent restaurants in dreamy settings and decidedly fewer family-style, lower-price eateries. As with most of the island, there's not much nightlife when restaurants close after dinner.

HOTEL AND RESTAURANT PRICES

Hotel prices in the reviews are the lowest cost of a standard double room in high season. Restaurant prices in the reviews are the average cost of a main course at dinner, or if dinner is not served, at lunch.

WHAT IT COSTS in U.S. Dollars			
$	$$	$$$	$$$$
RESTAURANTS			
under $18	$18–$26	$27–$35	over $35
HOTELS			
under $180	$180–$260	$261–$340	over $340

Safety

It's wise to get in the water only at lifeguarded beaches, especially if you are trying snorkeling or body boarding for the first time. Kauai currents are strong and surf conditions change, sometimes unpredictably, from season to season. Taking a surf lesson or adventuring with a guided group is a good idea. Always watch the water for a while before going in and never turn your back on the sea.

Tours

Kauai ATV / Aloha Kauai Tours

EXCURSIONS | FAMILY | You get *way* off the beaten track on these excursions. Choose from several options, including an ATV tour leading from the haul-cane roads behind the locked gates of Grove Farm Plantation to a waterfall, and another exploring the archaeology and ecosystem of Makauwahi Cave. The tour center, adjacent to a lively food truck scene, is also the place to book with SeaFun Ocean Adventures, for a four-hour snorkeling excursion, Koloa Zipline, for the chance to zip over Waita Reservoir, and Koloa Bass Fishing. ⊠ *3477A Weliweli Rd. (for check-in), Koloa* ☎ *808/742–2734* ⊕ *www.kauaiatv.com.*

Koloa

11 miles southwest of Lihue.

Hawaii's lucrative foray into sugar was born in this sleepy town, where the first sugar was milled back in 1830. You can still see the mill's old stone smokestack. Little else remains, save for the charming plantation-style buildings that have kept Koloa from becoming a tacky tourist trap for Poipu-bound visitors. The original small-town character has been preserved by converting historic structures along the main street into boutiques, restaurants, and shops. Placards describe the original tenants and life in the old mill town. Look for Koloa Fish Market, which offers poke and sashimi takeout, and Progressive Expressions, a popular local surf shop.

South Shore Festivals

Each July, the **Koloa Plantation Days** enlivens the area, with a parade, craft fair, concerts, historical tours, and a rodeo. In November, treat your tastebuds to the three-day **Poipu Food & Wine Festival**. It celebrates Kauai's diverse resources and talents, while supporting the culinary program at Kauai Community College.

◉ Sights

Koloa Heritage Trail

TRAIL | Throughout the South Shore, you'll find brass plaques with details of historical stops along the 10-mile Koloa Heritage Trail—bike it, hike it, or drive it, your choice. You'll learn about Koloa's whaling history, sugar industry, ancient Hawaiian cultural sites, the island's volcanic formation, and more. Pick up a free self-guided trail map at most any shop in Koloa Town. ⊠ *Koloa.*

★ Old Koloa Town

HISTORIC SITE | Koloa's first sugar mill opened in 1835, ushering in an era of sugar production throughout the islands, with more than 100 plantations established by 1885. Many of the workers came from the Philippines, Japan, China, Korea, and Portugal, creating Hawaii's multiethnic mélange. Today, many of Koloa's historic buildings beneath the shade of ancient monkeypod trees have been converted into fun shops and restaurants. You'll just want to stroll and take it all in; favorites include Island Soap and Candleworks, Crazy Shirts, and Lappert's, Hawaiian-inspired ice cream made daily in nearby Hanapepe. Try the Kauai Pie or

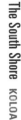

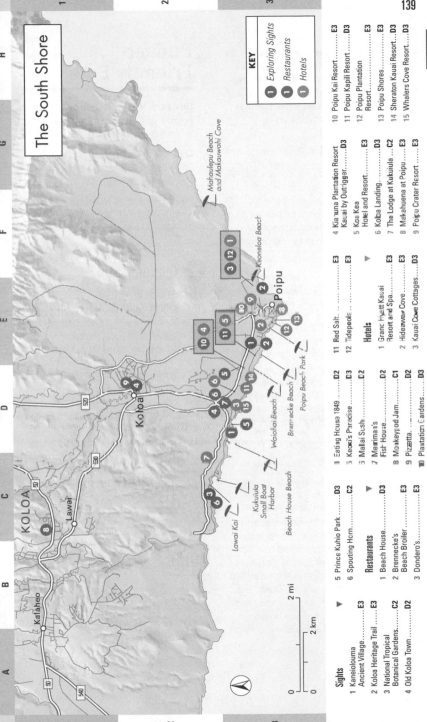

The South Shore

KEY

1 Exploring Sights
1 Restaurants
1 Hotels

Sights

1 Kaneiolouma Ancient Village E3
2 Koloa Heritage Trail E3
3 National Tropical Botanical Gardens C2
4 Old Koloa Town D2
5 Prince Kuhio Park D3
6 Spouting Horn C2

Restaurants

1 Beach House D3
2 Brennecke's Beach Broiler E3
3 Dondero's E3
4 Eating House 1849 .... D2
5 Keoki's Paradise D3
6 Mahai Sushi C2
7 Merriman's Fish House D2
8 Monkeypod Jam C1
9 Pizzetta D2
10 Plantation Gardens D3
11 Red Salt E3
12 Tidepools E3

Hotels:

1 Grand Hyatt Kauai Resort and Spa E3
2 Hideaway Cove E3
3 Kauai Cove Cottages D3
4 Kiahuna Plantation Resort Kauai by Outrigger D3
5 Koa Kea Hotel and Resort E3
6 Koloa Landing D3
7 The Lodge at Kukuiula ... C2
8 Makahuena at Poipu E3
9 Poipu Crater Resort E3
10 Poipu Kai Resort E3
11 Poipu Kapili Resort D3
12 Poipu Plantation Resort E3
13 Poipu Shores E3
14 Sheraton Kauai Resort ... D3
15 Whalers Cove Resort D3

5

The South Shore KOLOA

Luau Delight flavors, after a food truck lunch in nearby Knudsen Park. ■ TIP→ Be sure to approach Old Koloa Town via the Tree Tunnel, a romantic canopy of eucalyptus trees planted more than a century ago along a stretch of Maluhia Road. ✉ *Koloa Rd., Koloa* ⊕ *www.oldkoloa.com.*

Restaurants

Most eateries in Koloa are come-as-you-are casual, family-friendly, and modestly priced. Food trucks gather by the old sugar monument and in a lot behind the main street. Finer dining, sometimes with a view, can be found in Poipu, closer to the sea.

Monkeypod Jam

$ | HAWAIIAN | Part shop and part bistro, the highway storefront of Monkeypod Jam serves up healthy takeaway sandwiches, quiche, soup, baked goodies, and smoothies, and its shelves are packed with award-winning jams, curds, and chutneys made from tropical fruits. Travel-friendly samplers are available. **Known for:** preserves; quick lunches; cooking workshops. ⑤ *Average main: $10* ✉ *2-3687 Kaumualii Hwy., Lawai* ✢ *next to Lawai Post Office* ☎ *808/378–4208* ⊕ *www.monkeypodjam.com* ⊙ *Closed Sun.*

Pizzetta

$ | ITALIAN | FAMILY | This family-style Italian restaurant has an open-air deck where hearty portions of pasta, calzones, and thin-crust pizza are served, along with kalua pork and cabbage, grilled fish, and barbecue ribs, all of which can find their way into pizza toppings. Gluten-free crust and pasta are available. **Known for:** neighborhood delivery service; attentive wait staff; fresh, house-made bread. ⑤ *Average main: $17* ✉ *5408 Koloa Rd., Koloa* ☎ *808/742–8881.*

Budget-Friendly Eats

Da Crack Mexican Grinds ✉ *2827 Poipu Rd., Koloa* ☎ *808/742–9505* ⊕ *www.dacrackkauai.com.*

Little **Fish Coffee** ✉ *2290 Poipu Rd., Koloa* ☎ *808/742–2113* ⊕ *www.littlefishcoffee.com.*

Puka Dog ✉ *2650 Kiahuna Plantation Dr., Koloa* ☎ *808/742–6044* ⊕ *www.pukadog.com.*

🛍 Shopping

Warehouse 3540

LOCAL SPECIALTIES | An old warehouse to the west of Koloa in Lawai has new life as a marketplace for a dozen creative entrepreneurs and as a hub for food trucks. Hand-sewn and hand-printed clothing, authentic *lau hala* hats, boho chic jewelry, letterpressed cards, specialty food products, and locally crafted soaps are offered at the permanent micro-shops. These are joined by craft vendors, farmers, take-out food cooks, and musicians on Fridays and second Saturday evenings. Locals and visitors mingle at a large indoor library or enjoy communal seating outside. ✉ *3540 Koloa Rd., Kalaheo* ⊕ *www.warehouse3540.com* ⊙ *Closed Sun.*

Poipu

2 miles southeast of Koloa.

Thanks to its generally sunny weather and a string of golden-sand beaches dotted with oceanfront lodgings, Poipu is a top choice for many visitors. Beaches are user-friendly, with protected waters

Continued on page 144

BIRTH OF THE ISLANDS

How did the volcanoes of the Hawaiian Islands evolve here, in the middle of the Pacific Ocean? The ancient Hawaiians believed that the volcano goddess Pele's hot temper was the key to the mystery; modern scientists contend that it's all about plate tectonics and one very hot spot.

Plate Tectonics & the Hawaiian Question: The theory of plate tectonics says that the Earth's surface is comprised of plates that float around slowly over the planet's molten interior. The vast majority of earthquakes and volcanic eruptions occur near plate boundaries—the San Francisco earthquakes in 1906 and 1989, for example, were the result of activity along the nearby San Andreas Fault, where the Pacific and North American plates meet. Hawaii, more than 1,988 miles from the nearest plate boundary, is a giant exception. For years scientists struggled to explain the island chain's existence—if not a fault line, what caused the earthquakes and volcanic eruptions that formed these islands?

What's a hotspot? In 1963, J. Tuzo Wilson, a Canadian geophysicist, argued that the Hawaiian volcanoes must have been created by small concentrated areas of extreme heat beneath the plates. Wilson hypothesized that there is a hotspot beneath the present-day position of the Big Island. Its heat produced a persistent source of magma by partly melting the Pacific Plate above it. The magma, lighter than the surrounding solid rock, rose through the mantle and crust to erupt onto the sea floor, forming an active seamount. Each flow caused the seamount to grow until it finally emerged above sea level as an island volcano. Plausible so far, but why then, is there not one giant Hawaiian island?

HAWAIIAN CREATION MYTH

Holo Mai Pele, often played out in hula, is the Hawaiian creation myth. Pele sends her sister Hiiaka on an epic quest to fetch her lover Lohiau. Overcoming many obstacles, Hiiaka reaches full goddess status and falls in love with Lohiau herself. When Pele finds out, she destroys everything dear to her sister, killing Lohiau and burning Hiiaka's ohia groves. Each time lava flows from a volcano, ohia trees sprout shortly after, in a constant cycle of destruction and renewal.

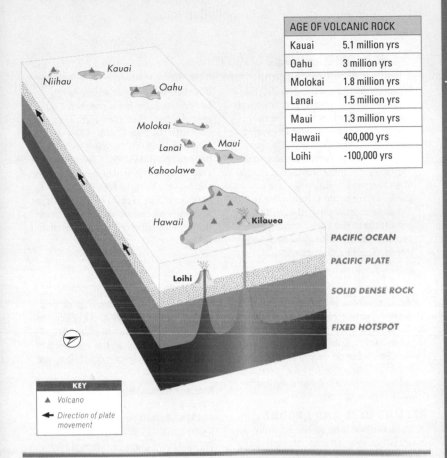

AGE OF VOLCANIC ROCK	
Kauai	5.1 million yrs
Oahu	3 million yrs
Molokai	1.8 million yrs
Lanai	1.5 million yrs
Maui	1.3 million yrs
Hawaii	400,000 yrs
Loihi	-100,000 yrs

PACIFIC OCEAN

PACIFIC PLATE

SOLID DENSE ROCK

FIXED HOTSPOT

KEY

▲ Volcano

← Direction of plate movement

Volcanoes on the Move: Wilson further suggested that the movement of the Pacific Plate itself eventually carries the island volcano beyond the hotspot. Cut off from its magma source, the island volcano becomes dormant. As the plate slowly moved, one island volcano would become extinct just as another would develop over the hotspot. After several million years, there is a long volcanic trail of islands and seamounts across the ocean floor. The oldest islands are those farthest from the hotspot. The exposed rocks of Kauai, for example, are about 5.1 million years old, but those on the Big Island are less than .5 million years old, with new volcanic rock still being formed.

An Island on the Way: Off the coast of the Big Island, the volcano known as Loihi is still submerged but erupting. Scientists long believed it to be a retired seamount volcano, but in the 1970s they discovered both old and new lava on its flanks, and in 1996 it erupted with a vengeance. It is believed that several thousand years from now, Loihi will be the newest addition to the Hawaiian Islands.

The Kauai Marathon

Heading into its second decade, the Kauai Marathon and its larger concurrent Half-Marathon attract runners and walkers from all over the world each September. Conch shells are blown to signal the start, and participants set off from the heart of Poipu, then turn up the Koloa Bypass Road as the sun rises behind the old sugar mill. Even the most competitive will stop for a selfie in the Tree Tunnel before continuing west along the highway (lanes closed for the occasion) and down through Omao where neighbors cheer from front porches. Full marathoners then turn right for a long loop into the tough hills of Lawai and Kalaheo; "halfers" turn left to head back to the waterfront. Hula dancers and Japanese *taiko* drummers pepper the route. The large free Health & Wellness Expo is open to the public, as are many marathon-related events at nearby shopping centers and sponsor hotels.

for *keiki* (children) and novice snorkelers, lifeguards, restrooms, covered pavilions, and a sweet coastal promenade ideal for leisurely strolls. Some experts have even ranked Poipu Beach Park number one in the nation. It depends on your preferences, of course, though it certainly does warrant high accolades.

GETTING HERE AND AROUND

Poipu is the one area on Kauai where you could get by without a car, though that could mean an expensive taxi ride from the airport and limited access to other parts of the island. To reach Poipu by car, follow Poipu Road south from Koloa. After the traffic circle, the road curves to follow the coast, leading to some of the popular South Shore beaches.

 Sights

Kaneiolouma Ancient Village

ARCHAEOLOGICAL SITE | Stone masons are rebuilding the walls of this largely intact 13-acre Hawaiian village dating back to the mid-1400s. Fish ponds, taro patches, a temple, and a festival arena eventually will be restored, serving as a cultural learning center for residents and visitors.

You can walk around the outside and check out the statues and signage; the interior is set to open in 2024. ⊠ *2000 Poipu Rd., Koloa* ✛ *at the intersection of Poipu Rd. and Hoowili Rd.* ⊕ *www.kaneiolouma.org.*

National Tropical Botanical Gardens (*NTBG*)

GARDEN | Tucked away in Lawai Valley, these gardens include lands and a cottage once used by Hawaii's Queen Emma for a summer retreat. Trams depart frequently to transport people from the visitor center to the gardens. The rambling 252-acre McBryde Garden has exhibits and easy trails to help visitors learn about biodiversity and plants collected throughout the tropics, including the Canoe Garden that features plants originally brought to Hawaii by early Polynesian voyagers. The 100-acre Allerton Garden, which can be visited only on a guided tour, artfully displays statues and water features originally developed as part of a private estate. Reservations and closed-toe shoes are required for all tours. The visitor center has a high-quality gift shop and a grab-and-go cafe. Besides propagating rare and endangered plants from Hawaii and elsewhere, NTBG functions as a scientific research and education center. The organization also operates gardens in Limahuli, on Kauai's North Shore, in Hana, on Maui's east shore, and in Florida. ⊠ *4425 Lawai Rd., Poipu* ☎ *808/742–2623* ⊕ *www.ntbg. org* ⊠ *McBryde self-guided tour $30, Allerton guided tour $60.*

Prince Kuhio Park

CITY PARK | A triangle of grass next to the Prince Kuhio condominiums honors the birthplace of Kauai's beloved Prince Jonah Kuhio Kalanianaole. Known for his kind nature and tireless work on behalf of the Hawaiian people, he lost his chance at the throne when Americans staged an illegal overthrow of Queen Liliuokalani in 1893 and toppled Hawaii's constitutional monarchy. He served as a delegate to the U.S. Congress for 19 years after Hawaii became a territory in 1900. An annual commemoration is held in March. This is a great place to watch wave riders surfing a popular break known as PKs or to watch the sun sink into the Pacific. ⊠ *Lawai Rd., Poipu.*

★ Spouting Horn

LOCAL INTEREST | When conditions are right, a natural blowhole in the rocky shoreline behaves like Old Faithful, shooting salt water high into the air and making a hollow, echoing sound. It's most dramatic during big summer swells, which jam large quantities of water through an ancient lava tube with great force. Most sidewalk vendors hawk inexpensive souvenirs, but a few carry locally set South Sea pearls or rare Niihau-shell creations, with prices ranging from affordable up to several thousand dollars. Look for green sea turtles bobbing in the adjacent cove. ⊠ *End of Lawai Rd., Poipu* ⊕ *www.kauai.com/spouting-horn.*

Beaches

Beach House Beach

BEACH—SIGHT | Don't pack the beach umbrella, beach mats, and cooler for this one—just your snorkel gear, when the seas are calm. The beach, named after the neighboring Beach House restaurant and located on the road to Spouting Horn, is a small slip of sand during low tide and a rocky shoreline when it's high; however, it is conveniently located by the road's edge, and its rocky edge and bottom make it great for snorkeling. (As a rule, sandy-bottom beaches are not great for snorkeling. Rocks provide safe hiding places and grow the food that fish and other marine life like to eat.) A sidewalk along the coastline on the restaurant side of the beach makes a great vantage point from which to peer into the water and look for *honu,* the Hawaiian green sea turtle. It's also a very popular gathering spot to watch the sun set. ■TIP→ **Make reservations for dinner at the Beach House in advance and time it around sunset.** You can park in the public lot across from the beach. **Amenities:** parking; showers; toilets. **Best for:** snorkeling; sunset; surfing. ⊠ *Lawai Rd., off Poipu Rd., Poipu.*

Brennecke Beach

BEACH—SIGHT | This beach is synonymous on Kauai with board surfing and bodysurfing, thanks to its shallow sandbar and reliable shore break. Because the beach is small and often congested, surfboards are prohibited near shore. The water on the rocky eastern edge of the beach is a good place to see the endangered green sea turtles noshing on plants growing on the rocks. **Amenities:** food and drink; parking. **Best for:** sunset; surfing. ⊠ *Hoone Rd., off Poipu Rd., Poipu.*

Keoneloa Beach (*Shipwreck Beach*)

BEACH—SIGHT | The Hawaiian name for this stretch of beach, Keoneloa, means "long sand," but many refer to this beach fronting the Grand Hyatt Kauai Resort

Did You Know?

Spouting Horn is a blowhole that shoots water through a lava tube up to 50 feet in the air.

and Spa by its common name: Shipwreck Beach. Both make sense. It is a long stretch of crescent beach punctuated by stunning sea cliffs on both ends, and, yes, a ship once wrecked here. With its rough onshore break, the waters off Shipwreck are best for body boarding and bodysurfing experts; however, the beach itself is plenty big for sunbathing, sand-castle building, Frisbee, and other beach-related fun. The eastern edge of the beach is the start of an interpretive cliff and dune walk (complimentary) held by the hotel staff; check with the concierge for days and times, and keep an eye out for snoozing monk seals below. **Amenities:** food and drink; parking; showers; toilets. **Best for:** sunrise; surfing; walking. ⊠ *Ainako Rd., continue on Poipu Rd. past Hyatt, turn makai on Ainako Rd., Poipu.*

Kukuiula Small Boat Harbor

BEACH—SIGHT | FAMILY | This is a great beach to sit and people-watch as diving and fishing boats, kayakers, and canoe paddlers head out to sea. Shore and throw-net fishermen frequent this harbor as well. It's not a particularly large harbor, so it retains a quaint sense of charm, unlike Nawiliwili Harbor or Port Allen. The lawn is a good picnic and ball-tossing spot and the bay is a nice, protected area for limited swimming, but with all the boat traffic kicking up sand and clouding the water, it's not good for snorkeling. Outside the breakwater, there is a decent surf spot. **Amenities:** parking; showers; toilets. **Best for:** picnics; sunset; swimming. ⊠ *Lawai Rd., off Poipu Rd., Poipu.*

Lawai Kai

BEACH—SIGHT | One of the most spectacular beaches on the South Shore is inaccessible by land unless you tour the National Tropical Botanical Garden's Allerton Garden, which we highly recommend. On the tour, you'll see the beach, but you won't step on the sand. The only way to legally access the beach on your own is by paddling a kayak 1 mile from Kukuiula Harbor. However, you have to rent the kayaks elsewhere and haul them on top of your car to the harbor. Also, the wind and waves usually run westward, making the in-trip a breeze but the return trip a workout against Mother Nature. ■ **TIP→ Do not attempt this beach in any manner during a south swell. Amenities:** none. **Best for:** solitude; sunset. ⊠ *4425 Lawai Rd., off Poipu Rd.* ☎ *808/712–2623 for tour information at the National Tropical Botanical Garden's Allerton Garden* ⊕ *www.ntbg.org.*

★ Mahaulepu Beach and Makauwahi Cave

BEACH—SIGHT | This 2-mile stretch of coast, with its sand dunes, limestone hills, sinkholes, and the Makauwahi Cave, is unlike any other on Kauai. Remains of a large, ancient settlement, evidence of great battles, and the discovery of a now-underwater petroglyph field indicate that Hawaiians lived in this area as early as AD 700. Mahaulepu's coastline is unprotected and rocky, which makes venturing into the ocean hazardous. There are three beach areas with bits of sandy-bottom swimming; however, the best way to experience Mahaulepu is simply to roam, especially in the morning, along the sand or heritage trail. Pack water and sun protection. ■ **TIP→ Access to this beach is via private property. Before driving or hiking here, check conditions as the unpaved road can be closed due to weather, grading, or movie filming. Access is during daylight hours only, so be sure to depart before sunset or risk getting locked in for the night. Amenities:** parking. **Best for:** solitude; sunrise; walking. ⊠ *Poipu Rd., Poipu* ✦ *past Hyatt Hotel and CJM Stables* ⊕ *www.cavereserve.org.*

★ Poipu Beach Park

BEACH—SIGHT | FAMILY | The most popular beach on the South Shore is Poipu Beach Park. During calm seas, the snorkeling and swimming are good, and when the surf's up, the body boarding and

South Shore beaches have good surf breaks. Head to Poipu Beach for board rentals or lessons.

surfing are good, too. Frequent sunshine, grassy lawns, play equipment, and easy access add to the appeal, especially with families. The beach is frequently crowded and great for people-watching. Even the endangered Hawaiian monk seal often makes an appearance. Take a walk west on a path fronting numerous resorts. **Amenities:** food and drink; lifeguards; parking; showers; toilets. **Best for:** parties; snorkeling; sunbathing; swimming. ⊠ Hoone Rd., off Poipu Rd., Poipu ☎ 808/742–7444.

Waiohai Beach

BEACH—SIGHT | The first hotel built in Poipu in 1962 overlooked this beach, adjacent to Poipu Beach Park. Actually, there's little to distinguish where this one ends and the other begins, other than a crescent reef at the eastern end of Waiohai Beach. That crescent, however, is important. It creates a small, protected bay—good for snorkeling and beginning surfers. If you're a beginner, this is the spot. However, when a summer swell kicks up, the near-shore conditions

become dangerous; offshore, there's a splendid surf break for experienced surfers. The beach itself is narrow and, like its neighbor, gets very crowded in summer. **Amenities:** parking. **Best for:** snorkeling; sunset; surfing; swimming. ⊠ Hoone Rd., off Poipu Rd., Poipu.

🍴 Restaurants

Beach House

$$$$ | MODERN HAWAIIAN | This busy restaurant has a dreamy ocean view, making it a good setting for a special dinner or a cocktail and appetizer while the sun sinks into the glassy blue Pacific and surfers slice the waves. The prices have gone up, but you can still find satisfaction in the pork belly appetizer or fresh catch of the day served with *lilikoi* (passion fruit) lemongrass beurre blanc. **Known for:** gluten-free and vegan entrees; small bar with a big view; indoor-outdoor dining. ⑤ Average main: $40 ⊠ 5022 Lawai Rd., Poipu ☎ 808/742–1424 ⊕ www.the-beach-house.com.

Sun Safety on Kauai

Hawaii's weather—seemingly never-ending warm, sunny days with gentle trade winds—can be enjoyed year-round with good sun sense. Because of Hawaii's subtropical location, the length of daylight here changes little throughout the year. The sun is particularly strong, with a daily UV average of 14. Visitors should take extra precaution to avoid sunburns and long-term cancer risks due to sun exposure.

While protecting your skin, protect Hawaii's reefs, too. Hawaii has banned the sale of sunscreens containing oxybenzone and octinoxate, ingredients that can harm coral reefs and marine ecosystems. Pack a reef-safe alternative, such as TropicSport.

The Hawaii Dermatological Society recommends these sun safety tips:

■ Plan your beach, golf, hiking, and other outdoor activities for the early morning or late afternoon, avoiding the sun between 10 am and 4 pm, when it's the strongest.

■ Apply a broad-band, reef-safe sunscreen with a sun protection factor (SPF) of at least 15. Cover areas that are most prone to burning, like your nose, shoulders, tops of feet, and ears. And don't forget your lips.

■ Apply sunscreen at least 30 minutes before you plan to be outdoors and reapply every two hours, even on cloudy days. Clouds scatter sunlight, so you can still burn on an overcast day.

■ Wear light, protective clothing, such as a long-sleeve shirt and pants, broad-brimmed hat, and sunglasses.

■ Stay in the shade whenever possible—especially on the beach—by using an umbrella. Remember that sand and water can reflect up to 85% of the sun's damaging rays.

■ Children need extra protection from the sun. Apply sunscreen frequently and liberally on children over six months of age and minimize their time in the sun. Sunscreen is not recommended for children under six months.

Brennecke's Beach Broiler

$$$ | AMERICAN | FAMILY | Casual and fun, with a busy mai tai bar and windows overlooking the beach, Brennecke's specializes in big portions in a wide range of offerings including rib-eye steak, burgers, fish tacos, pasta, shrimp, and the fresh catch of the day; create your own combination meal if you can't pick just one. This place is especially good for happy hour (3 to 5 pm and 8:30 pm to closing), as the drink and *pupu* (appetizer) menus bring the prices closer to reality. **Known for:** family-friendly setting; wide-ranging menu; take-out deli with shave ice.

⑤ *Average main: $27* ⊠ *2100 Hoone Rd., Poipu* ☎ *808/742–7588* ⊕ *www.brenneckes.com.*

★ Dondero's

$$$$ | ITALIAN | With a beautiful setting, good food, stunning ocean view, and impeccable service by career waiters, Dondero's is one of Kauai's better restaurants. The menu features housemade pastas, classics like grilled seafood cioppino and tender veal osso buco, and salad greens cut daily from the hotel's hydroponic farm. **Known for:** Italianate murals and elegant interior; romantic

Seal-Spotting on the South Shore

When strolling on one of Kauai's lovely beaches, don't be surprised if you find yourself in the rare company of Hawaiian monk seals. These are among the most endangered of all marine mammals, with perhaps fewer than 1,400 remaining. They primarily inhabit the northwestern Hawaiian Islands, although more are showing their sweet faces on the main Hawaiian Islands, especially on Kauai. They're fond of hauling out on the beach for a long snooze in the sun, particularly after a night of gorging on fish. They need this time to rest and digest, safe from predators.

Female seals regularly birth their young on the beaches around Kauai, where they stay to nurse their pups for upward of six weeks. It seems the seals enjoy particular beaches for the same reasons we do: the shallow, protected waters.

If you're lucky enough to see a monk seal, keep your distance and let it be. Although they may haul out near people, they still want and need their space. Stay several hundred feet away, and forget photos unless you've got a zoom lens. It's illegal to do anything that causes a monk seal to change its behavior, with penalties that include big fines and even jail time. In the water, seals may appear to want to play. It's their curious nature. Don't try to play with them. They are wild animals—mammals, in fact, with teeth.

If you have concerns about the health or safety of a seal, or just want more information, contact the **Hawaiian Monk Seal Conservation Hui** (☎ 808/651–7668).

outdoor dining experience; emphasis on local ingredients. ⑤ *Average main: $38* ✉ *Grand Hyatt Kauai Resort and Spa, 1571 Poipu Rd., Poipu* ☎ *808/240–6456* ⊕ *grandhyattkauai.com* ☉ *Closed Sun. and Mon. No lunch.*

★ Eating House 1849

$$$ | ASIAN FUSION | Hawaii's culinary superstar, Roy Yamaguchi, moved his signature Hawaiian-fusion-cuisine restaurant on Kauai's South Shore to a shopping village that suits the name and creative fare. Though billed as "plantation cuisine," the hot pot rice bowl, spicy ramen bowl, and burger that's half wild boar are about the only items that might have their roots in the days when sugar was king; otherwise, the menu is classic Asian fusion. **Known for:** innovative cuisine; use of local ingredients; lively atmosphere.

⑤ *Average main: $35* ✉ *Shops at Kukuiula, 2829 Ala Kalanikaumaka Rd., No. A-201, Poipu* ☎ *808/742–5000* ⊕ *www. eatinghouse1849.com.*

Keoki's Paradise

$$$ | ASIAN FUSION | FAMILY | Built to resemble a dockside boathouse, this active, semi-outdoor place fills up quickly at night thanks to a busy lounge and frequent live music. The day's fresh catch is available in various styles and sauces, from appetizers (Thai shrimp sticks) to mains (seafood risotto) to meat-lover options like the *imu*-roasted pork ribs. **Known for:** bustling bar with live music; keiki (kids) menu; fresh fish. ⑤ *Average main: $30* ✉ *Poipu Shopping Village, 2360 Kiahuna Plantation Dr., Poipu* ☎ *808/742–7534* ⊕ *www.keokisparadise.com.*

The Plate-Lunch Tradition

To experience island history first-hand, step up to the counter at one of Hawaii's ubiquitous "plate lunch" eateries, and order a segmented plate piled with beef, chicken, two scoops of rice, macaroni salad, and maybe a pickled vegetable condiment. On the sugar plantations, Native Hawaiians and immigrant workers from many different countries ate together in the fields, sharing food from their "kaukau tins," the utilitarian version of the Japanese *bento* lunchbox. From this "melting pot" came the vibrant language of Pidgin and its equivalent in food: the plate lunch.

Along roadsides, and at beaches and events, you will see food trucks, another excellent venue for sampling plate lunches. These portable restaurants are descendants of "lunch wagons" that began selling food to plantation workers in the 1930s. Try the deep-fried chicken *katsu* (rolled in Japanese panko bread crumbs and spices). The marinated beef teriyaki is another good choice, as is miso butterfish. The noodle soup, *saimin*, with its Japanese fish stock and Chinese red-tinted barbecue pork, is a distinctly local medley. Koreans have contributed spicy barbecue *kalbi* ribs, often served with chili-laden *kimchi* (pickled cabbage). Portuguese bean soup and tangy Filipino *adobo* stew are also favorites. The most popular Hawaiian contribution to the plate lunch is the *laulau*, a mix of meat and fish and young taro leaves, wrapped in more taro leaves and steamed.

★ **Makai Sushi**

$ | SUSHI | The menu is simple—poke bowls and a few types of sushi rolls—but the freshness of the fish and attention to quality preparation set this tiny sushi bar apart from the crowd and make it a star of the Poipu Beach food scene. Tucked into a corner of Kukuiula Market, it attracts a steady stream of customers who watch owner Matthew Oliver or another chef transform spicy ahi, blue crab, avocado, cucumber, and *tobiko* (roe) into the Hapa Roll or mix raw ahi, ono fish, salmon, cucumber, avocado, and sweet Maui onion into the Gorilla Bowl. **Known for:** superfresh fish; friendly sushi chefs; take-out options. ⑤ *Average main: $15* ✉ *Kukuiula Market, 2728 Poipu Rd., Koloa* ☎ *808/639–7219* ⊕ *makaisushi.com.*

Merriman's Fish House

$$$$ | MODERN HAWAIIAN | The regional food served up at chef Peter Merriman's namesake restaurant is enhanced by a sophisticated setting and lovely views from a pretty second-floor dining room. Start at the bar, where fine wines are offered by the glass, and then continue to the dinner menu, which states the origins of the fish, shrimp, lamb, beef, chicken, and veggies. **Known for:** upscale, romantic atmosphere; casual menu downstairs; partnerships with local fishermen and farmers. ⑤ *Average main: $45* ✉ *2829 Ala Kalanikaumaka St., G-149, Poipu* ☎ *808/742–8385* ⊕ *www. merrimanshawaii.com.*

Plantation Gardens

$$$ | HAWAIIAN | A historic plantation manager's home has been converted to a restaurant that serves seafood and meats with a Pacific Rim and Hawaiian

influence. Arrive early to stroll through the torch-lit orchid gardens and among lotus-studded koi ponds before settling in to the cozy European-style dining room or tropical veranda. **Known for:** veranda for outdoor dining; unique setting; inspired cocktails and bar menu. [$] *Average main: $30 ⊠ Kiahuna Plantation, 2253 Poipu Rd., Koloa ☎ 808/742–2121 ⊕ www. pgrestaurant.com ☻ No lunch.*

★ Red Salt
$$$$ | ECLECTIC | Smart, sophisticated decor, attentive and skilled service, and an exceptional menu that highlights Hawaiian seafood make Red Salt a great choice for leisurely fine dining. A breakfast buffet is also served, and the sushi lounge and pool bar offer more of the kitchen's great food at lower prices. **Known for:** dramatic presentation; $79 tasting menu; perfectly grilled meats. [$] *Average main: $48 ⊠ Koa Kea Resort, 2251 Poipu Rd., Poipu ☎ 808/742–4200 ⊕ meritagecollection.com/koa-kea.*

Tidepools
$$$$ | SEAFOOD | Of the Grand Hyatt's notable restaurants, Tidepools is definitely the most tropical and campy, with grass-thatch huts that seem to float on a koi-filled pond beneath starry skies while torches flicker in the lushly landscaped grounds nearby. The equally distinctive food has an island flavor that comes from the chef's advocacy of Hawaii regional cuisine and extensive use of island-grown products, including fresh herbs from the resort's organic garden. **Known for:** Hawaii regional cuisine; extensive use of island-grown products; excellent service. [$] *Average main: $50 ⊠ Grand Hyatt Kauai Resort and Spa, 1571 Poipu Rd., Poipu ☎ 808/240–6380 ⊕ grandhyattkau-ai.com ☻ No lunch.*

 # Hotels

★ Grand Hyatt Kauai Resort and Spa
$$$$ | RESORT | FAMILY | Dramatically handsome, this classic Hawaiian low-rise is built into the cliffs overlooking an unspoiled coastline; it's taken great strides to reduce its carbon footprint and boasts mouthwatering restaurants, which helps to make it Kauai's best mega-resort. **Pros:** fabulous pool; excellent restaurants; Hawaiian ambience. **Cons:** dangerous swimming beach during summer swells; small balconies; $40 daily resort fee. [$] *Rooms from: $424 ⊠ 1571 Poipu Rd., Poipu ☎ 808/742–1234 ⊕ www.grandhyattkauai.com ⤶ 604 rooms* ⑩ *No meals.*

Hideaway Cove
$$$ | RENTAL | Just one block from the ocean's edge in the heart of Poipu, Hideaway Cove has units ranging from studios to two bedrooms, each appointed with resort-quality furniture and original artwork. **Pros:** high-quality furnishings; private lanai; quiet road; rates drop with a weeklong stay. **Cons:** not on the ocean; better for couples than families; no pool. [$] *Rooms from: $275 ⊠ 2307 Nalo Rd., Poipu ☎ 808/635–8785, 866/849–2426 ⊕ www.hideawaycove.com ⤶ 7 units* ⑩ *No meals.*

Koloa Landing
$$$$ | RESORT | FAMILY | This family-friendly resort has incredible pools, an on-site spa, plenty of play space, and rooms the size of apartments. **Pros:** easy walk to dining and shopping; 350,000-gallon pool with waterslides; large units. **Cons:** beach not good for swimming; better for families than couples; restaurant is poolside with not much of a view. [$] *Rooms from: $450 ⊠ 2641 Poipu Rd., Koloa ☎ 808/725–2596 ⊕ koloalandingresort. com ⤶ 306 units* ⑩ *No meals.*

Romantic Dining

For divine sunsets, the **Beach House** (☎ 808/742–1424), in Koloa, is best, as it puts you right on the water. **Café Portofino** (☎ 808/245–2121), at the Kauai Marriott in Lihue, with its second-story view of Kalapaki Bay and harp music, practically caters to couples. Tops overall, though, is **Dondero's** (☎ 808/240–6456), in Koloa, where the food, service, and elegant setting come together to create a special evening. If the weather is nice, by all means opt for the terrace.

Be sure to make reservations, and don't plan on pinching pennies. If you're on a budget, pick up some take-out food and spread a blanket on the beach for a memorable sunset picnic and dessert beneath brilliant stars.

Kauai Cove Cottages

$$ | **RENTAL** | Located in a residential neighborhood, this property includes a quaint studio cottage at the mouth of Waikomo Stream, about two blocks from a nice snorkeling cove, as well as a full bedroom suite and a guest room with shared bath in a larger house a few miles away in the resort community at Poipu Kai. The airy tropical-theme studio has a cathedral ceiling, a complete kitchen, and a private patio with a gas grill. **Pros:** walk to shops and restaurants; great snorkeling nearby; quiet neighborhood. **Cons:** not on beach; $80–$90 cleaning fee upon departure; better for couples than families. ⑤ *Rooms from: $180* ✉ *2672 Puuholo Rd., Poipu* ☎ *808/631–9313 for cottage* ⊕ *www.kauaicove.com* ⇥ *3 units* ⑪ *No meals.*

Kiahuna Plantation Resort Kauai by Outrigger

$$ | **RENTAL** | **FAMILY** | This longtime Kauai condo project consists of 42 planta-tion-style, low-rise buildings with individ-ually owned one- and two-bedroom units that arc around a large, grassy field lead-ing to a lovely beach. **Pros:** great sunset and ocean views are bonuses in some units; convenient to restaurants and shops; swimmable beach and lawn for picnics and games. **Cons:** no air-condition-ing; be prepared for stairs; housekeeping

is extra. ⑤ *Rooms from: $180* ✉ *2253 Poipu Rd., Poipu* ☎ *808/742–6411, 866/994–1588 reservations* ⊕ *www.out-rigger.com* ⇥ *333 units* ⑪ *No meals.*

★ Koa Kea Hotel and Resort

$$$$ | **RESORT** | This boutique property offers a stylish, high-end experience without the bustle of many larger resorts, making it a great place to forget it all while relaxing at the spa or lounging by the pool on a honeymoon or babymoon. **Pros:** incredibly comfortable beds; friend-ly service; perfect romantic getaway. **Cons:** not much for children; all parking is valet, but it feels more like a convenience than a burden; very busy area. ⑤ *Rooms from: $429* ✉ *2251 Poipu Rd., Poipu* ☎ *808/742–4200 general information, 808/742–4271 reservations* ⊕ *www. koakea.com* ⇥ *121 rooms* ⑪ *No meals.*

The Lodge at Kukuiula

$$$$ | **RENTAL** | The private Lodge at Kuku-iula offers one- to four-bedroom luxury cottages and villas for rent to non-mem-bers; all homes have spacious lanai with expansive views, high-end kitchens, and both indoor and outdoor showers. **Pros:** top-tier luxury; golf, tennis, and a 32' boat; cultural activities. **Cons:** high price point; must drive to beach, shops, and eateries; in its own world, set apart from local scene. ⑤ *Rooms from: $850* ✉ *2700*

Ke Alaula St., Koloa ☎ *808/742–8000*
⊕ *www.lodgeatkukuiula.com* ⌁ *39
homes* ⧂ *Free Breakfast.*

Makahuena at Poipu

$$$ | RENTAL | Situated close to the center
of Poipu, on the southernmost point of
Kauai, the large, individually owned one-,
two-, and three-bedroom condos have
dramatic oceanfront views of both sunris-
es and sunsets. **Pros:** tennis court; scenic
walking path; right on the ocean. **Cons:**
no-swimming beach; no air-conditioning;
individually owned condos means the
decor and upkeep vary. ⑤ *Rooms from:
$309* ✉ *1661 Pee Rd., Poipu* ☎ *800/325–
5701 reservations* ⊕ *www.castleresorts.
com/kauai/makahuena-at-poipu* ⌁ *78
units* ⧂ *No meals.*

Poipu Crater Resort

$ | RENTAL | Set within an extinct volcanic
crater known as *Piha Keakua* , or "place
of the gods," these two-bedroom con-
dominium units in South Pacific–style
bungalows are fairly spacious, with large
windows, high ceilings, and full kitchens.
Pros: attractive and generally well-kept;
lush hilltop crater location; family friendly
with ping-pong, pool, and clubhouse.
Cons: beach isn't good for swimming;
few resort amenities; individually owned
units means upkeep and decor varies.
⑤ *Rooms from: $150* ✉ *2330 Hoohu Rd.,
Poipu* ☎ *808/742-7260* ⌁ *30 units* ⧂ *No
meals.*

Poipu Kai Resort

$$ | RENTAL | FAMILY | The condominiums
here, many with cathedral ceilings and
all with large furnished lanai and big
windows overlooking the lawns, give the
resort the feeling of a spacious, quiet
retreat inside and out. **Pros:** close to
ocean; full kitchens; good rates for the
location. **Cons:** some units don't have
air-conditioning; closest beaches not ideal
for swimming; two-night minimum stay
is required. ⑤ *Rooms from: $225* ✉ *1941
Poipu Rd., Koloa* ☎ *808/742–6464,
800/367–8020* ⊕ *villasatpoipukai.com*
⌁ *150 units* ⧂ *No meals.*

Poipu Kapili Resort

$$$ | RENTAL | FAMILY | White-frame
exteriors and double-pitched roofs
complement the tropical landscaping at
this resort, which offers spacious one-
and two-bedroom condo units—with
full kitchens, bedroom air-conditioning,
entertainment centers, and garden or
ocean views—that are minutes from
Poipu's restaurants and across the street
from a nice beach. **Pros:** units are roomy
and well-spaced; parking is close to the
unit; tennis and pickleball on site. **Cons:**
units are ocean-view but not oceanfront;
a three-night minimum stay is required;
minimal amenities. ⑤ *Rooms from: $300*
✉ *2221 Kapili Rd., Poipu* ☎ *808/742–
6449, 800/325–5701* ⊕ *www.poipukapili.
com* ⌁ *60 units* ⧂ *No meals.*

Poipu Plantation Resort

$ | B&B/INN | Plumeria, ti, and other trop-
ical foliage create a lush landscape for
this resort, which rents four suites in a
bed-and-breakfast–style plantation home
and nine one- and two-bedroom cottage
apartments. **Pros:** attractively furnished;
full breakfast at B&B; AC and free Wi-Fi.
Cons: three-night minimum; not on the
ocean; no resort amenities. ⑤ *Rooms
from: $165* ✉ *1792 Pee Rd., Poipu*
☎ *808/742–6757, 800/634–0263* ⊕ *www.
poipubeach.com* ⌁ *4 rooms, 9 cottages*
⧂ *Free Breakfast.*

Poipu Shores

$$$ | RENTAL | Perched on a rocky point
above pounding surf—perfect for whale-
or turtle-watching—three low-rise buildings have individually owned condos with
full kitchens and washer-dryers; there's
a pool in front of the middle one. **Pros:**
every unit faces the water; heated oceanfront pool; wildlife viewing. **Cons:** units
vary widely in style; no resort amenities;
swimming beach is 10-minute walk away.
⑤ *Rooms from: $298* ✉ *1775 Pee Rd.,
Koloa* ☎ *808/742–2200, 877/367–1912
reservations* ⊕ *www.castleresorts.com*
⌁ *39 units* ⧂ *No meals.*

★ Sheraton Kauai Resort

$$$ | RESORT | The Sheraton is a sprawling resort with rooms that offer views of the ocean and lovely landscaped gardens; it's worth splurging on the ocean-wing accommodations, which are so close to the water you can practically feel the spray of the surf as it hits the rocks below. **Pros:** ocean-view pool; restaurant with spectacular sunset views; good facilities for meetings, events, reunions. **Cons:** parking can be a ways from the room; renovated rooms but some dated infrastructure; $30 daily resort fee. ⑤ *Rooms from: $340* ✉ *2440 Hoonani Rd., Poipu Beach, Koloa* ☎ *808/742–1661, 888/627–8113* ⊕ *www.sheraton-kauai. com* ⤴ *378 rooms* ❖ *No meals.*

Whalers Cove Resort

$$$$ | RENTAL | Perched about as close to the water's edge as they can get, these condos are the most luxurious on the South Shore, available in one-, two-, or three-bedroom units. **Pros:** on-site staff and daily housekeeping; outstanding setting; spacious, with full kitchens. **Cons:** rocky beach not ideal for swimming; no air-conditioning; resort fee, but few amenities (parking, enhanced Wi-Fi). ⑤ *Rooms from: $430* ✉ *2640 Puuholo Rd., Poipu* ☎ *808/742–7571, 800/225–2683* ⊕ *www.whalerscoveresort.com* ⤴ *24 units* ❖ *No meals.*

Nightlife

Grand Hyatt Kauai Luau

THEMED ENTERTAINMENT | FAMILY | Excellent unlimited buffet food, an open bar, and exciting dance performances characterize this traditional luau, held twice weekly in a garden setting near majestic Keoneloa Bay. ✉ *Grand Hyatt Kauai Resort and Spa, 1571 Poipu Rd., Poipu* ☎ *808/240–6320* ⊕ *kauai.grand.hyatt.com/en/hotel/dining/grand-hyatt-kauai-luau.html* ✉ *From $135.*

Keoki's Paradise

BARS/PUBS | A young, energetic crowd makes this a lively spot on Friday and Saturday night. When the dining room clears out, there's a bit of a bar scene for singles. Live music every night and two happy hours—one 3–5 pm and the other from 9:30 until closing at 10:30 pm—keep the Bamboo Bar a happening place. ✉ *Poipu Shopping Village, 2360 Kiahuna Plantation Dr., Poipu* ☎ *808/742–7534* ⊕ *www.keokisparadise.com.*

Lava's on Poipu Beach

BARS/PUBS | This poolside bar and grill is a great place to be on the South Shore to celebrate sunset with a drink, because the ocean view is unsurpassed. Happy hour is from 3 to 5 pm, and there's live music Friday and Sunday night, as well as a hula show on Wednesday evenings. ✉ *Sheraton Kauai Resort, 2440 Hoonani Rd., Poipu* ☎ *808/742–1661* ⊕ *www. sheraton-kauai.com/dining.*

The Tasting Room

WINE BARS—NIGHTLIFE | Popular for a pre-dinner gathering or night out, this trendy new wine bar on Koloa's main street has great flights and small bites. It's a venture of the wine shop next door and offers non-snooty service. ✉ *5476 Koloa Rd., Koloa* ☎ *808/431–4311* ⊕ *www.tastingroomkauai.com.*

Shopping

Surprisingly, the South Shore doesn't have as many shops and restaurants as one might expect for such a popular resort region. However, it does have convenient shopping clusters, including Poipu Shopping Village, the upscale The Shops at Kukuiula, Koloa Town's main street, and the hip Warehouse 3540 nearby in Lawai. There are many high-priced shops, but some unique clothing and gift selections.

Halelea Gallery

ART GALLERIES | In addition to offering original works by Hawaii artists, this stylish gallery in Kukuiula Shopping Village doubles as a boutique that sells a unique sampling of clothing, jewelry, bags, and gifts by local designers. Their other locations focus on art and jewelry. ✉ *2829 Kalanikaumaka Rd., Ste. K, Koloa* ☎ *808/742–9525* ⊕ *www.haleleagallery. com.*

Poipu Shopping Village

SHOPPING CENTERS/MALLS | FAMILY | Convenient to nearby hotels and condos on the South Shore, the two dozen shops at Poipu Shopping Village sell resort wear, gifts, souvenirs, upscale jewelry, and art. This complex also has a number of food choices, from hot-dog or gelato stands to casual sit-down restaurants. Kauai Juice Co. has a loyal following. Watch a traditional hula show in the open-air courtyard Monday and Thursday at 5 pm, and shop at the bimonthly produce market. ✉ *2360 Kiahuna Plantation Dr., Poipu* ☎ *808/742– 2831* ⊕ *www.poipushoppingvillage.com.*

The Shops at Kukuiula

SHOPPING CENTERS/MALLS | This is the South Shore's upscale shopping center, with chic shops, exclusive galleries, several great restaurants, and a gourmet grocery store. The flagship of Malie Organics bath line, used by many top hotels and spas, is here. Check out the Kauai Culinary Market on Wednesday from 3:30 to 6, to see cooking demonstrations, listen to live music, visit the beer and wine garden, and shop from local vendors. This attractive open-air, plantation-style center is at the roundabout as you enter Poipu. ✉ *2829 Kalanikaumaka St., Poipu* ☎ *808/742–9545* ⊕ *www.theshopsat-kukuiula.com.*

Chapter 6

THE WEST SIDE

WITH WAIMEA CANYON

Updated by
Joan Conrow

👁 **Sights**
★★★★★

 Restaurants
★★☆☆☆

🛏 **Hotels**
★★☆☆☆

💲 **Shopping**
★☆☆☆☆

 Nightlife
★☆☆☆☆

WELCOME TO THE WEST SIDE

TOP REASONS TO GO

★ **Waimea Canyon.** Witness how the dramatic erosional forces of wind, water, and rain have left their mark in this 3,000-foot-deep colorful chasm that has been dubbed the Grand Canyon of the Pacific.

★ **Quiet Beaches.** Seemingly endless beaches, including Kekaha Beach Park and Polihale State Park, make up the distinctive, remote West Side scenery.

★ **Wilderness Trails.** With more than 45 miles of trails, Kokee State Park offers a chance to see native plants and sweeping views from Kalalau Lookout.

★ **Old Hawaii.** With its historic towns and slow way of life, the West Side still feels like the old Hawaii. It's a great place to escape the resort scene and experience nature at its finest.

★ **The Art Scene.** Hanapepe is home to impressive galleries, local crafts studios, and a lively street art fair on Friday nights.

1 Hanapepe. Brilliant bougainvillea blossoms cover the hillsides that mark the entry to Hanapepe, a cheerful little town with historical buildings and a burgeoning art scene.

2 Waimea and Waimea Canyon. Though Waimea is often billed as the gateway to the dramatic spectacle of Waimea Canyon, this pretty little town warrants its own visit. It's one of the few places in the Islands that still retains the look and lifestyle of old Hawaii.

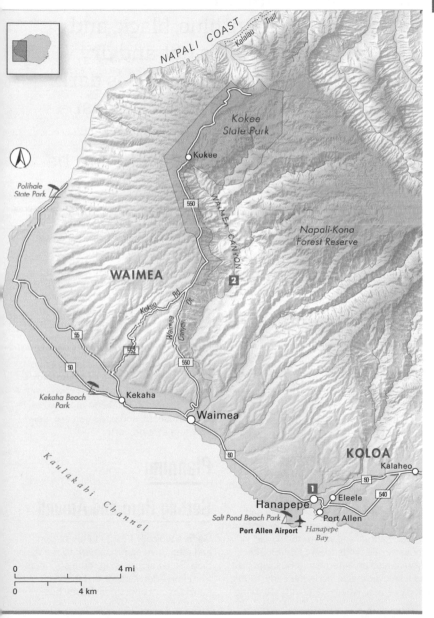

NAPALI COAST

Kalalau Trail

Kokee State Park

Kokee

550

Polihale State Park

WAIMEA CANYON

Napali-Kona Forest Reserve

2

WAIMEA

Kokee Rd.

Waimea Canyon Dr.

55

552

50

550

Kekaha Beach Park

Kekaha

Waimea

KOLOA

Kalaheo

60

Kaulakahi Channel

50

540

1

Eleele

Hanapepe

Salt Pond Beach Park

Port Allen Airport

Hanapepe Bay

Port Allen

0   4 mi

0   4 km

Exploring the West Side is akin to visiting an entirely different world. The landscape is dramatic and colorful—a patchwork of green, blue, black, and orange. The weather is hot and dry, the beaches are long, the sand is dark. Niihau, a private island and the last remaining place in Hawaii where Hawaiian is spoken exclusively, can be glimpsed offshore.

This is rural Kauai, where sugar is making its last stand and taro is still cultivated in the fertile river valleys. The lifestyle is slow, easy, and traditional, with many folks fishing and hunting to supplement their diets. Here and there modern industry has intruded into this pastoral scene: huge generators turn oil into electricity at Port Allen; seed companies cultivate experimental crops of genetically engineered plants in Kekaha and Waimea; the navy launches rockets at Mana to test the "Star Wars" missile defense system; and NASA mans a tracking station in the wilds of Kokee. It's a region of contrasts that simply shouldn't be missed.

Heading west from Lihue or Poipu, you pass through a string of tiny towns, plantation camps, and historic sites, each with a story to tell of centuries past. There's Hanapepe, whose coastal salt ponds have been harvested since ancient times; Kaumakani, where the sugar industry still clings to life; Fort Elizabeth, from which an enterprising Russian tried to take over the island in the early 1800s; and Waimea, where Captain Cook made his first landing in the Islands, forever changing the face of Hawaii.

From Waimea Town you can head up into the mountains, skirting the rim of magnificent Waimea Canyon and climbing higher still until you reach the cool, often-misty forests of Kokee State Park. From the vantage point at the top of this gemlike island, 3,200 to 4,200 feet above sea level, you can gaze into the deep, verdant valleys of the North Shore and Napali Coast. This is where the "real" Kauai can still be found: the native plants, insects, and birds that are found nowhere else on Earth.

Planning

Getting Here and Around

Visitors typically fly into Lihue Airport and then drive about an hour to the West Side. Some sightseeing tours are offered from Port Allen Airport in Hanapepe. Kauai County offers near-hourly bus service from Lihue to Kekaha, with stops in major towns along the way, from approximitely 5 am to 9 pm.

Beaches

The West Side of the island receives hardly enough rainfall year-round to water a cactus, and because it's also the lee-ward side, there are few tropical breezes. That translates to sunny and hot with long, languorous, and practically desert-ed beaches. You'd think the leeward waters—untouched by wind—would be calm, but there's no reef system, so the beach drops off quickly and currents are common. Rivers often turn the ocean water murky. Although there's some catering to visitors here, it's not much.

Hotels

To do a lot of hiking or immerse yourself in the island's history, get a room in Waimea. You won't find many resorts, restaurants, or shops, but you will encounter quiet days, miles of largely deserted beach, and a rural environment.

Restaurants

When it comes to dining on the West Side, pickings are mighty slim. Fortu-nately, the few eateries that are here are generally worth patronizing.

HOTEL AND RESTAURANT PRICES

Hotel prices in the reviews are the lowest cost of a standard double room in high season. Restaurant prices in the reviews are the average cost of a main course at dinner, or if dinner is not served, at lunch.

WHAT IT COSTS in U.S. Dollars			
$	$$	$$$	$$$$
RESTAURANTS			
under $18	$18-$26	$27-$35	over $35
HOTELS			
under $180	$180-$260	$261-$340	over $340

Shopping

The West Side is years behind the South Shore in development, offering minimal, simple shops with authentic local flavor.

Tours

Guided tours are convenient: you don't have to worry about finding a parking spot or getting admission tickets. Certi-fied tour guides have taken special class-es in Hawaiian history and lore. On the other hand, you won't have the freedom to proceed at your own pace, nor will you have the ability to take a detour trip if something else catches your attention.

Waimea Historic Walking Tour
WALKING TOURS | The West Kauai Visitor Center offers special group tours of historic Waimea Town by appointment only, as well as maps for self-guided tours. ⊠ *9565 Kaumualii Hwy., Waimea (Kauai County)* ☎ *808/338–1332* ⊕ *www.westkauaivisitorcenter.org* ⊠ *Donation.*

Visitor Information

For information about hiking and camping permits and rules and regulations for Napali Coast visit the Division of State Parks section of the ⊕ *hawaii.gov* website.

CONTACTS West Kauai Visitor Center.
⊠ *West Kauai Technology and Visitor Center Building, 9565 Kaumualii Hwy, Waimea (Kauai County)* ☎ *808/338–1332* ⊕ *www.westkauaivisitorcenter.org.*

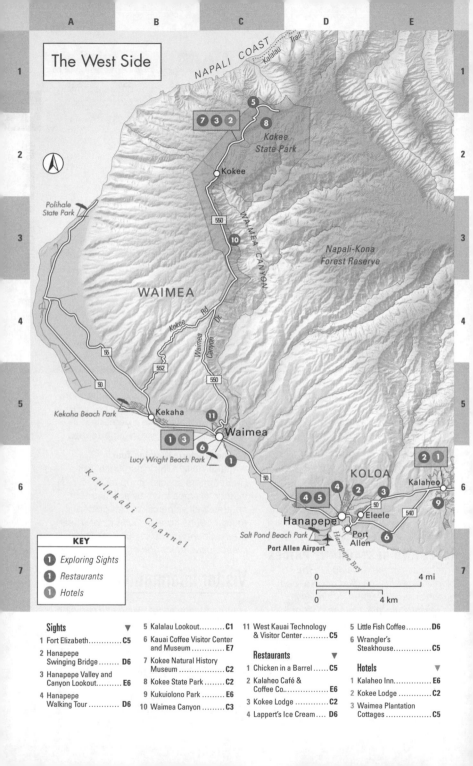

The West Side

Kokee State Park

Napali-Kona Forest Reserve

WAIMEA

Polihale State Park

Kekaha Beach Park

Kekaha

Waimea

Lucy Wright Beach Park

Kaulakahi Channel

KOLOA

Kalaheo

Eleele

Hanapepe

Salt Pond Beach Park

Port Allen Airport

Port Allen

Hanapepe Bay

| 0 | | | 4 mi |
| 0 | | | 4 km |

KEY

1 *Exploring Sights*
1 *Restaurants*
1 *Hotels*

Hanapepe

15 miles west of Poipu.

In the 1980s Hanapepe was fast becoming a ghost town, its farm-based economy mirroring the decline of agriculture. Today it's a burgeoning art colony with galleries, crafts studios, and a lively art-theme street fair on Friday nights. The main street has a new vibrancy enhanced by the restoration of several historic buildings. The emergence of Kauai coffee as a major West Side crop and expanded activities at Port Allen, now the main departure point for tour boats, also gave the town's economy a boost.

GETTING HERE AND AROUND

Hanapepe, locally known as Kauai's "biggest little town," is just past the Eleele Shopping Center on the main highway (Route 50). A sign leads you to the town center, where street parking is easy and there's an enjoyable walking tour.

Sights

Hanapepe Swinging Bridge

BRIDGE/TUNNEL | FAMILY | This bridge may not be the biggest adventure on Kauai, but it's enough to make your heart hop. It's considered a historic suspension bridge even though it was rebuilt in 1996 after the original was destroyed—like so much of the island—by Hurricane Iniki. It was also repaired and reopened following severe damages inflicted by flooding in 2019. What is interesting about this bridge is that it's not just for show; it actually provides the only access to taro fields across the Waimea River. If you're in the neighborhood, it's worth a stroll. ⊠ *Off Hanapepe Rd., next to Banana Patch Studios parking lot, Hanapepe* ⊕ *www.kauai.com/ hanapepe-swinging-bridge.*

Hanapepe Valley and Canyon Lookout

VIEWPOINT | This dramatic divide and fertile river valley once housed a thriving Hawaiian community of taro farmers, with some of the ancient fields still in cultivation today. From the roadside lookout, you can take in the farms on the valley floor with the majestic mountains as a backdrop. ⊠ *Rte. 50, Hanapepe.*

Hanapepe Walking Tour

TOUR—SIGHT | This 1½-mile self-guided walking tour takes you to 14 different plaques with historic photos and stories mounted on buildings throughout Hanapepe Town. Businesses and shops in town sell a map of the tour for $2; however, you can often pick one up free with a coupon found in many guidebooks on promotional-brochure rack stands. ⊠ *Hanapepe Town.*

Kauai Coffee Visitor Center and Museum

MUSEUM | Two restored camp houses, dating from the days when sugar was the main agricultural crop on the Islands, have been converted into a museum, visitor center, and gift shop. About 3,100 acres of McBryde sugar land have become Hawaii's largest coffee plantation, with its 4 million trees producing more than 50% of the state's beans. You can walk among the trees, view old grinders and roasters, watch a video to learn how coffee is processed, sample various estate roasts, and check out the gift store. The center offers free self-guided tours through a small coffee grove, a personalized "coffee on the brain" tour for $20 as well as two-hour guided tours that cost $60 for adults and $40 for children 8–18. From Kalaheo, take Highway 50 in the direction of Waimea Canyon (west) and veer left onto Highway 540. It's 2½ miles from the Highway 50 turnoff. ⊠ *870 Halewili Rd., Kalaheo* ☎ *808/335–0813* ⊕ *www.kauaicoffee. com* ✉ *Free.*

Flora and Fauna

Kauai offers some of the best birding in the state, due in part to the absence of the mongoose. Many nene (the endangered Hawaiian state bird) reared in captivity have been successfully released here, along with an endangered forest bird called the *puaiohi*. The island is also home to several species of migratory nesting seabirds and has three refuges protecting endangered Hawaiian waterbirds and seabirds. Kauai's most noticeable fowl, however, is the wild chicken. A cross between jungle fowl (*moa*) brought by the Polynesians and domestic chickens and fighting cocks that escaped during the last two hurricanes, they are everywhere, and the roosters crow when they feel like it, not just at dawn. Consider yourself warned.

Kukuiolono Park

CITY PARK | Translated as "Light of the God Lono," Kukuiolono has serene Japanese gardens, a display of significant Hawaiian stones, a meditation pavilion, and spectacular panoramic views. This quiet hilltop park is one of Kauai's most scenic areas and an ideal picnic spot. There's also a nine-hole golf course. ⊠ *Puu Rd., Kalaheo* ☎ *808/332–9151* ☎ *Free.*

Beaches

Salt Pond Beach Park

BEACH—SIGHT | **FAMILY** | A great family spot, Salt Pond Beach Park features a naturally made, shallow swimming pond behind a curling finger of rock where *keiki* (children) splash and snorkel. This pool is generally safe except during a large south swell, which usually occurs in summer, if at all. The center and western edge of the beach is popular with body boarders and bodysurfers. Pavilions with picnic tables offer shade, and there's a campground that tends to attract a rowdy bunch at the eastern end. On a cultural note, the flat stretch of land to the east of the beach is the last spot in Hawaii where ponds are used to harvest salt in the dry heat of summer. The beach park is popular with locals and it can get crowded on weekends and holidays.

Amenities: lifeguard; parking; showers; toilets. **Best for:** sunset; swimming; walking. ⊠ *Lolokai Rd., off Rte. 50, Hanapepe.*

 Restaurants

Kalaheo Café & Coffee Co.

$$ | **AMERICAN** | **FAMILY** | Folks love this roadside café—especially at breakfast, though it's good for lunch and dinner specials, too—for its casual neighborhood feel. It's frequently busy, especially on weekend mornings. **Known for:** fresh-baked pastries and bread; great local coffee; hearty portions like the Kahili Breakfast or the Longboard sandwich. ⑤ *Average main: $22* ⊠ *2-2560 Kaumualii Hwy. (Rte. 50), Kalaheo* ☎ *808/332–5858* ⊕ *www.kalaheo.com* ⊙ *No dinner Sun. and Mon.*

Lappert's Ice Cream

$ | **CAFÉ** | It's not ice cream on Kauai if it's not Lappert's Ice Cream. Guava, mac nut, pineapple, mango, coconut, banana—Lappert's is the ice-cream king of Kauai. **Known for:** Kauai Pie (coffee ice cream with chocolate fudge, coconut flakes, and macadamia nuts); super-premium ice cream made daily; homemade pastries and local coffee. ⑤ *Average main: $9* ⊠ *1-3555 Kaumualii Hwy., Hanapepe* ☎ *808/335–6121* ⊕ *www.lappertshawaii. com.*

Little Fish Coffee

$ | **CAFÉ** | **FAMILY** | For a wholesome breakfast or lunch on the West Side, this friendly, funky, and fun café—right down to the marking pens that allow you to leave your own graffiti on the bathroom wall—is the spot. The coffee is good, with each cup individually dripped, and the fresh bagels come with house-made cream cheese or a variety of toppings. **Known for:** casual setting; emphasis on wholesome ingredients; smoothies and fresh juices. **$** *Average main: $9* ⊠ *3900 Hanapepe Rd., Hanapepe* ☎ *808/335–5000* ⊕ *littlefishcoffee.com* ☺ *No dinner.*

Hotels

Kalaheo Inn

$ | **B&B/INN** | **FAMILY** | It isn't easy to find good lodgings on the southwest side of the island, but this old-fashioned budget inn with studios or one-, two-, and three-bedroom suites does an adequate, no-frills job in Kalaheo Town. **Pros:** some units have kitchens; walking distance to restaurants; coin-operated laundry on-site. **Cons:** property is a ways from the beach; no air-conditioning; dated furnishings. **$** *Rooms from: $93* ⊠ *4444 Papalina Rd., Kalaheo* ☎ *808/332–6023, 888/332–6023* ⊕ *www.kalaheoinn.com* ⌂ *16 units* ☽ *No meals.*

Nightlife

Port Allen Sunset Grill & Bar

BARS/PUBS | One of the few places for nightlife on the West Side, this casual eatery overlooks the harbor at Port Allen in Eleele and has a friendly bar, with karaoke, that stays open until 10:30 pm. It's a great spot to catch the sunset. ⊠ *4353 Waialo Rd., Eleele* ☎ *808/335–3188.*

Shopping

Eleele Shopping Center

SHOPPING CENTERS/MALLS | Kauai's West Side has a scattering of stores, including those at this no-frills strip mall. It has a post office, several banks, a hardware store, a laundromat, and a hair salon, and it's a good place to rub elbows with local folk at Longs Drugs or Big Save Times grocery store. There's a McDonald's, Subway, and a few little local eateries. ⊠ *4469 Waialo Rd., Eleele* ☎ *808/245–7238* ⊕ *www.eleeleshoppingcenter.com.*

Kauai Coffee Visitor Center and Museum

FOOD/CANDY | Kauai produces more coffee than any other island in the state. The local product can be purchased from grocery stores or here at the Kauai Coffee Visitor Center and Museum, where a sampling of the nearly two dozen coffees is available. Be sure to try some of the estate-roasted varieties. ⊠ *870 Halewili Rd., off Rte. 50, Kalaheo* ☎ *808/335–0813, 800/545–8605* ⊕ *www.kauaicoffee.com.*

Talk Story Bookstore

BOOKS/STATIONERY | Located in a historic building in quiet Hanapepe Town, this is the only bookstore on Kauai, with some 150,000 titles and a resident cat named Mochi Celeste. The cozy shop becomes a gathering place on busy Friday evenings, when local authors sign their books while live music and food trucks entertain meandering crowds during the weekly art nights. New, used, rare, and out-of-print books are sold here, as well as vinyl records. ⊠ *3785 Hanapepe Rd., Hanapepe* ☎ *808/335–6469* ⊕ *www.talkstorybookstore.com.*

Waimea and Waimea Canyon

Waimea is 7 miles northwest of Hanapepe; Waimea Canyon is approximately 10 miles northeast of Waimea.

Waimea is a serene, pretty town that has the look of the Old West and the feel of Old Hawaii, with a lifestyle that's decidedly laid-back. It's an ideal place for a refreshment break while sightseeing on the West Side. The town has played a major role in Hawaiian history since 1778, when Captain James Cook became the first European to set foot on the Hawaiian Islands. Waimea was also the place where Kauai's King Kaumualii acquiesced to King Kamehameha's unification drive in 1810, averting a bloody war. The town hosted the first Christian missionaries, who hauled in massive timbers and limestone blocks to build the sturdy Waimea Christian Hawaiian and Foreign Church in 1846. It's one of many lovely historic buildings preserved by residents who take great pride in their heritage and history.

North of Waimea town, via Route 550, you'll find the vast and gorgeous Waimea Canyon, also known as the Grand Canyon of the Pacific. The spectacular vistas from the lookouts along the road culminate in an overview of Kalalau Valley. There are various hiking trails leading to the inner heart of Kauai. A camera is a necessity in this region.

GETTING HERE AND AROUND

Route 50 continues northwest to Waimea and Kekaha from Hanapepe. You can reach Waimea Canyon and Kokee State Park from either town—the way is clearly marked. Some pull-off areas on Route 550 are fine for a quick view of the canyon, but the designated lookouts have bathrooms and parking.

Birdwatching on Kauai

It's easy to spot two islands, Niihau and Kaula, from the West Side. While Niihau is inhabited by Native Hawaiians, Kaula's only occupants are seabirds. More than 100,000 seabirds, ranging from sooty terns to brown boobies to wedge-tailed shearwaters, nest on Kaula. To help protect these birds, the state and conservation groups have conducted several eradication efforts aimed at eliminating the rodents that prey upon the eggs and chicks of the ground-nesting birds.

◉ Sights

Fort Elizabeth

ARCHAEOLOGICAL SITE | The ruins of this stone fort, built in 1816 by an agent of the imperial Russian government named Anton Scheffer, are a reminder of the days when Scheffer tried to conquer the island for his homeland, or so one story goes. Another claims that Scheffer's allegiance lay with King Kaumualii, who was attempting to regain leadership of his island nation from the grasp of Kamehameha the Great. The crumbling walls of the fort are not particularly interesting, but the signs loaded with historical information are. ⊠ *Rte. 50, Waimea (Kauai County).*

Kalalau Lookout

VIEWPOINT | At the end of the road, high above Waimea Canyon, Kalalau Lookout marks the start of a 1-mile (one-way) hike to **Puu o Kila Lookout.** On a clear day at either spot, you can see a dreamy landscape of gaping valleys, sawtooth ridges, waterfalls, and turquoise seas, where whales can be seen spouting and breaching during the winter months. If clouds block the view, don't despair—they tend to blow through fast, giving you time to snap that photo of a lifetime. You may spot wild goats clambering on the sheer rocky cliffs, and white-tailed tropic birds. If it's very clear to the northwest, drink in the shining sands of Kalalau Beach, gleaming like golden threads against the deep blue of the Pacific. ⊠ *Waimea Canyon Dr.* ✛ *4 miles north of Kokee State Park.*

Kokee Natural History Museum

MUSEUM | Kokee Natural History Museum is a great place to start your visit to Kokee State Park. The friendly staff is knowledgeable about trail conditions and weather, while informative displays and a good selection of reference books can teach you more about the unique attributes of the native flora and fauna. You may also find that special memento or gift you've been looking for. ⊠ *Rte. 550, Kokee* ☎ *808/335–9975* ⊕ *kokee.org* 🖃 *Donations accepted.*

Kokee State Park

NATIONAL/STATE PARK | This 4,345-acre wilderness park is 3,600 feet above sea level, an elevation that affords you breathtaking views and a cooler, wetter climate that's in marked contrast to the beach. You can gain a deeper appreciation of the island's rugged terrain and dramatic beauty from this vantage point. Large tracts of native ohia and koa forest cover much of the land, along with many varieties of exotic plants. Hikers can follow a 45-mile network of trails through diverse landscapes that feel wonderfully remote—until the tour helicopters pass overhead. *Note there's no cell phone service in the park.* ⊠ *Hwy. 50, Kekaha* ✛ *15 miles north of Kekaha* ⊕ *kokee.org.*

★ Waimea Canyon

CANYON | Carved over countless centuries by the Waimea River and the forces of wind and rain, Waimea Canyon is a dramatic gorge nicknamed the "Grand Canyon of the Pacific"—but not by Mark

Twain, as many people mistakenly think. Hiking and hunting trails wind through the canyon, which is 3,600 feet deep, 2 miles wide, and 10 miles long. The cliff sides have been sharply eroded, exposing swatches of colorful soil. The deep red, brown, and green hues are constantly changing in the sun, and frequent rainbows and waterfalls enhance the natural beauty. This is one of Kauai's prettiest spots, and it's worth stopping at both the **Puu ka Pele** and **Puu Hinahina** lookouts. Clean public restrooms and parking are at both lookouts. ⊠ *Hwy. 550 (Kokee Rd.), Waimea (Kauai County)* ☎ *808/274–3444* ⊕ *dlnr.hawaii.gov/dsp/parks/kauai/.*

West Kauai Technology & Visitor Center

INFO CENTER | Cultural information and local exhibits highlight this museum-style resource center in the middle of Waimea Town. This small center has a gift shop with island-made items, Niihau shell jewelry, color photographs of Kauai, books, and more. ⊠ *9565 Kaumualii Hwy., (Rte. 50), Waimea (Kauai County)* ☎ *808/338–1332* ⊕ *www.westkauaivisitorcenter.org/* 🖃 *Free* ☉ *Closed Wed., Sat., and Sun.*

Beaches

Kekaha Beach Park

BEACH—SIGHT | This is one of the premier spots on Kauai for sunset walks and the start of the state's longest beach. We don't recommend much water activity here without first talking to a lifeguard. The beach is exposed to open ocean and has an onshore break that can be hazardous any time of year. However, there are some excellent surf breaks—for experienced surfers only. Or, if you would like to run or stroll on a beach, this is the one—the hard-packed sand goes on for miles, all the way to Napali Coast, but you won't get past the Pacific Missile Range Facility and its post-9/11 access restrictions. Another bonus for this beach is its relatively dry weather year-round. If it's raining where you are, try Kekaha

Did You Know?

It's possible to see vast stretches of the Kalalau Valley from Kokee State Park, which is about 4,000 feet above sea level.

Beach Park. Toilets here are the portable kind. **Amenities:** lifeguards; parking; showers; toilets. **Best for:** sunset; surfing; walking. ⊠ *Rte. 50, near mile marker 27, Kekaha.*

Lucy Wright Beach Park

BEACH—SIGHT | Named in honor of the first Native Hawaiian schoolteacher, this beach is on the western banks of the Waimea River. It is also where Captain James Cook first came ashore in the Hawaiian Islands in 1778. If that's not interesting enough, the sand here is not the white, powdery kind you see along the South Shore. It's a combination of pulverized, black lava rock and lighter-color reef. It looks a bit like a mix of salt and pepper. Unfortunately, the intrigue of the beach doesn't extend to the waters, which are reddish and murky (thanks to river runoff) and choppy (thanks to an onshore break). Instead, check out the Waimea Landing State Recreation Pier, from which fishers drop their lines. It's located about 100 yards west of the river mouth. **Amenities:** parking; showers; toilets. **Best for:** sunset; surfing; walking. ⊠ *Pokile Rd., off Rte. 50, Waimea (Kauai County).*

★ Polihale State Park

BEACH—SIGHT | The longest stretch of beach in Hawaii starts in Kekaha and ends west about 15 miles away at the start of Napali Coast. On the far west end is the 5-mile-long, 140-acre Polihale State Park. In addition to being long, this beach is 300 feet wide in places and backed by sand dunes 50 to 100 feet tall. It is frequently very hot, with minimal shade and scorching sand in summer. Polihale is a remote beach accessed via a very rough and potholed, 5-mile haul-cane road (AWD or four-wheel drive recommended) at the end of Route 50 in Kekaha.

■ TIP→ **Be sure to start the day with a full tank of gas and a cooler filled with food and drink.** Though it's a popular camping and day-use beach location, the water here is typically rough and not recommended for recreation. No driving is allowed on the beach. The Pacific Missile Range Facility, operated by the U.S. Navy, is adjacent to the beach, and access to the coastline in front of the base is restricted. **Amenities:** parking; showers; toilets. **Best for:** solitude; sunset; walking. ⊠ *Dirt road at end of Rte. 50, Kekaha* ☎ *808/587–0300.*

🍽 Restaurants

Chicken in a Barrel

$ | BARBECUE | FAMILY | This casual eatery is located in the equally laid-back Waimea Plantation Cottages hotel; it's a great place to sit with a cocktail and watch the sun set or let the kids run around on the lawn. The fare is simple and hearty: barrel-smoked barbecue chicken, pork, brisket, or ribs; plus salads, tacos, and burgers. **Known for:** large portions; kid-friendly dining; great selection of sides. ⑤ *Average main: $15* ⊠ *9400 Kaumualii Hwy., Waimea (Kauai County)* ☎ *808/338–1625* ⊕ *www.coasthotels. com.*

Kokee Lodge

$ | AMERICAN | There's only one place to buy breakfast, hot food, drinks, and snacks in Kokee State Park, and that's the rustic Kokee Lodge. It's known for its Portugese bean soup and corn bread, of all things. **Known for:** Portuguese bean soup; pie and coffee; gift shop. ⑤ *Average main: $12* ⊠ *Kokee State Park, 3600 Kokee Rd., mile marker 15, Kokee* ☎ *808/335–6061* ⊕ *kokeelodge.com* ⊗ *No dinner.*

Wrangler's Steakhouse

$$$ | STEAKHOUSE | FAMILY | Denim-covered seating, decorative saddles, and a stagecoach in a loft helped to transform the historic Ako General Store in Waimea into a West Side steak house where you can eat under the stars on the deck out back or in the old-fashioned, wood-panel dining room. Open weekend evenings, the Saddle Room features a bar menu that includes seven styles of burgers

and there's live music on Saturday night. **Known for:** special lunch (rice, beef teriyaki, and shrimp tempura with kimchi) served in a three-tier kaukau tin; campy setting; local, grass-fed beef. ⑤ *Average main: $32 ⊠ 9852 Kaumualii Hwy., Waimea (Kauai County) ☎ 808/338–1218 ⊕ wranglerssteakhousehi.com ⊗ Closed Sun. No lunch Sat.*

Hotels

Kokee Lodge

$ | **RENTAL** | If you're an outdoors enthusiast, you can appreciate Kauai's mountain wilderness from the 12 rustic cabins—of varying age and quality—that make up this lodge. **Pros:** outstanding setting; more refined than camping; cooking facilities. **Cons:** wood-burning stove is the only heat; no restaurants for dinner; $45 cleaning fee. ⑤ *Rooms from: $89 ⊠ Kokee State Park, 3600 Kokee Rd., at mile marker 15, Kokee ☎ 808/652–6852 ⊕ www.westkauailodging.com/en-us ☞ 12 cabins* ⦿| *No meals.*

★ Waimea Plantation Cottages

$$ | **RENTAL** | Originally built in the early 1900s, these relocated and refurbished one- to five-bedroom sugar-plantation cottages are tucked among coconut trees along a lovely, walkable stretch of beach on the sunny West Side. **Pros:** unique lodging experience; quiet and low-key; lovely grounds. **Cons:** not a good swimming beach; rooms are simple; cottages can be hot in summer. ⑤ *Rooms from: $209 ⊠ 9400 Kaumualii Hwy., Box 367, Waimea (Kauai County) ☎ 808/338–1923, 800/716–6199 ⊕ www.coasthotels.com ☞ 61 cottages* ⦿| *No meals.*

Shopping

Waimea Canyon Plaza

SHOPPING CENTERS/MALLS | As the last stop for supplies before heading up to Waimea Canyon or out to Polihale Beach, Waimea Canyon Plaza has a Menehune Food Mart with limited groceries, snacks, beverages, fresh and prepared local foods, souvenirs, and island-made gifts for all ages. ⊠ *8171 Kekaha Rd., at Rte. 50, Kekaha ☎ 808/337–1335.*

Chapter 7

ACTIVITIES

Updated by
Charles E. Roessler

Kauai's outdoor recreation options extend well beyond the sand and surf, with plenty of activities to keep you busy on the ground and even in the air. You can hike the island's many trails, or consider taking your vacation into flight with a treetop zipline. You can have a backcountry adventure in a four-wheel drive, or relax in an inner tube floating down the cane-field irrigation canals.

Before booking tours, check with your concierge to find out what the forecast is for water and weather conditions. Don't rely on the Weather Channel for accurate weather reports, as they're often reporting Oahu weather, and variations in wind currents make for unreliable forecasts. If you happen to arrive during a North Shore lull in the surf, you'll want to plan to be on the ocean in a kayak or snorkeling on the reef. If it's raining, ATV tours are the activity of choice.

For the golfer in the family, Kauai's spectacular courses are rated among the most scenic, as well as the most technical. Princeville Golf Course has garnered accolades from numerous national publications, and Poipu Bay Golf Course hosted the prestigious season-end PGA Grand Slam of Golf for 13 years.

One of the most popular Kauai experiences is to see the island from the air. In an hour or so, you can see waterfalls, craters, and other places that are inaccessible even by hiking trails (some say that 70% or more of the island is inaccessible). The majority of flights depart from the Lihue airport and follow a clockwise pattern around the island. ■TIP→ If you plan to take an aerial tour, it's a good idea to fly when you first arrive, rather than saving it for the end of your trip. It will help you visualize what's where on the island, and it may help you decide what you want to see from a closer vantage point during your stay. Be prepared to relive your flight in dreams for the rest of your life. The most popular flight is 60 minutes long.

Ancient Hawaiians were water-sports fanatics—they invented surfing, after all—and that propensity hasn't strayed far from today's mindset. Even if you're not into water sports or sports in general, there's only a slim chance that you'll leave this island without getting out on the ocean, as Kauai's top attraction—Napali Coast—is something not to be missed.

For those who can't pack enough snorkeling, fishing, body boarding, or surfing time into a vacation, Kauai has it all—everything except parasailing, that is, as it's illegal to do it here (though not on Maui, the Big Island, or Oahu). If

Kauai's calmest water and best snorkeling is on the North Shore in summer and South Shore in winter.

you need to rent gear for any of these activities, you'll find plenty of places with large selections at reasonable prices. And no matter what part of the island you're staying on, you'll have several options for choice spots to enjoy playing in the water.

One thing to note, and we can't say this enough—the waters off the coast of Kauai have strong currents and can be unpredictable, so always err on the side of caution and know your limits. Follow the tagline repeated by the island's life-guards—"When in doubt, don't go out."

Aerial Tours

If you only drive around Kauai in your rental car, you will not see *all* of Kauai. There is truly only one way to see it all, and that's by air. Helicopter tours are the favorite way to get a bird's-eye view of Kauai—they fly at lower altitudes, hover above waterfalls, and wiggle their way into areas that a fixed-wing aircraft

cannot. That said, if you've already tried the helitour, how about flying in the open cockpit of a biplane, à la the Red Baron?

Air Tour Kauai

FLYING/SKYDIVING/SOARING | This company can hold up to six people in its Cessna 207 plane. The flights take off from the less crowded Port Allen Airport and will last 65 to 70 minutes. ⊠ *Port Allen Airport, 3441 Kuiloko Rd., Hanapepe* ☎ *808/639–3446* ⊕ *www.airtourkauai. com* ⊠ *$99 per person.*

Blue Hawaiian Helicopters

TOUR—SPORTS | This multiisland operator flies the latest in helicopter technology, the Eco-Star, costing $1.8 million. It has 23% more interior space for its six passengers, has unparalleled viewing, and offers a few extra safety features. As the name implies, the helicopter is also a bit more environmentally friendly, with a 50% noise-reduction rate. Even though flights run a tad shorter than others (50 to 55 minutes instead of the 55 to 65 minutes that other companies tout), they feel complete. A DVD of your tour is available for an additional $25. ✉ *3651 Ahukini Rd., Heliport 8, Lihue* ☎ *808/245–5800, 800/745–2583* ⊕ *www. bluehawaiian.com* ✉ *$289.*

★ Jack Harter Helicopters

TOUR—SPORTS | Jack Harter was the first company to offer helicopter tours on Kauai. The company flies the six-passenger ASTAR helicopter with floor-to-ceiling windows, and the four-person Hughes 500, which is flown with no doors. The doorless ride can get windy, but it's the best bet for taking reflection-free photos. Pilots provide information on the Garden Island's history and geography through two-way intercoms. The company flies out of Lihue. Tours are 60 to 65 minutes and 90 to 95 minutes. Receive a $30 discount when you book through their website. ✉ *4231 Ahukini Rd.* ☎ *808/245–3774, 888/245–2001* ⊕ *www.helicopters-kauai.com* ✉ *From $289.*

Sunshine Helicopter Tours

TOUR—SPORTS | If the name of this company sounds familiar, it may be because its pilots fly on all the main Hawaiian Islands except Oahu. On Kauai, Sunshine Helicopters departs out of two different locations: Lihue and Princeville. They fly the six-passenger FX STAR from Lihue or the super-roomy six-passenger WhisperSTAR birds. ■**TIP**➜ **Discounts can be substantial by booking online and taking advantage of the "early-bird" seating during off-hours.** ✉ *3416 Rice St., Ste. 203, Lihue* ☎ *808/240–2577, 866/501–7738* ⊕ *www.sunshinehelicopters.com* ✉ *From $244, Princeville $289.*

ATV Tours

Although all the beaches on the island are public, much of the interior land—once sugar and pineapple plantations—is privately owned. This is really a shame, because the valleys and mountains that make up the vast interior of the island easily rival the beaches in sheer beauty.

The good news is some tour operators have agreements with landowners that make exploration possible, albeit a bit bumpy—and unless you have back troubles, that's half the fun. ■**TIP**➜ **If it looks like rain, book an ATV tour ASAP. That's the thing about these tours: the muddier, the better.**

★ Kauai ATV Tours

TOUR—SPORTS | This is *the* thing to do when it rains on Kauai. Consider it an extreme mud bath. Kauai ATV in Koloa is the originator of the island's all-terrain-vehicle tours. The three-hour Koloa tour takes you through a private sugar plantation and historic haul-cane tunnel. The four-hour waterfall tour visits secluded waterfalls and includes a picnic lunch. This popular option includes a hike to secret WWII bunkers and a swim in a freshwater pool at the base of the falls—to rinse off all that mud. You must be 18 or older to operate your own ATV, but Kauai ATV also offers its four-passenger "Ohana Bug" and two-passenger "Mud Bugs" to accommodate families with kids ages five and older. ✉ *3477A Weliweli Rd., Koloa* ☎ *808/742–2734, 877/707–7088* ⊕ *www.kauaiatv.com* ✉ *From $358 for 2 people.*

Kipu Ranch Adventures

TOUR—SPORTS | This 3,000-acre property extends from the Huleia River to the top of Mt. Haupu. *Jurassic Park* and *Indiana Jones* were filmed here, and you'll see the locations for them on the three-hour Ranch Tour. The four-hour Waterfall Tour includes a visit to two waterfalls and a picnic lunch. Once a sugar plantation, Kipu Ranch today is a working cattle ranch, so you'll be in the company of bovines as well as pheasants, wild boars, and peacocks. If you're not an experienced ATV driver, they also offer guide-driven tour options. ✉ *235 Kipu Rd., off Hwy. 50, Lihue* ☎ *808/246–9288* ⊕ *www.kiputours.com* ✉ *From $148.*

Biking

Kauai is a labyrinth of cane-haul roads, which are fun for exploring on two wheels. The challenge is finding roads where biking is allowed and then not getting lost in the maze. Maybe that explains why Kauai is not a hub for the sport—yet. Still, there are some epic rides for those who are interested, both the adrenaline-rush and the mellower beach-cruiser kind. If you want to grind out some mileage, you could take the main highway that skirts the coastal area, but be careful: there are only a few designated bike lanes, the shoulders are often crowded with invasive guinea grass, and the terrain is hilly. You may find that keeping your eyes on the road rather than the scenery is your biggest challenge. "Cruisers" should head to Kapaa, where the Ke Ala Hele Makalae, a pedestrian and bicycle trail, runs along the East Side of Kauai for miles. You can rent bikes (with helmets) from the activities desks of certain hotels, but these are not the best quality. You're better off renting from Kauai Cycle in Kapaa, Outfitters Kauai in Poipu, or Pedal 'n' Paddle in Hanalei. Ask for the "Go Green Kauai" map for a full description of Kauai biking options.

BEST SPOTS

★ Ke Ala Hele Makalae (coastal path)

BICYCLING | This county beach park path follows the coastline on Kauai's East Side and is perfect for cruisers. Eventually, the path is projected to run some 20 miles, but an existing 8-mile-long stretch already offers scenic views, picnic pavilions, and restroom facilities along the way—all in compliance with the Americans with Disabilities Act. The path runs from Lydgate Beach Park to secluded Kuna Bay (aka Donkey Beach). An easy way to access the longest completed section of the path is from Kealia Beach. Park here and head north into rural lands with spectacular coastline vistas, or head south into Kapaa for a more immersive experience. ⊠ Kealia Beach, Kapaa ⊹ Trailhead: 1 mile north of Kapaa; park at north end of Kealia Beach ⊕ www.kauaipath.org/kauaicoastalpath.

Moalepe Trail

BICYCLING | This trail is perfect for intermediate to advanced trail-bike riders. The first 2 miles of this 5-mile double-track road wind steeply through pastureland. The real challenge begins when you reach the steep and rutted switchbacks, which during a rainy spell can be hazardous. Moalepe intersects the Kuilau Trail, which you can follow to its end at the Keahua Arboretum stream. ⊠ Wailua (Kauai County) ⊹ From Kuhio Hwy. in Kapaa drive mauka (toward mountains) on Kuamoo Rd. for 3 miles and turn right on Kamalu Rd., which dead-ends at Olohena Rd. Turn left and follow until road veers sharply to right.

Powerline Trail

BICYCLING | Advanced riders are challenged by this trail. It's actually an abandoned electric-company service road that splits the island. It's 13 miles long; the first 5 miles go from 620 feet in elevation to 2,000. The remaining 8 miles descend gradually over a variety of terrain, some technical. You'll have to carry your bike through some sections, but the views will stay with you forever. ■ TIP➔ When it's wet—in summer or winter—this trail is a mess. Check with a knowledgeable bike shop for trail conditions first and be prepared to improvise. ⊠ Powerline Rd., Kilauea ⊹ The trailhead is mauka (toward mountains), just past stream crossing at Keahua Arboretum, or at end of Powerline Rd. in Princeville, past Princeville Ranch Stables.

Spalding Monument

BICYCLING | For the novice rider, this ride offers a good workout and a summit ocean view that's not overly strenuous to reach. If you pick up a bike at Kauai Cycle in Kapaa, you can pedal a mile up Ke Ala

Bikers who prefer a leisurely cruise can pedal along the Ke Ala Hele Makalae Trail, an 8-mile path in Kapaa.

Hele Makalae to reach the start of the ride, and even make a snack stop at the corner food truck without a detour. From near the end of Kealia Beach, ride up a gradual incline 2 miles through horse pastures to Spalding Monument, named for a former plantation owner. Palms circle the lava-rock wall, where you can picnic while enjoying a 180-degree ocean view. Behind you is the glorious mountain backdrop of Kalalea. Coasting back down the road offers an almost hands-free, continual ocean view along with a peek into rural Kauai most visitors miss. ⊠ *The loop begins at end of Kealia Beach, past mile marker 10 on mauka (mountain) side of road, Kealia.*

Wailua Forest Management Road

BICYCLING | For the novice mountain biker, this is an easy ride, and it's also easy to find. From Route 56 in Wailua, turn *mauka* (toward the mountains) on Kuamoo Road and continue 6 miles to the picnic area known as Keahua Arboretum; park here. The potholed four-wheel-drive road includes some stream crossings—⚠ **stay away during heavy rains, because the streams flood**—and continues for 2 miles to a T-stop, where you should turn right. Stay on the road for about 3 miles until you reach a gate; this is the spot where the gates in the movie *Jurassic Park* were filmed, though it looks nothing like the movie. Go around the gate and down the road for another mile to a confluence of streams at the base of Mt. Waialeale. Be sure to bring your camera. ⊠ *Kuamoo Rd., Kapaa.*

Waimea Canyon Road

BICYCLING | For those wanting a very challenging road workout, climb this road, also known as Route 550. After a 3,000-foot climb, the road tops out at mile 12, adjacent to Waimea Canyon. From here it continues several miles (somewhat level) past the Kokee Museum and ends at the Kalalau Lookout. It's paved the entire way, uphill 100%, and curvy. ⚠ **There's not much of a shoulder on either road—sometimes none—so be extra** cautious. The road gets busier as the day wears on, so you may want to consider a sunrise ride. We suggest the slightly more moderate uphill climb on Kokee Road, Route 552, from Kekaha, which intersects with Route 550. Bicyclists can park their cars at Waimea ball park and ride over to Kekaha to begin the uphill climb. Bicycles aren't allowed on the hiking trails in and around Waimea Canyon and Kokee State Park, but there are miles of wonderful four-wheel-drive roads perfect for mountain biking. Check at Kokee Natural History Museum for a map and conditions. ⊠ *Off Rte. 50, near grocery store, Waimea (Kauai County).*

EQUIPMENT AND TOURS
Kauai Cycle

BICYCLING | This reliable, full-service bike shop rents, sells, and repairs bikes. Cruisers, mountain bikes (front and full suspension), and road bikes are available, with directions to trails. The Ke Ala Hele Makalae coastal path is right out the back door. ⊠ *4-934 Kuhio Hwy., across from Taco Bell, Kapaa* ☎ *808/821–2115* ⊕ *www.kauaicycle.com* ✉ *Rentals from $15 per day and $110 per wk.*

Outfitters Kauai

BICYCLING | Hybrid "comfort" and mountain bikes (both full suspension and hardtails) as well as road bikes are available at this shop in Poipu. You can ride right out the door to tour Poipu, or get information on how to do a self-guided tour of Kokee State Park and Waimea Canyon. The company also leads sunrise and evening coasting tours (under the name **Bicycle Downhill**) from Waimea Canyon past the island's West Side beaches. Stand-up paddle tours are also available. ⊠ *2827-A Poipu Rd., near turnoff to Spouting Horn, Poipu* ☎ *808/742–9667, 888/742–9887* ⊕ *www.outfitterskauai.com* ✉ *Downhill bike tours $114.*

Pedal 'n' Paddle

BICYCLING | This company rents old-fashioned, single-speed beach cruisers and hybrid road bikes. In the heart of Hanalei, this is a great way to cruise the town; the more adventuresome cyclist can head to the end of the road. Be careful, though, because there are no bike lanes on the twisting-and-turning road to Kee Beach. Be sure to obtain the $1 permit before entering the park either on bike or on foot. ⊠ *Ching Young Village, 5-5190 Kuhio Hwy., Hanalei* ☎ *808/826–9069* ⊕ *www.pedalnpaddle.com* ✉ *Rentals from $15 per day and $60 per wk.*

Boat Tours

Deciding to see Napali Coast by boat is an easy decision. Choosing the outfitter to go with is not. There are numerous boat-tour operators to choose from, and, quite frankly, they all do a good job. Before you even start thinking about whom to go out with, answer these three questions: What kind of boat do I prefer? Where am I staying? Do I want to go in the morning or afternoon? Once you settle on these three, you can easily zero in on the tour outfitter.

First, the boat. The most important thing is to match your personality and that of your group with the personality of the boat. If you like thrills and adventure, the rubber inflatable rafts—often called Zodiacs, which Jacques Cousteau made famous and which the U.S. Coast Guard uses—will entice you. They're fast, likely to leave you drenched and windswept, and quite bouncy. If you prefer a smoother, more leisurely ride, then the large catamarans are the way to go. The next boat choice is size. Both the rafts and catamarans come in small and large. Again—think smaller, more adventurous; larger, more leisurely. ■TIP➡ **Do not choose a smaller boat because you think**

there will be fewer people. There might be fewer people, but you'll be jammed together sitting atop strangers. If you prefer privacy over socializing, go with a larger boat, so you'll have more room to spread out. The smaller boats will also take you along the coast at a higher rate of speed, making photo opportunities a bit more challenging. One advantage to smaller boats, however, is that—depending on ocean conditions—some may slip into a sea cave or two. If that sounds interesting to you, call the outfitter and ask their policy on entering sea caves. Some won't, no matter the conditions, because they consider the caves sacred or because they don't want to cause any environmental damage.

Boats leave from three points around the island (Hanalei, Port Allen, and Waimea), and all head to the same spot: Napali Coast. Here's the inside skinny on which is the best: If you're staying on the North Shore, choose to depart out of the North Shore, except in wintertime when the boats can't navigate the big surf. If you're staying anywhere else, depart out of the West Side. It's that easy. Sure, the North Shore is closer to Napali Coast; however, you'll pay more for less overall time. The West Side boat operators may spend more time getting to Napali Coast, but they'll spend about the same amount of time along Napali, plus you'll pay less. Finally, you'll also have to decide whether you want to go on a morning tour, which includes a deli lunch and a stop for snorkeling, or an afternoon tour, which does not always stop to snorkel but does include a sunset over the ocean. The morning tours with snorkeling are more popular with families and those who love dolphins, as the animals enjoy the "waves" created by the front of the catamarans and might just escort you down the coast. The winter months will also be a good chance to spot some whales breaching, though surf is much rougher along Napali. You don't have to be an

Boat Tour Checklist

- Swimsuit
- Sunscreen
- Hat
- Sunglasses
- Beach towel
- Light jacket
- Camera (in waterproof bag, just in case)
- Motion sickness meds (take well before departure)
- Change of clothes (postcruise)

expert snorkeler or even have any prior experience, but if it is your first time, note that although there will be some snorkeling instruction, there might not be much. Hawaiian spinner dolphins are so plentiful in the mornings that some tour companies guarantee you'll see them, though you won't get in the water and swim with them. The afternoon tours are more popular with nonsnorkelers—obviously—and photographers interested in capturing the setting sunlight on the coast. ■TIP→ **No matter which tour you select, book it online whenever possible.** Most companies offer Web specials, usually around $10 to $20 off per person.

CATAMARAN TOURS
★ **Blue Dolphin Charters**
BOATING | Blue Dolphin operates 65-foot sailing (rarely raised and always motoring) catamarans designed with three decks of spacious seating with great visibility, as well as motorized rafts. ■TIP→ **The lower deck is best for shade seekers.** The most popular is a daylong tour of Napali Coast, which includes a detour across the channel to Niihau for

The best way to see Kauai's rugged coastline is by boat.

snorkeling and diving. Morning snorkel tours of Napali include a deli lunch. Sunset sightseeing tours include a Hawaiian-style buffet. North Shore and South Shore rafting tours are also available, as are daily sportfishing charters of four to eight hours for no more than six guests. Blue Dolphin promises dolphin sightings and the best mai tais "off the island." Book online for cheaper deals on every tour offered. ✉ *4353 Waialo Rd., #7B, Eleele* ☎ *808/335–5553, 877/511–1311* ⊕ *www.kauaiboats.com* ✉ *From $100; 2-hr whale-watching/sunset tours, winter only, $65.*

★ **Capt. Andy's Sailing Adventures**
BOATING | FAMILY | Departing from Port Allen and running 55- and 60-foot sailing catamarans, as well as 24-foot inflatables out of Kikiaola Harbor in Kekaha, Capt. Andy's offers something for every taste, from raft expeditions to Hawaiian yachting. They have several lunch and snorkeling packages and four-hour sunset tours along Napali Coast. The Zodiac rafts

have hydrophones to hear whales and other underwater sounds. The longtime Kauai company also operates a snorkel barbecue sail and a dinner sunset sail aboard its *Southern Star* yacht, originally built for private charters. This boat now operates as host for two of Capt. Andy's daily sailing trips for an upgraded feel. ■ **TIP➜ If the winds and swells are up on the North Shore, this company is usually a good choice—especially if you're prone to seasickness.** ✉ *4353 Waiola Rd., Suite 1A-2A, Eleele* ☎ *808/335–6833* ⊕ *www. napali.com* ✉ *From $99.*

Captain Sundown
BOATING | Sundown has one of the few permits to sail from Hanalei Bay and operates the only sailing catamaran there. Captain Bob has been cruising Napali Coast since 1971—six days a week, sometimes twice a day. (And right alongside Captain Bob is his son, Captain Larry.) To say he knows the area is an understatement. Here's the other good thing about this tour: they take

a maximum of 17 passengers on the 40-foot boat. The breathtaking views of the waterfall-laced mountains behind Hanalei and Haena start immediately, and then it's around Kee Beach and the magic of Napali Coast unfolds before you. All the while, the captains are trolling for fish, and if they catch any, guests get to reel 'em in. Afternoon sunset sails (summertime only) run three hours and check in around 3 pm—these are BYOB. Cancellations due to rough surf are more frequent in winter. ⊠ *5-5134 Kuhio Hwy., Hanalei* ☎ *808/826–5585* ⊕ *www.captainsundown.com* ⌚ *From $151.*

Catamaran Kahanu

BOATING | Hawaiian-owned and-operated, Catamaran Kahanu has been in business since 1985 and runs a 40-foot power catamaran with 18-passenger seating. It offers seasonal whale-watching and snorkeling cruises, ranging from two to five hours, and departs from Port Allen. The five-hour, year-round Na Pali Coast tour includes snorkeling at Nualolo Kai, plus a deli lunch and soft drinks. Check-in is at 7 am and the boat returns at approximately 1 pm. The boat is smaller than most and may feel a tad crowded, but the tour feels more personal, with a laid-back, *ohana* (family) style. There's no alcohol allowed. The two-hour whale-watching tour is available from late December through March and begins at 1 pm. ⊠ *4353 Waialo Rd., near Port Allen Marina Center, Eleele* ☎ *808/645–6176, 888/213–7711* ⊕ *www.catamarankahanu. com* ⌚ *From $75.*

HoloHolo Charters

BOATING | Choose between the 50-foot catamaran called *Leila* for a morning snorkel sail to Napali Coast, or the 65-foot *HoloHolo* seven-hour catamaran trip to the "forbidden island" of Niihau. Both boats have large cabins and little outside seating. HoloHolo also offers a four-hour seasonal voyage of Napali from Hanalei Bay on its rigid-hull inflatable

Best Boat Tours

Best for snorkeling: Z-Tourz

Best for romance: Capt. Andy's Poipu Sail

Best for thrill seekers: Napali Explorer (Zodiac 1)

Best for mai tais: Blue Dolphin Charters

Best for pregnant women: Capt. Andy's

Best for charters: Captain Sundown

Best for price: Napali Riders

rafts, specifically for diving and snorkeling. Originators of the Niihau tour, HoloHolo Charters built their 65-foot powered catamaran with a wide beam to reduce side-to-side motion and twin 425 HP turbo diesel engines specifically for the 17-mile channel crossing to Niihau. It's the only outfitter running daily Niihau tours. The *HoloHolo* also embarks on a daily sunset and sightseeing tour of Napali Coast. *Leila* can hold 37 passengers, while her big brother can take a maximum of 47. Check-in is at Port Allen Marina Center. ⊠ *4353 Waialo Rd., Suite 5A, Eleele* ☎ *808/335–0815, 800/848–6130* ⊕ *www.holoholocharters. com* ⌚ *From $139.*

Kauai Sea Tours

BOATING | This company operates the *Lucky Lady,* a 60-foot sailing catamaran designed almost identically to that of Blue Dolphin Charters, with all the same benefits, including great views and spacious seating. Snorkeling tours anchor near Makole (based on the captain's discretion). If snorkeling isn't your thing, try the four-hour sunset tour, with beer,

If you choose to sail by yourself in Kauai, be prepared for strong currents and know your limits.

wine, mai tais, *pupu* (appetizers), and a hot buffet dinner or a two-hour seasonal whale-watching cruise. Tours of Napali, one with a beach landing, are offered on inflatable rafts. Check in at Port Allen Marina Center. ⊠ *4353 Waialo Rd., Eleele* ☎ *808/335–5309, 800/733–7997* ⊕ *www. kauaiseatours.com* ✉ *From $95.*

Liko Kauai Cruises

BOATING | There are many things to like about Liko Kauai Cruises. The 49-foot powered catamaran will enter sea caves, ocean conditions permitting. Sometimes, Captain Liko himself—a Native Hawaiian—still takes the captain's helm. We particularly like the layout of his boat: most of the seating is in the bow, so there's good visibility. A maximum of 32 passengers make each trip, which lasts five hours and includes snorkeling, food, and soft drinks. Trips usually depart out of Kikiaola Harbor in Waimea, a bit closer to Napali Coast than those leaving from Port Allen. ⊠ *4516 Alawai Rd., Waimea (Kauai County)* ☎ *808/338–0333, 888/732–5456* ⊕ *www.liko-kauai.com* ✉ *$135.*

Napali Catamaran

BOATING | One of the few tour groups departing Hanalei, this company, formerly known as Whitey's, has been around since 1973. Once on board, it takes about 15 minutes before you're witnessing the magnificence of Napali Coast. Taking a maximum of 16 passengers, its new 35-foot powered catamaran is small enough—and with no mast, short enough—to dip into sea caves. Between March and October, they run two four-hour snorkeling tours per day, stopping at the best snorkeling site along Napali, Nualolo Kai. The rates are a bit pricey at $250 per person, but the four-hour tour includes a deli-style lunch. ⊠ *Ching Young Village, 5-5190 Kuhio Hwy., Hanalei* ☎ *808/826–6853, 866/255–6853* ⊕ *www. napalicatamaran.com* ✉ *From $250.*

Boat Tour Weather Cancellations

If it's raining where you're staying, that doesn't mean it's raining over the water, so don't shy away from a boat tour. Besides, it's not the rain that should concern you—it's the wind and waves. Especially from due north and south, wind creates surface chop and makes for rough riding. Larger craft are designed to handle winter's ocean swells, however, so unless monster waves are out there, your tour should depart without a hitch. If the water is too rough, your boat captain may reroute to calmer waters. It's a tough call to make, but your comfort and safety are always the foremost factor. ■TIP→ In winter **months, North Shore** departures are cancelled much **more** often **than those departing the** West Side. This is because the waves are often too big for the boats to leave Hanalei Bay, and as a result, some operators only work the summer season. If you want the closest thing to a guarantee of seeing Napali Coast in winter, choose a West Side outfitter. Oh, and even if your tour boat says it cruises the "entire Napali," keep in mind that "ocean conditions permitting" is always implied.

RAFT TOURS

Capt. Andy's Raft Expeditions

BOATING | Departing out of Kikiaola Harbor in Kekaha, Capt. Andy's Raft Expeditions offer both snorkeling and beach-landing excursions. The Zodiac rafts are on the smaller side—24 feet with a maximum of 14 passengers—and all seating is on the rubber hulls, so hang on. They operate three different rafts, so there's a good chance of availability. Trips include snorkeling at Nualolo Kai (ocean conditions permitting), sea caves, sightseeing along Napali Coast, a hiking tour through an ancient Hawaiian fishing village, and a buffet lunch on the beach. A shorter snorkeling tour is also offered. You're closer to the water on the Zodiacs, so you'll have great views of humpbacks, spinner dolphins, sea turtles, and other wildlife. ⊠ *Kikiaola Small Boat Harbor, Kaumualii Hwy., Kekaha* ☎ *808/335–6833, 800/535–0830* ⊕ *www.napali.com* ⊠ *From $99.*

Kauai Sea Tours

BOATING | This company holds a special permit from the state to land at Nualolo Kai along Napali Coast, ocean conditions permitting. Here, you'll enjoy a picnic lunch, as well as an archaeological tour of an ancient Hawaiian fishing village, ocean conditions permitting. Kauai Sea Tours operates four 24-foot inflatable rafts—maximum occupancy 14. These are small enough for checking out the insides of sea caves and the undersides of waterfalls. Four different tours are available, including snorkeling and whale-watching, depending on the season. ⊠ *Port Allen Marina Center, 4353 Waialo Rd., Eleele* ☎ *808/335–5309, 800/733–7997* ⊕ *www.kauaiseatours.com* ⊠ *From $145.*

★ Napali Explorer

BOATING | These tours operate out of Kikiaola Harbor, a tad closer to Napali Coast than most of the other West Side catamaran tours. The company runs two different sizes of inflatable rubber raft: a 48-foot, 36-passenger craft with an onboard toilet, freshwater shower, shade canopy, and seating in the stern (which is surprisingly smooth and comfortable) and bow (which is where the fun is); and a 26-foot, 14-passenger craft for the all-out fun and thrills of a white-knuckle ride in the bow. The smaller vessel stops at Nualolo Kai and ties up onshore for a tour of the ancient fishing village. Charters are available. ✉ *9814 Kaumalii Hwy., Waimea (Kauai County)* ☎ *808/338–9999* ⊕ *www. napaliexplorer.com* ✉ *From $149.*

Napali Riders

BOATING | This tour-boat outfitter distinguishes itself in two ways. First, it cruises the entire Napali Coast, clear to Kee Beach and back. Second, it has a reasonable price because it's a no-frills tour—no lunch provided, just beverages and snacks. The company runs morning and afternoon four-hour snorkeling, sightseeing, and whale-watching trips out of Kikiaola Harbor in Waimea on a 30-foot inflatable raft with a 28-passenger maximum—that's fewer than they used to take, but it can still be a bit cramped. ✉ *9600 Kaumualii Hwy., Waimea (Kauai County)* ☎ *808/742–6331* ⊕ *www.napaliriders.com* ✉ *$140.*

Z-Tourz

BOATING | What we like about Z-Tourz is that it's a boat company that makes snorkeling its priority. Its two- and three-hour tours focus solely on the South Shore's abundant offshore reefs. If you want to snorkel with Hawaii's tropical reef fish and turtles (pretty much guaranteed), this is your boat. The craft is a 26 foot rigid-hull inflatable (think Zodiac) with a maximum of 16 passengers. These snorkel tours are guided, so someone actually identifies what you're seeing. Rates include lunch and snorkel gear. ✉ *3417 Poipu Rd., Poipu* ☎ *808/742–7422, 888/998–6879* ⊕ *www.kauaiztours.com* ✉ *From $78.*

RIVERBOAT TOURS TO FERN GROTTO

Smith's Motor Boat Services

BOATING | This 2-mile trip up the lush and lovely Wailua River, the only navigable waterway in Hawaii, culminates at the infamous Fern Grotto, a yawning lava tube that is covered with fishtail ferns. During the boat ride, guitar and ukulele players regale you with Hawaiian melodies and tell the history of the river. It's a kitschy, but fun, bit of Hawaiiana and the river scenery is beautiful. Flat-bottom, 150-passenger riverboats (that rarely fill up) depart from Wailua Marina at the mouth of the Wailua River. ■**TIP**→ **It's extremely rare, but occasionally after heavy rains the tour doesn't disembark at the grotto; if you're traveling in winter, ask beforehand.** Round-trip excursions take 1½ hours, including time to walk around the grotto and environs. Tours run at 9:30, 11, 2, and 3:30 daily. ✉ *5971 Kuhio Hwy., Kapaa* ☎ *808/821–6895* ⊕ *www. smithskauai.com/fern-grotto/* ✉ *$30.*

Body Boarding and Bodysurfing

The most natural form of wave riding is bodysurfing, a popular sport on Kauai because there are many shore breaks around the island. Wave riders of this style stand waist deep in the water, facing shore, and swim madly as a wave picks them up and breaks. It's great fun and requires no special skills and absolutely no equipment other than a swimsuit. The next step up is body boarding, also called boogie boarding. In this case, wave riders lie with their upper body on a foam board about half the length of a traditional surfboard and kick as the wave propels them toward shore. Again, this is easy to pick up, and there are many places around Kauai to practice. The locals wear short-finned flippers to help them catch waves, which is a good idea to enhance safety in the water. It's worth spending a few minutes watching these experts as they spin, twirl, and flip—that's right—while they slip down the face of the wave. Of course, all beach-safety precautions apply, and just because you see wave riders of any kind in the water doesn't mean the water is safe for everyone. Any snorkeling-gear outfitter also rents body boards.

Some of our favorite bodysurfing and body-boarding beaches are **Brennecke, Wailua, Kealia, Kalihiwai,** and **Hanalei.**

Deep-Sea Fishing

Simply step aboard and cast your line for mahimahi, ahi, ono, and marlin. That's about how quickly the fishing—mostly trolling with lures—begins on Kauai. The water gets deep quickly here, so there's less cruising time to fishing grounds, which is nice, since Hawaii's seas are notoriously rough. Of course, your captain may elect to cruise to a hot location where they've had good luck lately.

There are oodles of charter fishermen around; most depart from Nawiliwili Harbor in Lihue, and most use lures instead of live bait. Inquire about each boat's "fish policy"; that is, what happens to the fish if any are caught. Some boats keep all; others will give you enough for a meal or two, even doing the cleaning themselves. On shared charters, ask about the maximum passenger count and about the fishing rotation; you'll want to make sure everyone gets a fair shot at reeling in the big one. Another option is to book a private charter. Shared and private charters run four, six, and eight hours in length.

BOATS AND CHARTERS
Captain Don's Sportfishing
FISHING | Captain Don is very flexible and treats everyone like family—he'll stop to snorkel or whale-watch if that's what the group (four to six) wants. Saltwater fly fishermen (bring your own gear) are welcome. He'll even fish for bait and let you keep part of whatever you catch, as long as the fish is less than 25 pounds. His *Happy Ryder* is a 39-foot Hatteras boat. ⊠ *Nawiliwili Small Boat Harbor, 2494*

Niumalu Rd., Nawiliwili ☎ *808/639–3012* ⊕ *www.captaindonsfishing.com* ☞ *From $150 (shared); from $750 (private).*

Kai Bear
FISHING | What's particularly nice about this company are the boats: the 38-foot Bertram, *Kai Bear,* and the 42-foot Bertram, *Grander,* which are well maintained and very roomy. The 41-foot Bertram, *Emma Nalani,* docks in Nawiliwili Small Boat Harbor, which is convenient for those staying on the East Side. The prices are reasonable ($160 per person for the four-hour shared charter or $699 for the eight-hour private charter), and they share the catch. ⊠ *Nawiliwili Small Boat Harbor, 2900 Nawiliwili Rd., Nawiliwili* ☎ *808/652–4556* ⊕ *www.kaibear.com* ☞ *From $160.*

Na Pali Explorer
BOATING | Operating since 1984, Na Pali Explorer is considered a pioneer of Napali Coast adventures. They offer snorkeling and sightseeing tours, including a coast landing on a secluded Napali beach, and whale-watching, in season. They leave from Kekaha, on the West Side of Kauai, and have two boats, a 26-foot Zodiac and a 48-foot Scarab. Private charters are also available ($5,000).

⊠ *Kikiaola Small Boat Harbor, 8932 Kekaha Rd, Kekaha* ☎ *808/338–9999* ⊕ *www.napaliexplorer.com* ☞ *From $159 per person.*

Golf

For golfers, the Garden Isle might as well be known as the Robert Trent Jones Jr. Isle. Four of the island's eight courses, including Poipu Bay—onetime home of the PGA Grand Slam of Golf—are the work of Jones, who maintains a home at Princeville. Combine these four courses with those from Jack Nicklaus, Robin Nelson, and local legend Toyo Shirai, and you'll see that golf sets Kauai apart from

The Makai course at Princeville Makai Golf Club has consistently been ranked a top course in the U.S.

the other Islands as much as the Pacific Ocean does. ■TIP→ Afternoon tee times at most courses can save you big bucks.

Kiahuna Plantation Golf Course

GOLF | A meandering brook, lava outcrops, and thickets of trees give Kiahuna its character. Robert Trent Jones Jr. was given a smallish piece of land just inland at Poipu, and defends par with smaller targets, awkward stances, and optical illusions. In 2003 a group of homeowners bought the club and brought Jones back to renovate the course (it was originally built in 1983), adding tees and revamping bunkers. The pro here boasts his course has the best putting greens on the island. This is the only course on Kauai with a complete set of junior's tee boxes. ⊠ 2545 Kiahuna Plantation Dr., Koloa ☎ 808/742–9595 ⊕ www.kiahunagolf. com ⊠ $105, including cart 🏌 18 holes, 6787 yards, par 70.

Ocean Course Hokuala Golf Club

GOLF | The Jack Nicklaus–designed Ocean Course Hokuala offers a beautiful and distinctly Hawaiian golf experience. With an assortment of plants and tropical birds adding to the atmosphere, this course winds through dark ravines and over picturesque landscape. The fifth hole is particularly striking as it requires a drive over a valley populated by mango and guava trees. The final holes feature unmatched views of Nawiliwili Bay, including the harbor, a lighthouse, and secluded beaches. ⊠ 3351 Hoolaulea Way, Lihue ☎ 808/241–6000, 800/634–6400 ⊕ www. hokualakauai.com/golf ⊠ From $150; after 2 pm $126 🏌 18 holes, 7156 yards, par 72.

Poipu Bay Golf Course

GOLF | Poipu Bay has been called the Pebble Beach of Hawaii, and the comparison is apt. Like Pebble Beach, Poipu is a links course built on headlands, not true links land. There's wildlife galore. It's not unusual for golfers to see monk seals sunning on the beach below, sea turtles bobbing outside the shore break, and humpback whales leaping offshore. From 1994 to 2006, the course (designed by Robert Trent Jones Jr.) hosted the annual PGA Grand Slam of Golf. Tiger Woods was a frequent winner here. Call ahead to take advantage of varying prices for tee times. ⊠ *2250 Ainako St., Koloa* ☎ *808/742–8711* ⊕ *www.poipubaygolf. com* ⊠ *$209 before noon, $185 after* ⚑ *18 holes, 6127 yards, par 72.*

★ Princeville Makai Golf Club

GOLF | The 27-hole Princeville Makai Golf Club was named for its five ocean-hugging front holes. Designed by golf-course architect Robert Trent Jones Jr. in 1971, the 18-hole championship Makai Course has consistently been ranked a top golf course in the United States. **■TIP→ Check the website for varying rates as well as other nongolf activities at the facility like the Sunset Golf Cart Tour, where you ride the course, sans clubs, and take in the spectacular ocean views.** ⊠ *4080 Lei O Papa Rd., Princeville* ⊕ *www. makaigolf.com* ⊠ *$305* ⚑ *18 holes, 7223 yards, par 72; Woods Course: 9 holes, 3445 yards, par 36.*

Wailua Municipal Golf Course

GOLF | Considered by many to be one of Hawaii's best public golf courses, this seaside course provides an affordable game with minimal water hazards, but it is challenging enough to have been chosen to host three USGA Amateur Public Links Championships. It was first built as a nine-holer in the 1930s. The second nine holes were added in 1961. Course designer Toyo Shirai created a course that is fun but not punishing. The trade winds blow steadily on the East Side of the island and provide a game with challenges. An ocean view and affordability make this one of the most popular courses on the island. Tee times are accepted up to seven days in advance and can be paid in cash, traveler's checks, and some

credit cards. ⊠ *3-5350 Kuhio Hwy., Lihue* ☎ *808/241–6666* ⊕ *www.kauai.gov/golf* ⊠ *$48 weekdays, $60 weekends; cart rental $20* ⚑ *18 holes, 6585 yards, par 72.*

Hiking

The best way to experience the *aina*—the land—on Kauai is to step off the beach and hike into the remote interior. You'll find waterfalls so tall you'll strain your neck looking, pools of crystal-clear water for swimming, tropical forests teeming with plant life, and ocean vistas that will make you wish you could stay forever.

■TIP→ For your safety wear sturdy shoes—preferably water-resistant ones. All hiking trails on Kauai are free, so far. There's a development plan in the works that could turn the Waimea Canyon and Kokee State Parks into admission-charging destinations. Whatever it may be, it will be worth it.

Hiking along the 11-mile Kalalau Trail will lead you from Kee Beach to Kalalau Beach.

BEST SPOTS
Hanalei-Okolehao Trail

HIKING/WALKING | *Okolehao* basically translates to "moonshine" in Hawaiian. This trail follows the Hihimanu Ridge, which was established in the days of Prohibition, when this backyard liquor was distilled from the roots of ti plants. The 2-mile hike climbs 1,200 feet and offers a 360-degree view of Hanalei Bay and Waioli Valley. Your ascent begins at the China Ditch off the Hanalei River. Follow the trail through a lightly forested grove and then climb up a steep embankment. From here the trail is well marked. Most of the climb is lined with hala, ti, wild orchid, and eucalyptus. You'll get your first of many ocean views at mile marker 1. ⊠ *Hanalei* ⊹ *Follow Ohiki Rd. (north of Hanalei Bridge) 5 miles to U.S. Fish and Wildlife Service parking area. Directly across street is small bridge that marks trailhead.*

Ho'opi'i Falls

HIKING/WALKING | Tucked among the winding roads and grassy pastures of Kapahi, 3 miles inland from Kapaa town, is an easy hike to two waterfalls. A 10 minute walk will deliver you to the creek. Follow it around to see the first set of falls. The more impressive second falls are a mere 25 minutes away. The swimming hole alone is worth the journey. Just climb the rooted path next to the first falls and turn left on the trail above. Turn left on the very next trail to descend back into the canyon and follow the leafy path that zigzags along the creek—the falls and the swimming hole lie below. ⊠ *Kapaa* ⊹ *On north end of Kapaa, ¼ mile past last lookout, is side road called Kawaihau. Follow road up 3 miles, then turn right on Kapahi Rd. into residential neighborhood. Kapahi Rd. dead-ends near trailhead. Look for yellow gate on your left.*

★ Kalalau Trail

HIKING/WALKING | Of all the hikes on the island, Kalalau Trail is by far the most famous and in many regards the most strenuous. A moderate hiker can handle the 2-mile trek to Hanakapiai Beach, and for the seasoned outdoorsman, the additional 2 miles up to the falls is manageable. But be prepared to rock-hop along a creek and ford waters that can get waist high during the rain. Round-trip to Hanakapiai Falls is 8 miles. This steep and often muddy trail is best approached with a walking stick. If there has been any steady rain, wait for drier days for a more enjoyable trek. The narrow Kalalau Trail delivers one startling ocean view after another along a path that is alternately shady and sunny. Wear hiking shoes or sandals, and bring drinking water since the creeks on the trail are not potable. Plenty of food is always encouraged on a strenuous hike such as this one. If you plan to venture the full 11 miles into Kalalau, you need to acquire a camping permit, either online or at the State Building in Lihue, for $20 per person per night. You should secure a permit well in advance of your trip. ⊹ *Drive north past Hanalei to end of road. Trailhead is directly across from Kee Beach* ⊕ *www.kalalautrail.com* ⊠ *$20 per person per night.*

Mahaulepu Heritage Trail

HIKING/WALKING | This trail offers the novice hiker an accessible way to appreciate the rugged southern coast of Kauai. A cross-country trail wends its way along the water, high above the ocean, through a lava field, and past a sacred *heiau* (stone structure) . Walk all the way to Mahaulepu, 2 miles north, for a two-hour round-trip. If conditions are right, you should be able to see dolphins, *honu* (green sea turtles), and whales. ⊹ *Drive north on Poipu Rd., turn right at Poipu Bay Golf Course sign. The street name is Ainako, but sign is hard to see. Drive down to beach and park in lot* ⊕ *www. hikemahaulepu.org.*

Lilikoi Alert

If you're hiking in May and June, you may come across *lilikoi*—often referred to as passion fruit—scattered like yellow eggs among the ferns. It tastes as sweet and floral as it smells—bite the tip of the rind off and you'll see speckled jelly with tiny black seeds; then slurp it right out of the skin. If you miss lilikoi season, scout out delicious lilikoi mustards and jams sold by local grocers. Lilikoi pie is also served at a few Hawaiian eateries.

Sleeping Giant Trail

HIKING/WALKING | An easily accessible trail practically in the heart of Kapaa, the moderately strenuous Sleeping Giant Trail—or simply Sleeping Giant—gains 1,000 feet over 2 miles. We prefer an early-morning—say, sunrise—hike up the east-side trailhead, with sparkling blue-water vistas, but there are other back-side approaches. At the top you can see a grassy grove with a picnic table. It is a local favorite, with many East Siders meeting here to exercise. ⊠ *Haleilio Rd., off Rte. 56, Wailua (Kauai County).*

Waimea Canyon and Kokee State Park

HIKING/WALKING | This park contains a 50-mile network of hiking trails of varying difficulty that take you through acres of native forests, across the highest-elevation swamp in the world, to the river at the base of the canyon, and onto pinnacles of land sticking their necks out over Napali Coast. All hikers should register at Kokee Natural History Museum, where you can find trail maps, current trail information, and specific directions.

The **Kukui Trail** descends 2,200 feet over 2½ miles into Waimea Canyon to the edge of the Waimea River—it's a steep climb. The **Awaawapuhi Trail,** with 1,600 feet of elevation gains and losses over

3¼ miles, feels more gentle than the Kukui Trail, but it offers its own huffing-and-puffing sections in its descent along a spiny ridge to a perch overlooking the ocean.

The 3½-mile **Alakai Swamp Trail** is accessed via the **Pihea Trail** or a four-wheel-drive road. There's one strenuous valley section, but otherwise it's a pretty level trail—once you access it. This trail is a bird watcher's delight and includes a painterly view of Wainiha and Hanalei Valleys at the trail's end. The trail traverses the purported highest-elevation swamp in the world via a boardwalk so as not to disturb the fragile plant and wildlife. It is typically the coolest of the hikes due to the tree canopy, elevation, and cloud coverage.

The **Canyon Trail** offers much in its short trek: spectacular vistas of the canyon and the only dependable waterfall in Waimea Canyon. The easy 2-mile hike can be cut in half if you have a four-wheel-drive vehicle. The late-afternoon sun sets the canyon walls ablaze in color. ⊠ *Kokee Natural History Museum, 3600 Kokee Rd., Kekaha* ☎ *808/335–9975 for trail conditions* ⊕ *www.kokee.org.*

EQUIPMENT AND TOURS
★ **Kauai Nature Tours**

HIKING/WALKING | Father-and-son scientists started this hiking tour business. As such, their emphasis is on education and the environment. If you're interested in flora, fauna, volcanology, geology, oceanography, and the like, this is the company for you. They offer daylong hikes along coastal areas, beaches, and in the mountains. ■ TIP→ **If you have a desire to see a specific location, just ask. They will do custom hikes to spots they don't normally hit if there is interest.** Hikes range from easy to strenuous. Transportation is often provided from your hotel. ⊠ *5162 Lawai Rd., Koloa* ☎ *808/742–8305, 888/233–8365*

⊕ *www.kauainaturetours.com* ✉ *From $155.*

Princeville Ranch Adventures

HIKING/WALKING | This company offers a 4-mile hike that traverses Princeville Ranch, crossing through a rain forest to a five-tier waterfall for lunch and swimming. Moderately strenuous hiking is required. ⊠ *Rte. 56, between mile markers 27 and 28, Princeville* ☎ *808/826–7669, 888/955–7669* ⊕ *www.princevilleranch.com* ✉ *$129.*

Horseback Riding

Most of the horseback-riding tours on Kauai are primarily walking tours with little trotting and no cantering or galloping, so no experience is required. Zip. Zilch. Nada. If you're interested, most of the stables offer private lessons. The most popular tours are the ones including a picnic lunch by the water. Your only dilemma may be deciding what kind of water you want—waterfalls or ocean. You may want to make your decision based on where you're staying. The "waterfall picnic" tours are on the wetter North Shore, and the "beach picnic" tours take place on the South Shore.

CJM Country Stables

HORSEBACK RIDING | Just past the Hyatt in Poipu, CJM Stables offers a three-hour picnic ride with noshing on the beach, as well as their more popular two-hour trail ride without the picnic break. The landscape here is rugged and beautiful, featuring sand dunes and limestone bluffs. CJM can get you as close as anyone to the secluded Mahaulepu Bay. They sponsor seasonal rodeos that are free and open to the public, and participate in other popular community events. ⊠ *Poipu Rd., Koloa* ⊹ *1½ miles from Grand Hyatt Kauai* ☎ *808/742–6096* ⊕ *www.cjmstables.com* ✉ *From $130.*

★ **Princeville Ranch Adventures**

HORSEBACK RIDING | A longtime *kamaaina* (resident) family operates Princeville Ranch. They originated the waterfall picnic tour, which runs three and a half hours and includes a short but steep hike down to Kalihiwai Falls, a dramatic three-tier waterfall, for swimming and picnicking. Princeville also has shorter, straight riding tours and private rides. A popular option is the three-hour combination Ride 'N Glide tour with three ziplines. ⊠ *Kuhio Hwy., off Kapaka Rd., between mile markers 27 and 28, Princeville* ☎ *808/826–7669* ⊕ *www.princevilleranch. com* ⊠ *Ride only from $129; private tours from $189.*

Kayaking

Kauai is the only Hawaiian island with navigable rivers. As the oldest inhabited island in the chain, Kauai has had more time for wind and water erosion to deepen and widen cracks into streams and streams into rivers. Because this is a small island, the rivers aren't long, and there are no rapids, which makes them generally safe for kayakers of all levels, even beginners, except when rivers are flowing fast from heavy rains.

For more advanced paddlers, there aren't many places in the world more beautiful for sea kayaking than Napali Coast. If this is your draw to Kauai, plan your vacation for the summer months, when the seas are at their calmest. ■**TIP→ Tour and kayak-rental reservations are recommended at least two weeks in advance during peak summer and holiday seasons.** In general, tours and rentals are available year-round, Monday through Saturday. Pack a swimsuit, sunscreen, a hat, bug repellent, water shoes (sport sandals, aqua socks, old tennis shoes), and motion sickness medication if you're planning on sea kayaking.

RIVER KAYAKING

Tour outfitters operate on the Huleia, Wailua, and Hanalei Rivers with guided tours that combine hiking to waterfalls, as in the case of the first two, and snorkeling, as in the case of the third. Another option is renting kayaks and heading out on your own. Each has its advantages and disadvantages, but it boils down as follows:

If you want to swim at the base of a remote 100-foot waterfall, sign up for a five-hour kayak (4-mile round-trip) and hiking (2-mile round-trip) tour of the **Wailua River.** It includes a dramatic waterfall that is best accessed with the aid of a guide, so you don't get lost. ■**TIP→ Remember— it's dangerous to swim under waterfalls no matter how good a water massage may sound. Rocks and logs are known to plunge down, especially after heavy rains.**

If you want to kayak on your own, choose the **Hanalei River.** It's most scenic from the kayak itself; there are no trails to hike to hidden waterfalls. And better yet, a rental company is right on the river—no hauling kayaks on top of your car.

If you're not sure of your kayaking abilities, head to the **Huleia River**; 3½-hour tours include easy paddling upriver, a nature walk through a rain forest with a cascading waterfall, a rope swing for playing Tarzan and Jane, and a ride back downriver—into the wind—on a motorized, double-hull canoe.

As for the kayaks themselves, most companies use the two-person sit-on-top style that is quite buoyant—no Eskimo rolls required. The only possible danger comes in the form of communication. The kayaks seat two people, which means you'll share the work with a guide (good), or with your spouse, child, parent, or friend (the potentially dangerous part). On the river, the two-person kayaks are known as "divorce boats." Counseling is not included in the tour price.

Wailua River, Hanalei River, and Huleia River are Kauai's most scenic spots to river kayak.

SEA KAYAKING

In its second year and second issue, *National Geographic Adventure* ranked kayaking Napali Coast second on its list of America's Best 100 Adventures, right behind rafting the Colorado River through the Grand Canyon. That pretty much says it all. It's the adventure of a lifetime in one day, involving eight hours of paddling. Although it's good to have some kayaking experience, feel comfortable on the water, and be reasonably fit, it doesn't require the preparation, stamina, or fortitude of, say, climbing Mt. Everest. Tours run May through September, ocean conditions permitting. In the winter months sea-kayaking tours operate on the South Shore—beautiful, but not as dramatic as Napali.

EQUIPMENT AND TOURS

Kayak Kauai

KAYAKING | This company pioneered kayaking on Kauai. It offers guided tours on the Wailua River, and sea kayak tours in Hanalei Bay and along Napali Coast, in season. It has consolidated operations and is now conveniently located in the Wailua Marina. From there, it can launch kayaks right into the Wailua River for its five-hour Secret Falls hike-paddle tour and three-hour paddle to a swimming hole. Kayak Kauai also offers 12-hour escorted summer sea kayak tours and camping trips on Napali Coast. Stand-up paddleboard instruction and sea-kayak whale-watching tours round out its repertoire. The company will shuttle kayakers as needed, and, for rentals, it provides the hauling gear necessary for your rental car. Snorkel gear, body boards, and stand-up paddleboards also can be rented. ⊠ *Wailua Marina, 3-5971 Kuhio Hwy., Wailua (Kauai County)* ☎ *808/826–9844, 888/596–3853* ⊕ *www.kayakkauai.com* 🖃 *From $85 (river tours) and $240 (sea tours); kayak rentals from $95 per day.*

Kayak Wailua

KAYAKING | We can't quite figure out how this family-run business offers pretty much the same Wailua River kayaking tour as everyone else—except for lunch and beverages, which are BYO—for the

Leptospirosis in Kauai

Before you go wading into a stream or river in Kauai, take note: leptospirosis, a bacterial disease that is transmitted from animals to humans, may be present. It can survive for long periods of time in freshwater and mud contaminated by the urine of infected animals, such as pigs, rats, and goats.

The bacteria enter the body through the eyes, ears, nose, mouth, and broken skin. To avoid infection, don't drink untreated water from streams, and don't wade in brown water or submerge skin with cuts and abrasions in streams or rivers.

Symptoms are often mild and resemble the flu—fever, diarrhea, chills, nausea, headache, vomiting, and body pains—and may occur 2 to 20 days after exposure. If you think you have these symptoms, see a doctor right away.

---

lowest price, but it does. They say it's because they don't discount and don't offer commissions to activities and concierge desks. Their trip, a 4½-hour kayak, hike, and waterfall swim, is offered six times a day, with the last at 1 pm. With the number of boats going out, large groups can be accommodated. No tours are allowed on Wailua River on Sunday. ⊠ *4565 Haleilio Rd., behind old Coco Palms hotel, Kapaa* ☎ *808/822–3388* ⊕ *www.kayakwailua.com* ⊠ *$60.*

★ Napali Kayak

KAYAKING | A couple of longtime guides ventured out on their own to create this company, which focuses solely on a 17-mile sea-kayaking paddle along Napali Coast from April to October for small groups, or private and honeymoon tours. These guys are highly experienced and still highly enthusiastic about their livelihood—so much so that REI Adventures hires them to run their multiday, multisport tours. If you're an experienced kayaker and want to try camping on your own at Kalalau (you'll need permits), Napali Kayak will provide kayaks outfitted with dry bags, extra paddles, and seat backs, while also offering transportation drop-off and pickup. They also do Napali Coast day tours from Hanalei to Polihale, with a lunch break at Milolii, and rent camping equipment and first-aid kits. ⊠ *5-5075 Kuhio Hwy., next to Postcards Café, Hanalei* ☎ *808/826–6900* ⊕ *www. napalikayak.com* ⊠ *From $250.*

Outfitters Kauai

KAYAKING | FAMILY | This well-established tour outfitter operates year-round river-kayak tours on the Huleia and Wailua rivers, as well as sea-kayaking tours along Napali Coast in summer and the South Shore in winter. Outfitters Kauai's specialty, however, is the Kipu Safari. This all-day adventure starts with kayaking up the Huleia River and includes a rope swing over a swimming hole, a wagon ride through a working cattle ranch, a picnic lunch by a private waterfall, hiking, and two "zips" across the rain-forest canopy (strap on a harness, clip into a cable, and zip over a quarter of a mile). They then offer a one-of-a-kind Waterzip Zipline at their mountain stream–fed blue pool. The day ends with a ride on a motorized double-hull canoe. It's a great tour for the family, because no one ever gets bored. ⊠ *2827-A Poipu Rd., Poipu* ☎ *808/742–9667, 888/742–9887* ⊕ *www. outfitterskauai.com* ⊠ *Kipu Safari $189.*

Wailua Kayak & Canoe

KAYAKING | This purveyor of kayak rentals is right on the Wailua River, which means no hauling your kayak on top of your car (a definite plus). Guided waterfall tours are also offered. This outfitter promotes itself as "Native Hawaiian owned and operated." No Wailua River tours are offered on Sunday. ⊠ *162 Wailua Rd., Kapaa* 🕾 *808/821–1188* ⊕ *www.wailu-ariverkayaking.com* 🖃 *$50 for a single, $100 for a double; guided tours from $75.*

Kiteboarding

Several years ago, the latest wave-riding craze to hit the Islands was kiteboarding, and the sport is still going strong. As the name implies, there's a kite and a board involved. The board you strap on your feet; the kite is attached to a harness around your waist. Steering is accomplished with a rod that's attached to the harness and the kite. Depending on conditions and the desires of the kiteboarder, the kite can go some 30 to 100 feet in the air. The result is a cross between waterskiing—without the boat—and windsurfing. Speeds are fast and aerobatic maneuvers are involved. Though lessons are available, you can also enjoy watching the pros who can put on a pretty spectacular show. The most popular year-round spots for kiteboarding are **Kapaa Beach Park, Anini Beach Park,** and **Mahaulepu Beach.** ■**TIP→ Many visitors come to Kauai dreaming of parasailing. If that's you, make a stop at Maui or the Big Island. There's no parasailing or commercial jet skiing on Kauai.**

Kiteboard Kauai

HANG GLIDING/PARAGLIDING/PARASAILING | Certified instructor Adam Finn is committed to helping students quickly and safely master basic techniques so they can enjoy maximum time on the waves. To that end, he uses waterproof radio helmets to communicate with students in the water. Lessons by appointment only. ⊠ *Kapaa* ⊕ *www.kiteboardkauai.com.*

Mountain Tubing

For the past 40 years, Hawaii's sugar-cane plantations have closed one by one. In the fall of 2009, Gay & Robinson announced the closure of Kauai's last plantation, leaving only one in the state, in Maui. The sugarcane irrigation ditches remain, striating these Islands like spokes in a wheel. Inspired by the Hawaiian *auwai,* which diverted water from streams to taro fields, these engineering feats harnessed the rain. One ingenious tour company on Kauai has figured out a way to make exploring them an adventure: float inflatable tubes down the route.

Kauai Backcountry Adventures

LOCAL SPORTS | FAMILY | Both zipline and tubing tours are offered. Popular with all ages, the tubing adventure can book up two weeks in advance in busy summer months. Here's how it works: you recline in an inner tube and float down fern lined irrigation ditches that were built more than a century ago—the engineering is impressive—to divert water from Mt Waialeale to sugar and pineapple fields around the island. They'll even give you a headlamp so you can see as you float through five covered tunnels. The scenery from the island's interior at the base of Mt. Waialeale on Lihue Plantation land is superb. Ages five and up are welcome. The tour takes about three hours and includes a picnic lunch and a swim in a swimming hole. ■**TIP→ You'll definitely want to pack water-friendly shoes (or rent some from the outfitter), sunscreen, a hat, bug repellent, and a beach towel.** Tours are offered up to a dozen times daily. ⊠ *3-4131 Kuhio Hwy., across from gas station, Hanamaulu* 🕾 *808/245–2506, 888/270–0555* ⊕ *www.kauaibackcountry.com* 🖃 *$125 per person.*

Scuba Diving

The majority of scuba diving on Kauai occurs on the South Shore. Boat and shore dives are available, although boat sites surpass the shore sites for a couple of reasons. First, they're deeper and exhibit the complete symbiotic relationship of a reef system, and second, the visibility is better a little farther offshore.

The dive operators on Kauai offer a full range of services, including certification dives, referral dives, boat dives, shore dives, night dives, and drift dives. Be sure to inquire about a company's safety record and precautions if you are new to the activity. ■TIP→ **As for certification, we recommend completing your confined-water training and classroom testing before arriving on the island.** That way, you'll spend less time training and more time diving.

BEST SPOTS

The best and safest scuba-diving sites are accessed by boat on the South Shore of the island, right off the shores of Poipu. The captain selects the actual site based on ocean conditions of the day. Beginners may prefer shore dives, which are best at **Koloa Landing** on the South Shore year-round and **Makua (Tunnels) Beach** on the North Shore in the calm summer months. Keep in mind, though, that you'll have to haul your gear a ways down the beach.

For the advanced diver, the island of Niihau—across an open ocean channel in deep and crystal-clear waters—beckons and rewards, usually with some big fish. Seasport Divers, Fathom Five, and Bubbles Below venture the 17 miles across the channel in summer when the crossing is smoothest. Divers can expect deep dives, walls, and strong currents at Niihau, where conditions can change rapidly. To make the long journey worthwhile, three dives and Nitrox are included.

EQUIPMENT, LESSONS, AND TOURS

Bubbles Below

SCUBA DIVING | Marine ecology is the emphasis here aboard the 36-foot, eight-passenger *Kai Manu*. This longtime Kauai company discovered some pristine dive sites on the West Side of the island where white-tip reef sharks are common—and other divers are not. Thanks to the addition of a 32-foot powered catamaran—the six-passenger *Dive Rocket*—the group also runs Niihau, Napali, and North Shore dives year-round (depending on ocean conditions, of course). They're still known for their South Side trips and lead dives at the East Side walls as well, so they truly do circumnavigate the island. A bonus on these tours is the wide variety of food served between dives. Open-water certification dives, check-out dives, and intro shore dives are available upon request. ✉ *Port Allen Small Boat Harbor, 4353 Waialo Rd., Eleele* ☎ *808/332–7333* ⊕ *www.bubblesbelowkauai.com* 🖃 *$140 for 2-tank boat dive; $90 for rider/snorkeler; Niihau charter $400.*

Kauai Down Under Dive Team

SCUBA DIVING | This company offers boat dives and specializes in shore diving for beginners, typically at Koloa Landing (year-round). They're not only geared toward beginning divers—for whom they provide a thorough and gentle certification program as well as the Discover Scuba program—but also offer night dives and scooter (think James Bond) dives for certified divers. Their main emphasis is a detailed review of marine biology, such as pointing out rare dragon eel and harlequin shrimp tucked away in pockets of coral. ■TIP→ **Hands down, we recommend Kauai Down Under for beginners, certification (all levels), and refresher dives.** One reason is that their instructor-to-student ratio does not exceed 1:4 for beginners. For certified divers the ratio can be 6:1.

Continued on page 202

SNORKELING IN HAWAII

Molokini Crater

The waters surrounding the Hawaiian Islands are filled with life   from giant manta rays cruising off the Big Island's Kona Coast to humpback whales giving birth in the waters around Maui. Dip your head beneath the surface to experience a spectacularly colorful world: pairs of milletseed butterflyfish dart back and forth, redlipped parrotfish snack on coral algae, and spotted eagle rays flap past like silent spaceships. Sea turtles bask at the surface while tiny wrasses give them the equivalent of a shave and a haircut. The water quality is typically outstanding; many sites afford 30-foot-plus visibility. On snorkel cruises, you can often stare from the boat rail right down to the bottom.

Certainly few destinations are as accommodating to every level of snorkeler as Hawaii. Beginners can tromp in from sandy beaches while more advanced divers descend to shipwrecks, reefs, craters, and sea arches just offshore. Because of Hawaii's extreme isolation, the island chain has fewer fish species than Fiji or the Caribbean—but many of the fish that live here exist nowhere else. The Hawaiian waters are home to the highest percentage of endemic fish in the world.

The key to enjoying the underwater world is slowing down. Look carefully. Listen. You might hear the strange crackling sound of shrimp tunneling through coral, or you may hear whales singing to one another during winter. A shy octopus may drift along the ocean's floor beneath you. If you're hooked, pick up a waterproof fishkey from Long's Drugs. You can brag later that you've looked the Hawaiian turkeyfish in the eye.

Picasso Triggerfish

Milletseed Butterflyfish*

Yellow Tang

Moorish Idol

Hawaiian Whitespotted Toby*

Saddleback Wrasse*

Redlip Parrotfish

Hawaiian Turkeyfish*

Zebra Moray Eel

Stocky Hawkfish

Green Sea Turtle (Honu)

Spotted Eagle Ray

*endemic to Hawaii

POLYNESIA'S FIRST CELESTIAL NAVIGATORS: HONU

Honu is the Hawaiian name for two native sea turtles, the hawksbill and the green sea turtle. Little is known about these dinosaur-age marine reptiles, though snorkelers regularly see them foraging for *limu* (seaweed) and the occasional jellyfish in Hawaiian waters. Most female honu nest in the uninhabited Northwestern Hawaiian Islands, but a few sociable ladies nest on Maui and Big Island beaches. Scientists suspect that they navigate the seas via magnetism—sensing the earth's poles. Amazingly, they will journey up to 800 miles to nest—it's believed that they return to their own birth sites. After about 60 days of incubation, nestlings emerge from the sand at night and find their way back to the sea by the light of the stars.

SNORKELING

Many of Hawaii's reefs are accessible from shore.

The basics: Sure, you can take a deep breath, hold your nose, squint your eyes, and stick your face in the water in an attempt to view submerged habitats . . . but why not protect your eyes, retain your ability to breathe, and keep your hands free to paddle about when exploring underwater? That's what snorkeling is all about.

Equipment needed: A mask, snorkel (the tube attached to the mask), and fins. In deeper waters (any depth over your head), life jackets are advised.

Steps to success: If you've never snorkeled before, it's natural to feel a bit awkward at first, so don't sweat it. Breathing through a mask and tube, and wearing a pair of fins take getting used to. Like any activity, you build confidence and comfort through practice.

If you're new to snorkeling, begin by submerging your face in shallow water or a swimming pool and breathing calmly through the snorkel while gazing through the mask.

Next you need to learn how to clear water out of your mask and snorkel, an essential skill since splashes can send water into tube openings and masks can leak. Some snorkels have built-in drainage valves, but if a tube clogs, you can force water up and out by exhaling through your mouth. Clearing a mask is similar: lift your head from water while pulling forward on mask to drain. Some masks have built-in purge valves, but those without can be cleared underwater by pressing the top to the forehead and blowing out your nose (charming, isn't it?), allowing air to bubble into the mask, pushing water out the bottom. If it sounds hard, it really isn't. Just try it a few times and you'll soon feel like a pro.

Now your goal is to get friendly with fins—you want them to be snug but not too tight—and learn how to propel yourself with them. Fins won't help you float, but they will give you a leg up, so to speak, on smoothly moving through the water or treading water (even when upright) with less effort.

Flutter stroking is the most efficient underwater kick, and the farther your foot bends forward the more leg power you'll be able to transfer to the water and the farther you'll travel with each stroke. Flutter kicking movements involve alternately separating the legs and then drawing them back together. When your legs separate, the leg surface encounters drag from the water, slowing you down. When your legs are drawn back together, they produce a force pushing you forward. If your kick creates more forward force than it causes drag, you'll move ahead.

Submerge your fins to avoid fatigue rather than having them flailing above the water when you kick, and keep your arms at your side to reduce drag. You are in the water—stretched out, face down, and snorkeling happily away—but that doesn't mean you can't hold your breath and go deeper in the water for a closer look at some fish or whatever catches your attention. Just remember that when you do this, your snorkel will be submerged, too, so you won't be breathing (you'll be holding your breath). You can dive head-first, but going feet-first is easier and less scary for most folks, taking less momentum. Before full immersion, take several long, deep breaths to clear carbon dioxide from your lungs.

If your legs tire, flip onto your back and tread water with inverted fin motions while resting. If your mask fogs, wash condensation from lens and clear water from mask.

TIPS FOR SAFE SNORKELING

■ Snorkel with a buddy and stay together.

■ Plan your entry and exit points prior to getting in the water.

■ Swim into the current on entering and then ride the current back to your exit point.

■ Carry your flippers into the water and then put them on, as it's difficult to walk in them, and rocks may be slippery.

■ Make sure your mask fits properly and is not too loose.

■ Pop your head above the water periodically to ensure you aren't drifting too far out, or too close to rocks.

■ Think of the water as someone else's home—don't take anything that doesn't belong to you, or leave any trash behind.

■ Don't touch any sea creatures; they may sting.

■ Wear a T-shirt over your swimsuit to help protect you from being fried by the sun.

■ When in doubt, don't go without a snorkeling professional; try a guided tour.

■ Don't go in if the ocean seems rough.

Green sea turtle (Honu)

Scuba Q&A

Q: Do I have to be certified to go scuba diving?

A: No. You can try Discover Scuba, which allows you to dive up to 40 feet after an introductory lesson in a pool. Most dive outfitters on Kauai offer this introductory program.

Q: Can I dive if I have asthma?

A: Only if your doctor signs a medical release—the original of which you must present to your dive outfitter.

Q: Can I get certified on Kauai?

A: Yes. Start to finish, it'll take three days. Or, you can complete your classroom and confined-water training at home and just do your check-out dives on Kauai.

Q: How old do you have to be to learn how to dive?

A: Most certifying agencies require that you be at least 12 years old (with PADI it's 10) when you start your scuba-diving course. You will normally receive a junior certification, which can be upgraded to a full certification when you are 15 years old.

Q: Can I wear contact lenses or glasses while diving?

A: You can either wear contact lenses with a regular mask or opt for a prescription mask—just let your dive outfitter know in advance.

Q: What if I forget my certification card?

A: Let your dive outfitter know immediately; with advance notice, they can usually dig up your certification information online.

All dive gear is included. ✉ *Sheraton Kauai Resort, 2440 Hoonani Rd., Koloa* ☎ *877/538–3483, 808/742–9534* ⊕ *www. kauaidownunderscuba.com* ✆ *From $155 for a 2-tank certified dive; $550 for certification.*

★ **Ocean Quest Watersports/Fathom Five**
SCUBA DIVING | This operator offers it all: boat dives, shore dives, night dives, certification dives. They pretty much do what everyone else does with a few twists. First, they offer a three-tank premium charter for those really serious about diving. Second, they operate a Nitrox continuous-flow mixing system, so you can decide the mix rate. Third, they add on a twilight dive to the standard, one-tank night dive, making the outing worth the effort. Fourth, their shore diving isn't an afterthought. Finally, we think their dive masters are pretty darn good, too.

They even dive Niihau in the summer aboard their 38-foot *Force*. In summer, book well in advance. ✉ *3450 Poipu Rd., Koloa* ☎ *808/742–6991, 800/972–3078* ⊕ *www.fathomfive.com* ✆ *From $155 for boat dives; from $100 for shore dives; $45 for gear rental, if needed.*

Seasport Divers
SCUBA DIVING | Rated highly by readers of *Scuba Diving* magazine, Seasport Divers' 48-foot *Anela Kai* tops the chart for dive-boat luxury. But owner Marvin Otsuji didn't stop with that. A second boat—a 32-foot catamaran—is outfitted for diving, but we like it as an all-around charter. The company does brisk business, which means it won't cancel at the last minute because of a lack of reservations, like some other companies, although they may book up to 18 people per boat.
■ **TIP→ There are slightly more challenging trips in the morning; mellower dive sites**

are in the afternoon. The company runs a good-size dive shop for purchases and rentals, as well as a classroom for certification. Night dives are offered, and Niihau trips are available in summer. There's also an outlet in Kapaa. ⊠ *2827 Poipu Rd., look for yellow submarine in parking lot, Poipu* ☎ *808/742–9303, 808/742–9303* ⊕ *www.seasportdivers. com* ⊠ *From $145, plus $37 for gear; $105 1-tank shore dive, plus gear charge.*

Snorkeling

Generally speaking, the calmest water and best snorkeling can be found on Kauai's North Shore in summer and South Shore in winter. The East Side, known as the windward side, has year-round, prevalent northeast trade winds that make snorkeling unpredictable, although there are some good pockets. The best snorkeling on the West Side is accessible only by boat.

A word on feeding fish: don't. As Captain Ted with HoloHolo Charters says, fish have survived and populated reefs for much longer than we have been donning goggles and staring at them. They will continue to do so without our intervention. Besides, fish food messes up the reef and—one thing always leads to another—can eliminate a once-pristine reef environment. As for gear, if you're snorkeling with one of the Napali boat-tour outfitters, they'll provide it; however, depending on the company, it might not be the latest or greatest. If you have your own, bring it. On the other hand, if you're going out with SeaFun or Z-Tourz, the gear is top-notch. If you need to rent, hit one of the "snorkel-and-surf" shops such as Snorkel Bob's in Koloa and Kapaa, Nukumoi in Poipu, or Seasport in Poipu and Kapaa, or shop Walmart if you want to drag it home. Typically, though, rental gear will be better quality than that found

at Walmart or Kmart. ■**TIP**➜ **If you wear glasses, you can rent prescription masks at the rental shops—just don't expect them to match your prescription exactly.**

BEST SPOTS

Just because we say these are good places to snorkel doesn't mean that the exact moment you arrive, the fish will flock—they are wild, after all.

Beach House (Lawai Beach). Don't pack the beach umbrella, beach mats, or cooler for snorkeling at Beach House. Just bring your snorkeling gear. The beach—named after its neighbor the Beach House restaurant—is on the road to Spouting Horn. It's a small slip of sand during low tide and a rocky shoreline during high tide; however, it's right by the road's edge, and its rocky coastline and somewhat rocky bottom make it great for snorkeling. Enter and exit in the sand channel (not over the rocky reef) that lines up with the Lawai Beach Resort's center atrium. Stay within the rocky points anchoring each end of the beach. The current runs east to west. ⊠ *5017 Lawai Rd., makai (ocean) side of Lawai Rd., park on road in front of Lawai Beach Resort, Koloa.*

Kee Beach. Thanks to a permit system that limits the number of visitors, Kee Beach doesn't get as crowded as it used to, and it's quite often a good snorkeling destination if the water conditions are right. The snorkeling is best early in the morning or later in the afternoon. ■**TIP**➜ **Snorkeling here in winter can be hazardous. Summer is the best and safest time, although you should never swim beyond the reef.** A parking area allows for 100 vehicles at a time. Get your permit ahead of time on ⊕ *www.gohaena.com.* ⊠ *At end of Rte. 560, Haena.*

Lydgate Beach Park. Lydgate Beach Park is typically the safest place to snorkel on Kauai, though not the most exciting. With its lava-rock wall creating a protected swimming pool, it's a good spot for beginners, young and old. The fish are so tame here it's almost like swimming in a saltwater aquarium. There is also a lifeguard, a playground for children, plenty of parking, and full-service restrooms with showers. ⊠ *4470 Nalu Rd.* ⊹ *Just south of Wailua River, turn makai (toward ocean) off Rte. 56 onto Lehu Dr. and left onto Nalu Rd., Kapaa.*

Niihau. With little river runoff and hardly any boat traffic, the waters off the island of Niihau are some of the clearest in all Hawaii, and that's good for snorkeling and excellent for scuba diving. Like Nualolo Kai, the only way to snorkel here is to sign on with one of the tour boats venturing across a sometimes rough open-ocean channel: Blue Dolphin Charters and HoloHolo.

Nualolo Kai. Nualolo Kai was once an ancient Hawaiian fishpond and is now home to the best snorkeling along Napali Coast (and perhaps on all of Kauai). The only way to access it is by boat, including kayak. Though many boats stop offshore, only a few Napali snorkeling-tour operators are permitted to come ashore. We recommend Napali Explorer and Kauai Sea Tours.

Poipu Beach Park. You'll generally find good year-round snorkeling at Poipu Beach Park, except during summer's south swells (which are not nearly as frequent as winter's north swells). The best snorkeling fronts the Marriott Waiohai Beach Club. Stay inside the crescent created by the sandbar and rocky point, and within sight of the lifeguard tower. The current runs east to west. ⊠ *Hoone Rd.* ⊹ *From Poipu Rd., turn right onto Hoone Rd.*

Tunnels (Makua). The search for Tunnels (Makua) is as tricky as the snorkeling. Park at Haena Beach Park and walk east—away from Napali Coast—until you see a sand channel entrance in the water, almost at the point. Once you get here, the reward is fantastic. The name of this beach comes from the many underwater lava tubes, which always attract marine life. The shore is mostly beach rock interrupted by three sand channels. You'll want to enter and exit at one of these channels (or risk stepping on a sea urchin or scraping your stomach on the reef). Follow the sand channel to a dropoff; the snorkeling along here is always full of nice surprises. Expect a current running east to west. Snorkeling here in winter can be hazardous; summer is the best and safest time for snorkeling. ⊠ *Haena Beach Park* ⊹ *Near end of Rte. 560, across from lava-tube sea caves, after stream crossing.*

TOURS
★ SeaFun Kauai

SNORKELING | FAMILY | This guided snorkeling tour, for beginners and intermediates alike, is led by a marine expert who not only provides snorkeling instruction but also actually gets into the water with you and identifies marine life. You're guaranteed to spot tons of critters you'd never see on your own. This is a land-based operation and the only one of its kind on Kauai. (Don't think those snorkeling cruises are guided snorkeling tours— they rarely are. A member of the boat's crew serves as lifeguard, not a marine life *guide*.) A morning or afternoon tour includes all your snorkeling gear—and a wet suit to keep you warm—and stops at one or two snorkeling locations, chosen based on ocean conditions. They will pick up customers at some of the resorts, depending on locale and destination. ⊠ *3477A Weliweli Rd., Koloa* ☎ *808/245– 6400, 800/452–1113* ⊕ *www.seafunkauai. com* ⊠ *$89.*

Spas

THE NORTH SHORE
Hanalei Day Spa

SPA/BEAUTY | As you travel past tony Princeville, life slows down. The single-lane bridges may be one reason. Another is the Hanalei Day Spa, a boutique day spa on the grounds of the Hanalei Colony Resort in Haena with in-spa and beach-side spa services. Owner Darci Frankel is an Ayurveda practitioner with more than 27 years of experience. Spa treatments include body wraps, scrubs, and packages for individuals and couples. Its specialty is the massage: *lomilomi* (a traditional Hawaiian-style massage), deep tissue, relaxation, and a special four-hands massage.

✉ *Hanalei Colony Resort, Rte. 560, Haena* ⊹ *6 miles past Hanalei* ☎ *808/826–6621* ⊕ *www.hanaleidayspa.com* ✉ *Massage from $110* ☽ *Closed Sun. and Mon.*

THE EAST SIDE
Alexander Day Spa & Salon at the Kauai Marriott

SPA/BEAUTY | This spa focuses on body care rather than exercise, so don't expect any fitness equipment or exercise classes, just pampering and beauty treatments. The Alexander Day Spa & Salon at the Kauai Marriott is a sunny, pleasant facility. Massages are available in treatment rooms, your room, and on the beach, although the beach locale isn't as private as you might imagine. Wedding-day and custom spa packages can be arranged. ✉ *Kauai Marriott Resort & Beach Club, 3610 Rice St., Suite 9A, Lihue* ☎ *808/246–4918* ⊕ *www.alexanderspa.com* ✉ *Massage from $130.*

Angeline's Muolaulani Wellness Center

SPA/BEAUTY | It doesn't get more authentic, or rustic, than this. In the mid-1980s Aunty Angeline Locey opened her Anahola home to offer traditional Hawaiian

Try a Lomi Massage

Life in ancient Hawaii wasn't about sunbathing and lounging at the beach. Growing taro was hard work, as was building canoes, fishing for dinner, and pounding *tapa* cloth for clothing, sails, and blankets. Enter *lomilomi*—Hawaiian-style massage. It's often described as being more vigorous, more rhythmic, and faster than Swedish massage, and it incorporates more elbow and forearm work. It might even involve chanting, music, and four hands (in other words, two people).

healing practices. Though she passed on, her son and granddaughter carry on the tradition. There's a two-hour treatment ($175) that starts with a steam, followed by a sea-salt-and-clay body scrub and a four-handed massage. The real treat, however, is relaxing on Aunty's open-air garden deck. The Center's mission is to promote a healthy body image. Detailed directions are given when you book a treatment. ■ TIP→ This is cash only and you need to bring your own towel. ✉ *Kamalomaloo Pl., Anahola* ☎ *808/822–3235* ⊕ *www.angelineslomikauai.com.*

Golden Lotus Studio

AEROBICS/YOGA | This small studio, tucked off the main road in Kapaa, offers a variety of yoga and dance classes daily, including heated power vinyasa yoga and aerial yoga. Various types of massage are available by appointment, including traditional Hawaiian *lomilomi*, Ayurveda, deep tissue, and Thai yoga style, starting at $95 an hour. Check their website for special events and workshops, offered frequently. ✉ *4-941A Kuhio Hwy., Kapaa* ☎ *808/823–9810* ⊕ *www.goldenlotuskauai.org.*

Questions for a Surf Instructor

Thinking about taking surf lessons? These are a few good questions to ask your potential surf instructor:

■ Are you legally permitted to operate on the beach?

■ What equipment do you provide? (If you're a beginner, you'll want to hear about their soft-top beginner boards. You'll also want to know if they'll provide rash guards and aqua socks.)

■ Who will be my instructor? (It's not always the name on the company logo. Ask about your instructor's qualifications.)

■ How do you select the location? (Ideally, you'll be assured that they pick the location because of its gentle waves, sandy beach bottom, and good year-round conditions.)

■ What if the waves are too big? (Under the best circumstances, they'll select another location or reschedule for another day.)

■ How many students do you take at a time? (Don't book if it's more than four students per instructor. You'll definitely want some personal attention.)

■ Are you CPR- and lifeguard-certified? (It's good to know your instructor will be able to help if you get into trouble.)

THE SOUTH SHORE

★ Anara Spa

SPA/BEAUTY | The luxurious Anara Spa has all the equipment and services you expect from a top resort spa, along with a pleasant, professional staff. Best of all, it has indoor and outdoor areas that capitalize on the tropical locale and balmy weather, further distinguishing it from the Marriott and St. Regis spas. Its 46,500 square feet of space includes the lovely Garden Treatment Village, an open-air courtyard with private thatched-roof huts, each featuring a relaxation area, misters, and open-air shower in a tropical setting. Ancient Hawaiian remedies and local ingredients are featured in many of the treatments, such as a pineapple-papaya body hydration, and a traditional *lomilomi* massage. The open-air lava-rock showers are wonderful, introducing many guests to the delightful island practice of showering outdoors. The spa, which includes a full-service salon, adjoins the Hyatt's legendary swimming pool. ⊠ *Hyatt Regency Kauai Resort and Spa,* *1571 Poipu Rd., Poipu* ☎ *808/240–6440* ⊕ *www.anaraspa.com* ✉ *Massages from $180.*

THE WEST SIDE

Sweet Lomi Massage

SPA/BEAUTY | Sweet Lomi Massage offers a variety of services, from Swedish and hot stone massages to an especially good reflexology treatment. The two-hour Sweet Lomi Blend includes a variety of massage techniques and is truly divine. ⊠ *4492 Moana Rd., Waimea (Kauai County)* ☎ *808/651–8857* ⊕ *www.sweetlomi. com* ✉ *Massages from $100* ☷ *Closed Sun. and Mon.*

Stand-Up Paddling

This is an increasingly popular sport that even a novice can pick up—*and* have fun doing. Beginners start with a heftier surfboard and a longer-than-normal canoe paddle. And, just as the name implies, stand-up paddlers stand

Winter brings big surf to Kauai's North Shore. You can see some of the sport's biggest celebrities catching waves at Haena and Hanalei Bay.

on their surfboards and paddle out from the beach—no timing a wave and doing a push-up to stand. The perfect place to learn is a river (think **Hanalei** or **Wailua**) or a calm lagoon (try **Anini** or **Kalapaki**). But this sport isn't just for beginners. Tried-and-true surfers turn to it when the waves are not quite right for their preferred sport, because it gives them another reason to be on the water. Stand-up paddlers catch waves earlier and ride them longer than longboard surfers. In the past couple of years, professional stand-up paddling competitions have popped up, and surf shops and instructors have adapted to its quick rise in popularity.

EQUIPMENT AND LESSONS

Not all surf instructors teach stand-up paddling, but more and more are, like Blue Seas Surfing School and Titus Kinimaka Hawaiian School of Surfing *(see Surfing).*

Back Door Surf Co.

WATER SPORTS | Along with its sister store across the street—Hanalei Surf Shop—Back Door Surf Co. provides just about all the rentals necessary for a fun day at Hanalei Bay, along with clothing and new boards. ⌷ *Ching Young Village, 5-5190 Kuhio Hwy., Hanalei* ☎ *808/826–9000* ⊕ *www.hanaleisurf.com/our-sister-stores.*

Hawaiian Surfing Adventures

WATER SPORTS | This Hanalei location has a wide variety of stand-up boards and paddles for rent, with a few options depending on your schedule. Check in at the storefront and then head down to the beach, where your gear will be waiting. Lessons are also available on the scenic Hanalei River or in Hanalei Bay, and include 30 minutes of ocean safety, paddling, and wave-reading instruction and an hour in the water to practice with the board. This Native Hawaiian–owned company also offers surfboard and kayak rentals and surfing lessons. ✉ *5134 Kuhio*

What's That Whale Doing?

Although humpbacks spend more than 90% of their lives underwater, they can be very active above water while they're in Hawaii. Here are a few maneuvers you may see:

■ Blow: the expulsion of air that looks like a geyser of water.

■ Spy hop: the raising of just the whale's head out of the water, as if to take a look around.

■ Tail slap: the repetitive slap of the tail, or fluke, on the surface of the water.

■ Pec slap: the repetitive slap of one or both fins on the surface of the water.

■ Fluke up dive: the waving of the tail above water as the whale slowly rolls underwater to dive.

■ Breach: the launching of the entire whale's body out of the water.

Hwy., Hanalei ☎ *808/482–0749* ⊕ *www. hawaiiansurfingadventures.com* ✉ *Paddleboard rental from $30; surfboard rentals from $20; lessons from $65.*

Kauai Beach Boys
WATER SPORTS | This outfitter is right on the beach at Kalapaki, so there's no hauling your gear on your car. Classes are also held at Poipu Beach, at the Marriott Waiohai. In addition to stand-up paddle lessons, they offer sailing and surfing lessons, too. ✉ *3610 Rice St., Lihue* ☎ *808/246–6333, 808/742–4442* ⊕ *www. kauaibeachboys.com* ✉ *$79 for 90-min surf or SUP lesson.*

Surfing

Good ol' stand-up surfing is alive and well on Kauai, especially in winter's high-surf season on the North Shore. If you're new to the sport, we highly recommend taking a lesson. Not only will this ensure you're up and riding waves in no time, but instructors will provide the right board for your experience and size, help you time a wave, and give you a push to get your momentum going. ■ **TIP→ You don't need to be in top physical shape to take a lesson. Because your instructor helps** push you into the wave, you won't wear yourself out paddling. If you're experienced and want to hit the waves on your own, most surf shops rent boards for all levels, from beginners to advanced.

BEST SPOTS
Perennial-favorite beginning surf spots include **Poipu Beach** (the area fronting the Marriott Waiohai Beach Club), **Hanalei Bay,** and the stream end of **Kalapaki Beach.** More advanced surfers move down the beach in Hanalei to an area fronting a grove of pine trees known as **Pine Trees,** or paddle out past the pier. When the trade winds die, the north ends of **Wailua** and **Kealia** beaches are teeming with surfers. Breaks off **Poipu** and **Beach House/Lawai Beach** attract intermediates year-round. During high surf, the break on the cliff side of **Kalihiwai** is for experts only. Advanced riders will head to Polihale to face the heavy West Side waves when conditions are right.

EQUIPMENT AND LESSONS
Blue Seas Surfing School
SURFING | FAMILY | Surfer and instructor Charlie Smith specializes in beginners (especially children), and though he operates primarily at Poipu Beach, lessons

Humpback whales arrive at Kauai in November and stick around until early April. You can see these majestic creatures breach and spout from shore, or take a boat tour.

are offered elsewhere on the island. His soft-top longboards are very stable, making it easier to stand up. He specializes in one-on-one or family lessons, so personal interaction is a priority. He has also added stand-up paddling to his operation. Transportation is provided, if needed. ⊠ 1959 Hoono Rd., Koloa 🕾 808/634-6979 🖃 From $75 for a 90 min lesson.

Hanalei Surf Company

SURFING | You can rent boards here and shop for rash guards, wet suits, and some hip surf-inspired apparel. ⊠ Hanalei Center, 5-5161 Kuhio Hwy., Hanalei 🕾 808/826-9000 ⊕ www.hanaleisurf. com.

Nukumoi Surf Co.

SURFING | Owned by the same folks who own Brennecke's restaurant, this shop arranges surfing lessons and provides board (surfing, body, and stand-up paddle), snorkel, and beach-gear rental, as well as casual clothing. Their primary surf spot is the beach fronting the Sheraton.

⊠ 2100 Hoone Rd., across from Poipu Beach Park, Koloa 🕾 808/742-8019 ⊕ www.nukumoi.com 🖃 $75 for groups for 90 min; $250 for private sessions.

Progressive Expressions

SURFING | This full-service shop has a choice of rental boards and a whole lotta shopping for clothes, swimsuits, and casual beach wear. ⊠ 5428 Koloa Rd., Koloa 🕾 808/742-6041 ⊕ www.progressiveexpressions.com.

Tamba Surf Company

SURFING | This is Kauai's homegrown surf shop, and your best bet for surfboard and snorkel gear rentals, new boards, and surfing lessons on the East Side. Tamba is a big name in local surf apparel. ⊠ 4-1543 Kuhio Hwy., Kapaa 🕾 808/823-6942 ⊕ www.tamba.com.

Titus Kinimaka Hawaiian School of Surfing

SURFING | Famed as a pioneer of big-wave surfing, this Hawaiian believes in giving back to his sport. Beginning, intermediate, and advanced lessons are available

On the North Shore, adventure seekers will find a nine-zipline course run by Princeville Ranch Adventures.

at Hanalei, with a maximum of three students. If you want to learn to surf from a living legend, this is the man. Advanced surfers can also take a tow-in lesson with a Jet Ski. ■**TIP➜ He employs other instructors, so if you want Titus, be sure to ask for him. (And good luck, because if the waves are going off, he'll be surfing, not teaching.)** Customers are able to use the board for a while after the lesson is complete. ✉ *Quicksilver, 5-5088 Kuhio Hwy., Hanalei* ☎ *808/652–1116* ⊕ *www. hawaiianschoolofsurfing.com* ✉ *$75, 90-min group; $250 Jet Ski surf; $130, 90-min stand-up paddle.*

Whale-Watching

Every winter North Pacific humpback whales swim some 3,000 miles over 30 days, give or take a few, from Alaska to Hawaii. Whales arrive as early as November and sometimes stay through April, though they seem to be most populous in February and March. They come to Hawaii to breed, calve, and nurse their young.

TOURS

Of course, nothing beats seeing a whale up close. During the season, any boat on the water is looking for whales; they're hard to avoid, whether the tour is labeled "whale-watching" or not. Consider the whales a benefit to any boating event that may interest you. If whales are definitely your thing, though, you can narrow down your tour-boat decision by asking a few whale-related questions, like whether there's a hydrophone on board, how long the captain has been running tours in Hawaii, and if anyone on the crew is a marine biologist or trained naturalist.

Several boat operators will add two-hour afternoon whale-watching tours during the season that run on the South Shore (not Napali). Operators include **Blue Dolphin, Catamaran Kahanu, HoloHolo,** and **Napali Explorer** *(see Boat Tours)*. Trying one of these excursions is a good option for those who have no interest in snorkeling or sightseeing along Napali Coast, although keep in mind, the longer you're on the water, the more likely you'll be to see the humpbacks.

One of the more unique ways to (possibly) see some whales is atop a kayak. For such an encounter, try **Outfitters Kauai's** South Shore kayak trip (see Kayaking Tours). There are a few lookout spots around the island with good land-based viewing: Kilauea Lighthouse on the North Shore, the Kapaa Scenic Overlook just north of Kapaa Town on the East Side, and the cliffs to the east of Keoniloa (Shipwreck) Beach on the South Shore.

Zipline Tours

The latest adventure on Kauai is "zipping," or "ziplining." Regardless of what you call it, chances are you'll scream like a rock star while trying it. Strap on a harness, clip onto a cable running from one side of a river or valley to the other, and zip across. The step off is the scariest part. ■ TIP➔ **Pack knee-length shorts or pants, athletic shoes, and courage for this adventure.**

Outfitters Kauai

TOUR—SPORTS | This outfitter's most popular adventure, the Kipu Zipline Safari Tour, features an 1,800-foot tandem zip—that's right, you don't have to go it alone. You can also paddle the Wailua River or take the downhill bike ride along the Waimea Canyon road. They also offer The Flyline, the state's longest zipline, which has a "run" of 4,000 feet. ⊠ 2827-A Poipu Rd., Poipu ☎ 808/742–9667, 888/742–9887 ⊕ www.outfitterskauai.com ☑ From $109.

Princeville Ranch Adventures

TOUR—SPORTS | The North Shore's answer to ziplining is a nine-zipline course with a bit of hiking and suspension-bridge-crossing thrown in for a half-day adventure. The four-and-a-half-hour Zip 'N Dip tour includes a picnic and swimming at a waterfall pool, while the Zip Express whizzes you through the entire course in three hours. Both excursions conclude with a 1,200-foot tandem zip across a valley. Guides are energetic and fun. This is as close as it gets to flying; just watch out for the albatross. ⊠ Rte. 56, between mile markers 27 and 28, Princeville ☎ 808/826–7669, 888/955–7669 ⊕ www.princevilleranch.com ☑ From $139.

7

Activities ZIPLINE TOURS

Index

W

Z

Photo Credits

Front Cover: Credit: Joe Belanger / Alamy [Description: An aerial view of the Na Pali coast's Open Ceiling Cave, Kauai, Hawaii, USA]. **Back cover, from left to right:** Bennymarty/Dreamstime, Marek © Hawaii Tourism Authority (HTA), MNStudio/Dreamstime. **Spine:** Panachai Cherdchucheep/Shutterstock. **Interior, from left to right:** Steveheap/Dreamstime (1). Danwatt417/Dreamstime (2). SergiyN / Shutterstock (5) **Chapter 1: Experience Kauai:** Mfron/Dreamstime (6-7). Jodielee/Dreamstime (8). SCHREIER Fotografie/agefotostock (9). Jeff Whyte/Shutterstock (9). Hawaii Tourism Authority (10). Tor Johnson/Hawaii Tourism Authority (10). Anson Chappell/Flickr, [CC BY-ND 2.0] (10). MH Anderson Photography/Shutterstock (10). Trudywsimmons/Dreamstime (11). MNStudio/Dreamstime (12). Kyrien/Dreamstime (12). Bonniemarie/Dreamstime (12). Dejjf82/Dreamstime (12). Nikkigensert/Dreamstime (13). Fleurdly/Dreamstime (13). Jeff Whyte/Shutterstock (13). Bonniemarie/Dreamstime (13). Izanbar/Dreamstime (14). MNStudio/Dreamstime(14). Luau Kalamaku (15). Brian G. Oar - Fairways Photography (16). Tim Saunders (16). Steve Mitchell (16). Flyingwolf/Dreamstime (16). Steveheap/Dreamstime (17). Ralf Broskvar/Dreamstime (22). Hawaii Tourism Authority/Tor Johnson (22). Hawaii Tourism Authority (HTA) (22). julianufer/Shutterstock (23). Hawaii Tourism Authority/Tor Johnson (23). Hawaii Tourism Authority (HTA) / Daeja Fallas (24). Bill Florence/Shutterstock (24). Steve Heap/Shutterstock (24). nstanev/iStockphoto (24). Fominayaphoto/Shutterstock (24). maximkabb/iStockphoto (25). Fominayaphoto/Shutterstock (25). MNStudio/Shutterstock (25). Danita Delmont/Shutterstock (25). L.A. Nature Graphics/Shutterstock (25). Pr2is/Dreamstime (26). Ancha Chiangmai/Shutterstock (26). Marilyn Gould/Dreamstime (26). Tpower70/Dreamstime (26). Vfbjohn/Dreamstime (26). Big Island Visitors Bureau (BIVB) / Kirk Lee Aeder (27). Eddygaleotti/Dreamstime (27). Caner CIFTCI/Dreamstime (27). Elmar Langle/iStockphoto (27). Koondon/Shutterstock (27). Martinmark/Dreamstime (28). Dana Edmunds 2014 (28). Hawaii Tourism (28). Magdanatka/Shutterstock (29). Big Island Visitors Bureau (BIVB) / Kirk Lee Aeder (29). Temanu/Dreamstime (30). Hawaii Tourism Authority (HTA) / Brooke Dombroski (30). Lost Mountain Studio/Shutterstock (30). Alla Machutt/iStockphoto (30). Mongkolchon Akesin/Shutterstock (30). Hawaii Tourism Authority (HTA) / Heather Goodman (31). Hawaii Tourism Authority (HTA) / Heather Goodman (31). Hawaii Tourism Authority (HTA) / Dana Edmunds (31). Hawaii Tourism Authority (31). olgakr/iStockphoto (31). Cathy Locklear/Dreamstime (35). HVCB (36). Thinkstock LLC (37). Linda Ching/HVCB (39). Sri Maiava Rusden/HVCB (39). Leis Of Hawaii @ leisofhawaii.com (40). www.kellyalexanderphotography.com (40). Leis Of Hawaii @ leisofhawaii.com (40). Leis Of Hawaii @ leisofhawaii.com (40). Leis Of Hawaii @ leisofhawaii.com (40). www.kellyalexanderphotography.com(40). Tim Wilson/Flickr, [CC BY-NC 2.0] (41). Polynesian Cultural Center (42, 1-5). Dana Edmunds/Polynesian Cultural Center's/Alii Luau (43,1-3). Hawaii Visitors Bureau (43). **Chapter 3: The North Shore With Napali Coast:** meseberg/iStockphoto (65). Nickolay Stanev/Shutterstock (72-73). Joel Carillet/iStockphoto (77). Stevengaertner/Dreamstime (78). STLJB/Shutterstock (81). Backyard Productions LLC/iStockphoto (86). Sergiyn/Dreamstime (88-89). SergiyN / Shutterstock (90-91). Marisa Estivill/Shutterstock (91). Rob Marmion/Shutterstock (91). Kikuko Nakayama/Flickr, [CC BY-SA 2.0] (92-93). Photo Resource Hawaii / Alamy (93). Na Pali Coast (93). Mark A. Johnson / Alamy (94-95). Photo Resource Hawaii / Alamy (95). Dallas & John Heaton/agefotostock (95). **Chapter 4: The East Side:** Tommy Song/Dreamstime (97). Juergen_Wallstabe/Shutterstock (107). Roger Fletcher / Alamy (117). Steve Heap/Shutterstock (122-123). Cphoto/Dreamstime (125). Kauai Visitors Bureau (126). Jack Jeffrey (127). muhawi001/Flickr (129). raisbeckfoto /istockphoto (131). **Chapter 5: The South Shore:** Everett Atlas/Shutterstock (133). Alexander Demyanenko/Shutterstock (141). Estivillml/Dreamstime (142). Adam-Springer/iStockphoto (146). Hawaii Tourism Authority (HTA) / Tor Johnson (148). **Chapter 6: The West Side With Waimea Canyon:** SVongpra/Shutterstock (157). SMJoness/iStockphoto (168). MNStudio/Shutterstock (170-171). **Chapter 7: Activities:** jim kruger/iStockphoto (173). YinYang/iStockphoto (175). Hawaii Tourism Authority (HTA) / Tor Johnson (178). Helio San Miguel (181). Americanspirit/Dreamstime (183). Courtesy of St. Regis Princeville (187). Galyna Andrushko/Shutterstock (189). Bob Pool/Shutterstock (193). HVCB/Ron Dahlquist (197). Shane Myers Photography/Shutterstock (198). Gert Vrey/iStockphoto (200). SPrada/iStockphoto (200). sweetlifephotos/iStockphoto (201). jarvis gray/Shutterstock (207). Robert Plotz/iStockphoto (209). Princeville Ranch Adventures (210). **About Our Writers:** All photos are courtesy of the writers.

Every effort has been made to trace the copyright holders, and we apologize in advance for any accidental errors. We would be happy to apply the corrections in the following edition of this publication.

Notes

Notes

Notes

Notes

Notes

Notes

Fodor's KAUAI

Publisher: Stephen Horowitz, *General Manager*

Editorial: Douglas Stallings, *Editorial Director;* Jill Fergus, Jacinta O'Halloran, Amanda Sadlowski, *Senior Editors;* Kayla Becker, Alexis Kelly, Rachael Roth, *Editors*

Design: Tina Malaney, *Director of Design and Production;* Jessica Gonzalez, *Graphic Designer;* Mariana Tabares, *Design and Production Intern*

Production: Jennifer DePrima, *Editorial Production Manager;* Elyse Rozelle, *Senior Production Editor;* Monica White, *Production Editor*

Maps: Rebecca Baer, *Senior Map Editor;* Mark Stroud and Henry Colomb (Moon Street Cartography), David Lindroth, *Cartographers*

Photography: Viviane Teles, *Senior Photo Editor;* Namrata Aggarwal, Ashok Kumar, Carl Yu, *Photo Editors;* Rebecca Rimmer, *Photo Intern*

Business and Operations: Chuck Hoover, *Chief Marketing Officer;* Robert Ames, *Group General Manager;* Devin Duckworth, *Director of Print Publishing;* Victor Bernal, *Business Analyst*

Public Relations and Marketing: Joe Ewaskiw, *Senior Director Communications and Public Relations;* Esther Su, *Senior Marketing Manager*

Fodors.com: Jeremy Tarr, *Editorial Director;* Rachael Levitt, *Managing Editor*

Technology: Jon Atkinson, *Director of Technology;* Rudresh Teotia, *Lead Developer;* Jacob Ashpis, *Content Operations Manager*

Writers: Marla Cimini, Joan Conrow, Charles E. Roessler, Mary F. Williamson

Editor: Kayla Becker

Production Editor: Jennifer DePrima

8th Edition

ISBN 978-1-64097-292-6

ISSN 1934–550X

All details in this book are based on information supplied to us at press time. Always confirm information when it matters, especially if you're making a detour to visit a specific place. Fodor's expressly disclaims any liability, loss, or risk, personal or otherwise, that is incurred as a consequence of the use of any of the contents of this book.

SPECIAL SALES
This book is available at special discounts for bulk purchases for sales promotions or premiums. For more information, e-mail SpecialMarkets@fodors.com.

PRINTED IN CANADA

10 9 8 7 6 5 4 3 2 1

MIX
Paper from responsible sources
FSC
www.fsc.org
FSC® C016245

About Our Writers

 Marla Cimini is an award-winning writer with a passion for travel, music, beaches, and culinary adventures. As an avid globetrotter and frequent Hawaii visitor, she has covered topics ranging from luxury hotels to surf culture. Her articles have appeared in publications worldwide, including *USA Today, Robb Report, Travel Age West,* and many others. Marla wrote parts of the Experience chapter for this edition. Her website is ⊕ *www.marlacimini.com.*

 Joan Conrow is an independent journalist who splits her time between Kauai and New Mexico. She has written about Hawaii politics, culture, environment, and lifestyles for many regional and national publications. She helped write the original Fodor's guide to Kauai and updated the West Side chapter of this edition.

 Charles E. Roessler is a longtime Kauai resident who was an editor for the *Japan Times* and the *Buffalo News* after teaching English and journalism for 10 years. He contributes to the *New York Times* as a stringer/freelancer and loves Kauai, especially playing tennis and swimming at Anini Beach. Charles updated the Experience, Travel Smart, the North Shore, the East Side, and Activities chapters sections of this guide.

 Mary F. Williamson grew up in Honolulu and lives on Kauai, where her husband's family moved in the late 1800s. A former nonprofit director, she now organizes bicycle races and helps small businesses and organizations with public communication and events. She updated the South Shore chapter of this guide.